The First Age of Industrial Globalization

NEW APPROACHES TO INTERNATIONAL HISTORY

Series editor: Thomas Zeiler, Professor of American Diplomatic History, University of Colorado Boulder, USA

New Approaches to International History covers international history during the modern period and across the globe. The series incorporates new developments in the field, such as the cultural turn and transnationalism, as well as the classical high politics of state-centric policymaking and diplomatic relations. Written with upper level undergraduate and postgraduate students in mind, texts in the series provide an accessible overview of international, global and transnational issues, events and actors.

Published

Decolonization and the Cold War, Leslie James and Elisabeth Leake (2015)

Cold War Summits, Chris Tudda (2015)

The United Nations in International History, Amy Sayward (2017)

Latin American Nationalism, James F. Siekmeier (2017)

The History of United States Cultural Diplomacy, Michael L. Krenn (2017)

International Cooperation in the Early Twentieth Century,
Daniel Gorman (2017)

Women and Gender in International History, Karen Garner (2018)

The Environment and International History, Scott Kaufman (2018)

International Development, Corrina Unger (2018)

Forthcoming

Canada and the World since 1867, Asa McKercher

An International History of Modern Colonial Labour: Debates and Case Studies, Miguel Bandeira Jerónimo and José Pedro Monteiro

The International LGBT Rights Movement, Laura Belmonte

Reconstructing the Postwar World, Francine McKenzie

Scandinavia and the Great Powers, Michael Jonas

The First Age of Industrial Globalization

An International History 1815–1918

MAARTJE ABBENHUIS AND GORDON MORRELL

BLOOMSBURY ACADEMIC

LONDON · NEW YORK · OXFORD · NEW DELHI · SYDNEY

BLOOMSBURY ACADEMIC
Bloomsbury Publishing Plc
50 Bedford Square, London, WC1B 3DP, UK
1385 Broadway, New York, NY 10018, USA

First published in Great Britain 2020

For legal purposes the Acknowledgements on p. x constitute an
extension of this copyright page.

Series design by Catherine Wood
Cover image: Illustration of warships in the Suez Canal
(© Stefano Bianchetti / CORBIS / Getty Images)

A catalogue record for this book is available from the British Library.

A catalog record for this book is available from the Library of Congress.

ISBN: HB: 978-1-4742-6710-6
PB: 978-1-4742-6709-0
ePDF: 978-1-4742-6712-0
eBook: 978-1-4742-6711-3

Series: New Approaches to International History

Typeset by Newgen KnowledgeWorks Pvt. Ltd., Chennai, India
Printed and bound in Great Britain

To find out more about our authors and books visit www.bloomsbury.com
and sign up for our newsletters.

Who but a lunatic would try to bring the endless information about contemporary life into a single focus? – Theodore H. von Laue (1987)

Contents

Illustrations

Figures

Tables

Acknowledgements

This book is the product of many years of daily conversation and not a few heated debates (over coffee, while doing the dishes, going grocery shopping and cooking dinner) about what constitutes nineteenth-century globalization and why that globalization is historically relevant. Mostly, it is a book that aims to explain the seeming oxymoron that the 'world became a more global place' during the nineteenth century and that the rising sense of global connectiveness mattered in fundamental ways to contemporaries and to the nineteenth-century international environment. It is a book written for our students, who continue to grapple with some essential questions relating to the global impact of the industrial revolution, capitalist imperialism and the evolution of the modern world.

Books like these are never finished, they are artefacts of a particular moment, and they speak to the many influences in their authors' lives as academics, historians and teachers and, in our case, as partners in all walks of life. We are grateful to the many inspirational historians who came before us, who framed the nineteenth century as a globally integrated space and who carved out ways of interpreting and understanding the nineteenth-century world as one of immense and intense change. Without them, this book would not exist. We walk in the footsteps of giants, stumbling all the way.

Alongside these historians and our students at the University of Auckland and Nipissing University (Ontario), we would also like to take this opportunity to thank some key individuals who enabled this project to take form as it did, including: Sam Jaffe for his bibliographic work; Hazel Petrie, Preeti Chopra, Genevieve de Pont, Annalise Higgins, Sara Buttsworth, Matthew Hoye, Remco Raben and Angelie Sens for their feedback and reading suggestions; Igor Drecki for the maps; and the School of Humanities at the University of Auckland and Bloomsbury Publishing for their financial and material support.

A Note on Sources

We wrote this book for our students, aiming to offer an accessible international history of the nineteenth century as an 'age of globalization'. Each chapter presents an argument on a particular theme relating to the impact of the industrial revolution as it went global after 1815. It is a book of synthesis, integrating several existing approaches to the history of nineteenth-century globalization, industrialization, warfare, diplomacy and imperialism. We have kept our references to a minimum, focusing on the most useful or accessible sources when possible. Each chapter finishes with a series of study questions, which may be useful to instructors and students alike. We also conclude each chapter with a list of recommended readings, mostly chapters and journal articles that we found particularly lucid, illuminating or interrogative. We hope that they supplement readers' understanding of the text and lead them in interesting and exciting directions.

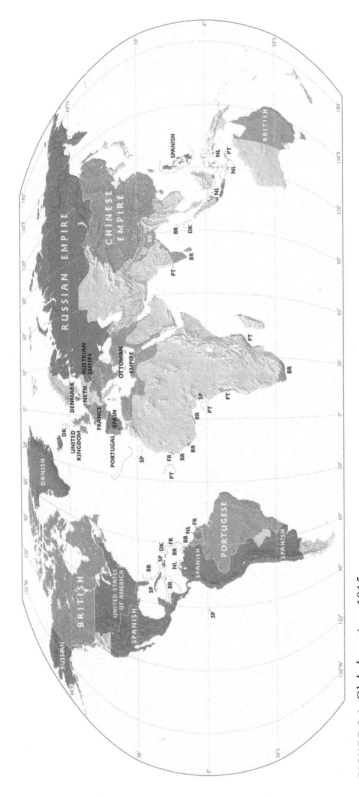

FIGURE 0.1 *Global empires, 1815.*
Source: Igor Drecki (designer), 2018.

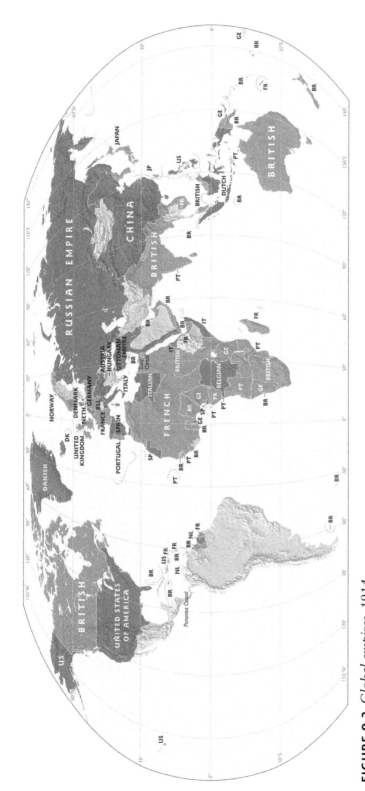

FIGURE 0.2 *Global empires, 1914.*
Source: Igor Drecki (designer), 2018.

1

Introducing the contours of the first age of industrial globalization, 1815–1918

It is a truism to state that two hundred years ago the world was quite a different place than it is today. But it really was. In 1815, where we begin our history, wherever you looked in the world, most people lived in agricultural societies supported by the produce that came off the land or out of the sea. As they had for centuries, their daily lives were influenced by seasonal calendars: by the needs of planting, growing, harvesting, or of fishing, hunting, gathering. Even if they lived in a city (as about 3 percent of them did), their livelihoods were locally or regionally focused. Their social customs, mores and religious practices were influenced by the community in which they resided and the political authority that was in charge (be it an empire, kingdom, tribe or republic). Power was generally wielded by a small caste of elites, whose lives and livelihoods tended to be served by the rest. For most, the pace of change was slow and measured. Barring extraordinary events – such as those occasioned by wars, invasions, regime changes, famines, plagues and natural disasters – people's lives were relatively predictable, if often precarious. In one lifetime, most would not travel further than a few miles from the place where they were born.

There were, of course, exceptions. Merchants, traders, sealers, whalers, bankers, entrepreneurs, bureaucrats, diplomats, adventurers, colonizers, missionaries, soldiers, labourers (both free and unfree) and those seeking a new life crossed the oceans and continents, exchanging luxury goods, precious metals, new inventions, new knowledge, plants, pathogens and diseases as they moved themselves and other people, at times against their will. Long-distance travel was slow, costly, weather-dependent and often dangerous. For example, a journey from London to New York could take three or four weeks, sometimes longer; from London to India around six months. News, information and letters travelled equally slowly: by foot, horseback or camel on land, by sail at sea.

Still, over the course of nearly three hundred years, a vast interdependent economy had formed across the Atlantic Ocean region as European settlers in their thousands brought sugar, coffee, cotton, indigo and rice crops into the Americas, waged war and displaced the local indigenous peoples, established plantations and settlements and imported African slaves and European indentured labourers to work for them. The produce of this labour crossed back across the Atlantic to Europe and Africa, often carried on the same ships that brought the slaves to this 'new world'. An estimated 12 million Africans journeyed across the Atlantic against their will and under bestial conditions between the sixteenth and nineteenth centuries.[1] Their unfree labour grew the wealth of Europe and sat at the heart of what historians call the 'Atlantic world'.

Across the same time period, the Chinese Qing dynasty, which ruled a massive territory in central Asia, also grew enormously wealthy extorting tribute from weaker neighbours and reaping taxes on the sale of silks, tea, spices, gold, ceramics, carpets and other luxury items for the consumption of elites around Asia, the Middle East and Europe. By 1815, China operated the world's largest economy and benefitted greatly from its sales to eager merchants who came to its ports to buy its bounteous wares. Almost a third of Europe's silver, much of it sourced from Latin America, finished up in China to pay for these luxuries.

The Indian Ocean region supported a sizeable trade-based economy as well, much of it out of the wealthy Mughal empire that ruled the Indian subcontinent and had done so since the sixteenth century. Indian-origin spices, silks, textiles and exotic goods traversed the world. In the Pacific, the Polynesian peoples also journeyed across the expansive waters between the ocean's many islands to expand their dynasties and trading networks. Meanwhile, through what historians call the 'early modern period' (dated from about 1500), a number of European monarchies acquired 'blue water' empires as they established colonial outposts and settlements in the Americas, South Asia, Australasia, the East Indian archipelago and coastal Africa. Altogether these colonial outposts and shipping connections ensured that the world was an interconnected place in 1815.[2] At this point of time, Anglo-Europeans claimed sovereignty over 35 percent of the world's land mass.[3] China occupied about 10 percent, which was just a little more than the Russian Romanov empire that straddled Eurasia.[4]

This was not a peaceful world. Since the onset of the French Revolution in 1789, much of Europe was in constant strife. The wars fought between

1789 and 1815 brought Europe to the brink of economic ruin, cost more than 4 million people their lives and witnessed extensive military campaigns on four continents (in Europe, the Americas, northern Africa and South and South East Asia) as well as on the Atlantic Ocean. These wars caused the collapse of the centuries-old Holy Roman Empire, confirmed the independence of the recently established United States of America, inspired a break-away republic of ex-slaves in Haiti and substantiated the global naval supremacy of the British empire, the military supremacy of the Russian empire and the commercial supremacy of the Chinese who had, by dint of their geographic distance and general good sense, kept out of these 'foreign' affairs.

Our story starts in 1815, at the end of the Napoleonic Wars, a moment that marked the convergence of three decisive and interdependent developments that would have a profound impact on the future of the whole world, namely: a general peace agreement among the great European powers, the opening up of the world's seas and oceans to commerce and migration and the expansion of the industrial revolution from its place of origin in Great Britain into Europe, the Americas and across the globe. Within the next hundred years, the combination of these three developments affected the social, cultural, political and economic fabric of most societies and had a serious environmental impact on the world's flora and fauna. As a consequence, this period witnessed the phenomenal ascendancy of the economic, diplomatic and political power of what we call 'Anglo-European' societies (and what other scholars might describe as 'the West') over the rest.[5] The years between 1815 and 1914, when the First World War erupted, also brought modernity into being, creating a world that is more familiar to many of us today than that of the pre-industrial agricultural past, a world whose people were more globally connected, interdependent and aware of their interconnectedness than ever before. This book describes the contours of these nineteenth-century global transformations. We call it the 'first age of industrial globalization'.[6]

For those familiar with the large literature on the broad sweep of the nineteenth century, the reference to an 'age' will remind them of the profound works by such scholars as Eric Hobsbawm, William H. McNeill, Christopher Bayly, Richard Evans, Paul Schroeder, Paul Kennedy, Eric Jones, Jürgen Osterhammel and many others. Indeed, this book owes much to the breadth and depth of this collective scholarship and cannot, in such a short space, hope to cover the range of issues and elements of the period that these longer, more complex and erudite works examine. For example, Eric Hobsbawm wrote three whole volumes on a similar subject, each an 'age' in themselves, namely the *Age of Revolution* (1789–1848), *Age of Capital* (1848–75) and *Age of Empire* (1875–1914).[7] Hobsbawm's volumes provide a powerful dimension to the arguments on offer in this book.

What we call the 'first age of industrial globalization' is described by the other scholars almost interchangeably as the 'ascendancy of Europe' (Martin Anderson), the 'rise of the West' (McNeill), the 'birth of the modern world' (Bayly), the 'great divergence' (Kenneth Pomeranz), the 'pursuit of power' (Evans), the 'eclipse of the non-European world' (Kennedy), the 'rise of western power' (Jonathan Daly), the 'transformation of the world' (Osterhammel), the 'European miracle' (Jones) and as a 'world connecting' (Emily Rosenberg). While each of these authors accentuate different elements of the nineteenth-century past, they all acknowledge the key importance of that century to consolidating the processes of industrialization.

As we shall see, the power of the industrial revolution was critical to the advance of globalization as it accelerated the transformation of the already interconnected world of trade, production and commerce that existed in 1815 into a far more potent set of economic and political relationships. Industrialization is a process involving the widespread adoption of technological and scientific innovation, replacing manual labour with mechanical labour and speeding up manufacturing processes. The industrial revolution began in Great Britain in the eighteenth century. It globalized swiftly after 1815. The nineteenth century saw the invention and use of a swathe of new machines, materials and manufacturing methods. It witnessed the advent of locomotives, steamships, railway lines, telegraphy (which enabled messages to be passed along wired networks), electricity, synthetic dyes, quick-loading rifles, photography, cheap printing methods and (a little later) automobiles, telephone systems and aeroplanes. Industrial production relied on factories, powered by coal furnaces, bringing workers and raw materials into manufacturing hubs, around which sizeable cities grew. Industrialization accelerated the production of goods, making them cheaper and more abundant and inspiring the rise and spread of consumer and wage-labour societies. It also sped up transportation and communications, enabling people, goods, money and ideas to travel farther and faster than ever before. By 1914, a journey from London to New York by steamship took a matter of days; a trip to India via the Suez Canal took less than three weeks. A telegraph message could cover the same distances within a matter of minutes. Moving people and goods around the world had become faster, cheaper, more reliable and thus more commonplace.

Industrialization then was an inherently globalizing phenomenon, which offers one reason why this book describes the nineteenth-century industrial age as an 'age of globalization'. Effective factory production relied on the steady supply of raw materials and fuels: local sources rarely met manufacturing needs. Sourcing raw materials was a global enterprise, providing a catalyst for the establishment of vast agricultural plantations and the extraction of mineral and animal resources from across the planet, which were then shipped in large quantities across great distances back to the industrial metropoles for manufacturing. Finding markets for the resulting manufactured products was also a global exercise.

Industrialization, then, grew the global economy, redefined monetary systems, regulated rates of trade and exchange and inspired the standardization of global timekeeping. These global elements of industrialization also relied on easy access to the seas, the expansion of shipping routes, the opening up of ports, the building of railway lines and the extension of telegraph cables. By 1900, the world was more connected than it had ever been. As Figure 1.1 shows, by the turn of the twentieth century very few communities were not affected by the reach of industrialization.

Industrialization was also an imperial enterprise: it relied on the expansion of a state's power and control over territory, people and resources. Most often, industrial production occurred at home in the metropole. The rest of the empire both supplied these industrial centres with primary produce and offered markets for the resulting manufactures to be sold. Merchant ships plied the seas moving raw materials from colonial outpost to industrial metropole, and manufactured goods from metropole back to market. After 1815, the states that industrialized early or those that industrialized rapidly were also the century's most successful empires in terms of exercising control over much of the planet. By 1914, the industrial heartlands of Britain, Europe, the United States and Japan claimed dominion over more than 84 percent of the world's land mass and people. In contrast, the Chinese were latecomers to industrialization and fell victim to the imperial expansion of the other powers. By 1914, the size of the Chinese empire had shrunk to less than 10 percent of the world's land mass while Russia's had expanded, now occupying 14 percent.[8] The Mughals too were late to industrialize and rapidly fell victim to British expansionism and economic exploitation, so much so that in 1858 Britain claimed sovereignty over much of South Asia.

Just as importantly, nineteenth-century industrial power also depended on the control and expansion of global economic, commercial and communications infrastructures. In 1850 there were already 14,500 miles of railway track laid down in Europe. Within thirty years that network expanded to 101,700 miles, which equated to more than four times the circumference of the globe. By 1900, India had the fourth largest railway network in the world, consisting of more than 24,000 miles of track. Oceanic submarine telegraph cables were also laid throughout the period and by 1870 telegraphic communication spanned the globe.[9] The British dominated the overseas shipping networks throughout the nineteenth century. By 1890, its shipping tonnage was greater than all the rest of the world combined. As late as 1910, that is *after* the emergence of the United States and Germany as industrial naval powers, British shipping still controlled 40 percent of the world's trade.[10] The flow of money out of the industrial metropoles of Europe, the United

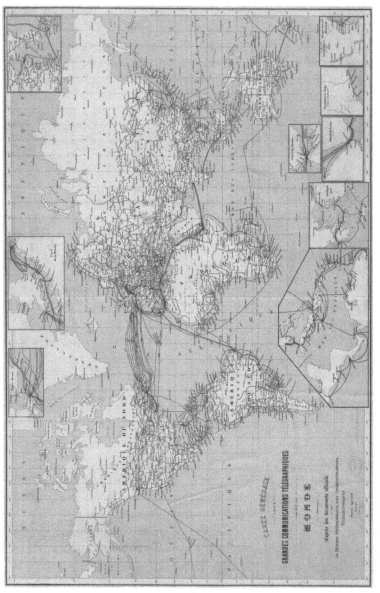

FIGURE 1.1 *Global telegraph cables, 1903. This map, created in 1903 by the International Telegraph Bureau (situated in Bern, Switzerland), shows up the network of telegraph cables that crossed the world both under the seas and oceans and across the continents. These cables enabled individuals to send messages across the planet quickly and efficiently.*

Source: C. van Hoven, 'Carte générale des grandes communications télégraphiques du monde' Bern, International Telegraph Bureau, 1903, Norman B. Leventhal Map Center at the Boston Public Library.

States and Japan through the century also ensured a financial domination by these societies over the rest. Britain dominated that process too. By 1914, 40 percent of investments in foreign countries originated in Britain, much of the rest came out of Europe, the United States and, in Asia, from Japan.[11] The British pound was the world's primary trading currency.[12]

Other signals of the fundamental impact of industrialization are clear from the following statistics. The world's population increased from about 1.1 billion to 1.8 billion between 1815 and 1914.[13] One in seven people (about 14 percent) now lived in an urban centre (as opposed to 3 percent in 1815). The size of these cities ballooned creating new social, political and welfare challenges. Perhaps even more astoundingly, more than a hundred million people traversed the world's oceans and continents in the nineteenth century, settling in new places, establishing new enterprises, bringing cultures into contact and into conflict. Invariably, these developments affected the social fabric and political cohesion of societies. It also ensured that an expectation of change and innovation (as opposed to predictability and stasis) became normalized. Industrialization effectively made the world a smaller place, easier to navigate, to communicate around and ultimately to manipulate. Because the world industrialized after 1815, it also globalized. And it was the particular way in which the world industrialized that can tell us a lot about the rise of global power, global economics and global values.

Industrialization is the most important development to affect humanity since the invention of agriculture. It is also a process that has not stopped. It continues to shape the contours of our present. Some scholars call today's highly integrated world of computers, artificial intelligence, satellite communications and social media the 'fourth industrial age', an age in which China is leading the world.

Our highly globalized present is quite clearly the product of the nineteenth-century industrial past and the rise to global power of the Anglo-European states in that century (including the United States). English is the *lingua franca* of the world today because the British people were the first to industrialize and maximized the advantages their industrialization gave. Through the nineteenth century, Britain acquired the largest empire the world has ever seen (covering almost 24 percent of the world's land surface). As owners of the world's largest navy, the British could also police the oceans and keep them relatively free for their (and everyone else's) commerce to thrive. The nineteenth century was, in so many ways, Britain's century.

It was in an attempt to replicate these British successes that industrialization quickly spread after 1815 into Europe and the United States, although it took an era of relative international peace to do so. At least at its outset, industrialization was a Eurocentric development. It would not remain so. Still, because Anglo-Europeans dominated the first waves of industrialization, they also came to dominate the world economy, its political systems and many (although by no means all) of its global cultural values. As societies became increasingly more globalized after 1815, they adopted more uniform standards of trade, exchange, even language, social customs, legal norms, property rights and dress sense. Many of these developments were influenced by what we today would describe as 'Western' (Anglo-American-European) ideas and values. The history of the 'first age of industrial globalization' then is also a story of why these Western norms still dominate our 'fourth industrial age'. Thus, it is also a tragic and destructive story, for the rise of the 'the West' came at the expense of many other people and cultures.

The dominance of Europe in terms of global power and industrial advances was not lost on contemporaries. In the 1890s, the Chinese scholar T'an Ssu T'ung described the stakes involved in 'Westernizing' China and incorporating China fully in the international economic and diplomatic system. He was desperately concerned that if China did not industrialize in line with what was happening in Europe, Japan and the Americas, then China would disappear. His words are worth quoting at length:

> We [Chinese] should extend the telegraph lines, establish post offices ... supply water, and burn electric or gas lamps for the use of the people. When the streets are well kept, the sources of pestilence will be cut off; when hospitals are numerous, the medical treatment will be excellent. We should have parks for public recreation and health. We should have a holiday every seven days to enable civil and military officials to follow the policy of (alternation between) pressure and relaxation. We should thoroughly learn the written and spoken languages of all countries so as to translate Western books and newspapers, in order to know what other countries are doing all around us; and also to train men of ability as diplomats. ... We should send people to travel to all countries to enlarge their points of view and enrich their store of information, to observe the strengths and weaknesses, the rise and fall, of other countries; to adopt all the goods points of other nations and to avoid their bad points from the start. As a result there will be none of the ships and weapons of any nation which we shall not be able to make, and none of the machines of implemento which we shall not be able to improve.[14]

T'an Ssu T'ung's fear for China's future was its subjugation to 'the West'. His hope was that the Qing empire could modernize quickly and overcome its loss of international status and power. To do that, the Chinese had to accept that they had to replicate these foreign methods and adapt them to their own needs (some scholars call this process 'defensive modernization'). That same realization inspired the rulers of Meiji Japan to embark on a rapid and highly successful process of industrialization from the 1870s on. By 1900, Japan was considered a major power, a potential rival to China and to the growing number of European empires establishing colonies and trade ports in the Asia-Pacific region.

These Chinese and Japanese examples also tell us that the story of nineteenth-century industrialization and globalization was not only about the West nor was the domination of the West over the rest a singular, uniform or even one-sided process. Modernization had many faces as well as numerous applications, agents and consequences. Every community related to the processes and impacts of modernization in different ways. Stressing the multiplicity of modernization processes and impacts on communities around the world during the nineteenth century is important.[15] Those multiplicities, however, take nothing away from the fact that what all these communities had in common was their incorporation into and interaction with an increasingly globally connected international environment: an environment dominated by extraordinary wealth and power differentials and an environment in which the agents of industrialization increasingly dominated the rest.

Among Anglo-Europeans in the nineteenth century, the rise of their industrial, economic and imperial power was a source of much reflection and self-congratulation, which many of them endowed with racial overtones.[16] The idea that white Europeans were superior (and more 'civilized') than all other peoples permeated the Anglo-European cultural landscape of the time. The prevalence of such racial conceptions is clear, for example, from an academic address made in 1904 to the Royal Geographic Society in London by Professor Halford J. MacKinder. In his seminar, which he titled 'The Geographical Pivot of History', MacKinder argued that four hundred years after Columbus 'discovered' the continent of America, the age of Columbus had finally come to an end. In 1900, almost no part of the planet was left unexplored or remained unappropriated by the forces of 'civilization'. He meant that no part of the globe was left unaffected by the spread of white Christian Europeans who had, by means of superior technology, industrialization and a will to conquer, displaced what he called the 'unknown space and barbaric chaos' of non-European communities. According to MacKinder, the dawn of the twentieth century recognized the social-economic unity of the world, which was dominated by and ruled from the heartland of industrializing Europe. Thanks to the conquest of much of the world by Europeans, in MacKinder's eyes, the globe now functioned as a single organism, its people connected by networks of railways, steamships, newspapers, telegraph cables, the exchange of money and the rapid movement of people.[17]

MacKinder was a typical European scholar of his time. He was utterly convinced of the progressive and civilizing function of European culture and dismissive of all other societies, their values and influences, which he considered alien and barbaric. He was also a highly influential scholar, appointed as the first director of the London School of Economics and Political Science. He was the founder of the academic field of geopolitics, the study of international relations and power dynamics through the lens of geographic factors. Few scholars today accept MacKinder's parochial Eurocentric version of global history and more recently historians have done much to recover the diversity and profundity of the wide range of human societies that existed in the nineteenth century. These historians also register just how destructive and revolutionary the processes of nineteenth-century industrialization were across the globe. Marilyn Lake and Henry Reynolds, for example, argue for the importance of this century in establishing the cultural dominance of 'whiteness' around the world (for more, see the Recommended Readings). Nineteenth-century industrial globalization was not a benign or kind-hearted process, it involved an extraordinary amount of violence, acculturation and adaptation.

Quite in contrast, when people like Halford J. MacKinder considered the rapid spread of Anglo-European peoples, values and empires, they saw mainly success and progress in aid of a 'civilizing' project. Their idea of 'progress' was marked by scientific and technological inventions, by the rapid growth of populations, by an upsurge in medical advances, by the expansion of industrial production and military might, by the rise of a global economy and by Europe's expanding dominion over much of the world. Had they known that much of this handiwork had important legacies in our world today, these Anglo-Europeans would doubtlessly have felt confirmed in their convictions that anything that could last so long must be 'good'.[18] There is, of course, a lot to say for the power of science and technology to improve people's lives. But there were enormous costs to creating this nineteenth-century form of 'civilization', not least to non-European communities and cultures but also to the environment and the world's flora and fauna. In other words, what at the time was considered 'progress' for some was never progress for all, or even for the majority, of the world's inhabitants.

Yet MacKinder was not wrong in asserting that there was a phenomenal rise of Anglo-European power during the nineteenth century that did indeed transform the globe. The origins of what we today consider 'first world' and 'third world' (also sometimes described as the 'global north' and 'global south') can be found in the 1800s. This book then attempts to answer the same kinds of questions as MacKinder asked in 1904, namely: How and why did the world become a more globalized place in the nineteenth century? How and why did the industrial revolution that took off in the Anglo-European world (including in the United States) after 1815 expand networks of migration and trade and transform sociopolitical and economic relationships around the world? How and why did Anglo-European systems and cultural values come to dominate that global space by the turn of the twentieth century?

Like MacKinder, we situate our explanations in the field of geopolitics. Unlike MacKinder, our answers do not emphasize the supposed superiority of European culture, nor do they suggest that all that mattered to contemporaries were these European values. Our focus is rather on the ways in which industrialization was a globalizing process that began in Europe and use that process to explain how and why Anglo-Europeans were able to dominate the international environment. In this book we acknowledge that industrialization as it went global both created and destroyed, produced new winners and many losers and transformed international power relations. In many respects, then, this book offers a prequel to Theodore H. von Laue's powerful 1987 study entitled *The World Revolution of Westernization: The Twentieth Century in Global Perspective*, by highlighting how nineteenth-century geopolitical and economic power drove the cultural and political dominance of the 'West' over the rest.[19]

Our story begins with geopolitics. Critical to the geopolitical order that helped to propel industrial globalization were the principles and practices established at the Congress of Vienna of 1815, which ended the Napoleonic Wars. The compact struck between the European great powers at Vienna aimed first and foremost at preserving their monarchies against the revolutionary forces unleashed around Europe and the Atlantic world after the American War of Independence (1775–83) and the French Revolution of 1789. In protecting these monarchies against domestic threats, the powers at Vienna also understood the urgent need to stabilize their international relations. Wars were dangerous, costly and destructive. Preventing the rise of another Napoleon was also paramount. Thus, the treaties struck at Vienna looked to redraw the map of Europe and its empires, balancing power between them, setting up buffer zones to prevent conflict and crisis and confirming the principle of war avoidance. In so doing, the architects of Vienna established what historians call the 'congress' or 'concert system', which was essentially an agreement that the great powers take responsibility for the stability of the international system and for the general peace in Europe. Though there were wars in Europe in the century after 1815, the death toll in European battles was one-seventh of the death toll from the previous century.[20]

To help contain potential conflict in Europe, the Vienna architects set up buffer zones between the great powers. They even neutralized some of these buffers, including Switzerland, Cracow and (later) Belgium, with an eye to removing a reason to go to war over them. Over time, the role of neutrality expanded. Strong and weak European powers adopted neutrality when others went to war so that they could protect their economic, imperial and foreign policy interests.[21] Neutrality aided industrialization because by avoiding war with other states, neutrals could continue to access the world economy. For most nineteenth-century governments, warfare was considered costly, neutrality was not. The 'first age of industrial globalization' then was not only an 'age of empire' and an 'age of revolution' but it was also an 'age of neutrals'.[22] The outbreak of the First World War in 1914 interrupted this 'age of neutrality' and through the course of the war brought the 'first age of industrial globalization' to an end.

This book, then, explains how the great power agreements and practices begun in 1815 enabled the industrial revolution to go global. When the European states were not focused on their continental rivalries, their people and resources could be redistributed and refocused on imperial and commercial enterprises. It was, then, in the aftermath of the Congress of Vienna that British industrialization gave Britons clear advantages in the global economy. In recognizing those advantages, other people and their governments looked to replicate the British example. The Viennese peace agreement enabled Anglo-Europeans to dominate the globalization of industrialization. In avoiding the danger of general war within the erstwhile 'Atlantic world', these powers could focus on expanding their power globally, including by military means. Where European wars were considered dangerous and to be avoided, wars against non-Europeans in aid of imperial expansion (both *formal* and *informal*) were often deemed necessary. In other words, peace at home enabled industrial imperialism to thrive abroad. Or, as the English journalist W. T. Stead explained in the 1890s, expanding 'civilization' among the Anglo-European states depended on concepts of peace, stability and prosperity, while expanding 'civilization' outwards depended on the often violent repression of non-European peoples and cultures.[23]

This is not to say, however, that the industrializing processes of the nineteenth century overturned all the old ways of past societies or that the majority of people lived in sprawling industrial cities by the turn of the century. The historian Arno Mayer is quite right to remind us of the social and cultural continuities that connected the pre-industrial era to the world of 1900 (although he may have overstated their importance to the causes of the First World War).[24] Historians of the non-European world and indigenous communities are also right to stress how local cultures continued to dominate people's belief systems and priorities. Hundreds of millions continued to live in non-industrialized agricultural communities, which was even true within the heartlands of industrial Europe. Overwhelmingly, the vast majority of people lived in states that were monarchies of one variant or another. But these realities take nothing away from the fact that at the turn of the twentieth century, the tentacles of the industrial revolution, often augmented by intense imperial rivalry, reached into every community connected to the ever-growing global network of commerce, migration and communications. These networks included all seaports, all stops on the growing number of railway routes that crossed the continents and all places with a telegraph exchange, which as Figure 1.1 highlights included much of the planet.

This book uses the framework of geopolitics (that concept which MacKinder helped to formulate in 1904) to describe the industrial and globalization processes in play during the nineteenth century. Geopolitics also explains why we end 'the first age of industrial globalization' in 1918 at the formal conclusion of the tumultuous First World War. That war shattered the principles that dominated the international diplomatic system since 1815. The war, which began in Europe in July 1914, pulled the world's industrial empires into a maelstrom of a global industrial conflict from which almost no community (be they European or non-European) could escape. The First World War devastated the global economy, cost tens of millions of people their lives and millions more their livelihoods. Even more people would die in the civil wars that followed. The war witnessed the collapse of four European empires that had played a prominent role in the establishment and operation of the 1815 international system (namely Russia, Austria-Hungary, Germany/ Prussia and the Ottomans) and it gravely weakened the other two (Britain and France). Only the rapidly rising industrial powers of the United States and Japan benefitted from this Great War. They did so, in part, because the former stayed out of the war for so long as a neutral and the latter fought a much more limited war against the weakly held German outposts in Asia-Pacific. In this sense, both states successfully practiced policies that were at the core of the nineteenth-century international system.

In 1917, the contours of a new 'second age of industrial globalization' began to emerge with the United States' entry into the war as an 'associated' (not allied) power and the astonishing success of the militant communist Bolsheviks in Russia, who claimed to offer the global masses of workers and peasants an alternative future to that of imperialism, capitalism and nationalism. The Russian Revolutions of 1917 and the Bolshevik exit from the Great War in 1918 marked a decisive break with the international system that the Romanovs had helped to create in 1815. The first appearance of American troops in force in the western European theatre of war in that same year, 1918, marked another break with the system the European powers had dominated since 1815. Together, these two actions initiated the 'short' twentieth century as the 'second age of industrial globalization', and one in which the superpowers of the United States and the Soviet Union played a dominant role. That century would finish in 1991 with the collapse of the Soviet Union and the end of the Cold War.

In setting up its periodization of 1815–1918, this book utilizes two types of history: that of 'top-down' international historians (who focus on states, their governance, their interrelationships and their elites, and the political, economic and cultural systems in which they functioned and used to sustain their power) and that of 'bottom-up' social-economic and cultural historians (who focus on individuals, groups and the various masses within societies as they defined and presented themselves and interacted with and affected the power structures imposed by governments and elites). In explaining the trajectories that defined the nineteenth century, traditional international historians prioritize explanations that account for the decisions of states and their leaders, especially considerations of how and why they went to war, how they managed international crises and dealt with or shaped the international diplomatic system.[25] International histories of the nineteenth century often begin in 1815. They describe the establishment of the Congress system in Vienna that aimed at sustaining peace and stability and then recount how that system ultimately failed in 1914 with the outbreak of the First World War. We might describe these types of histories as 'war-to-war' explanations, which privilege a narrative of diplomatic crisis and focus primarily on the agents of state and global power.

Social-economic and cultural historians tend to be critical of diplomatic historians. In contrast, they privilege historical explanations that account for sociopolitical power shifts and cultural perceptions and reduce the role of states in their analysis. They often begin their accounts of the nineteenth century with the French revolution of 1789 and stress the vital importance of ideas and identities in explaining shifting power dynamics. Social histories of the nineteenth century are rarely 'war-to-war' ones. Instead they focus on the concept of revolution, fundamental societal change and the violence that ensued in the struggle for the seizure of social, political and economic power within a state or empire. These histories foreground representations and identities in their narratives and categorize the 1800s as a century of immense upheaval and as a century that brought into being the modern world. Just as traditional international histories rarely explain the social and cultural impact of diplomatic developments, social-economic and cultural historians rarely reflect on the dynamics of the international diplomatic system to account for the shifts of nineteenth-century power. Even Bayly's phenomenal 2004 book *The Birth of the Modern World*, which is essential reading for anyone who wishes to truly understand nineteenth-century modernity, barely mentions the Congress of Vienna or the international system birthed in Europe in 1815 that enabled the processes of Anglo-European industrialization and modernization to succeed.[26]

From our perspective, it is impossible to explain the first age of industrial globalization that appeared after 1815 without understanding the role played by the political-diplomatic power system. It is equally impossible to do justice to the importance of that age without recognizing the fundamental socio-economic, political and cultural impact of industrializing processes around the world. To that end, the following nine chapters offer a synthesis of different historical approaches, not only political and diplomatic but also social, economic, environmental, intellectual and cultural. Like the inspirational historian S. A. M. Adshead, we prioritize explanations that focus on the rise of institutions and networks that connected people across the globe and integrated their everyday lives.[27]

Above all, the following nine chapters present the history of the nineteenth century as one of fundamental change at almost every level of human interaction. Almost no community escaped the consequences of the industrializing processes that exploded in the 1800s. Of course, some were more powerfully affected by those changes than others, but even the secluded peoples living in the jungles of the Amazon or present-day Papua New Guinea were impacted by the environmental changes wrought by nineteenth-century industrialization. As such, this book is a history of conflict and the physical, emotional and conceptual violence that occurred as 'old' met 'new' and as individuals, societies, states and empires were confronted with industrialization in its variety of guises.

By necessity, this book is also a history of contradictions, juxtapositions and paradoxes. Industrialization wreaked rapid change in all societies that encountered it. Some of this change was planned and intended. Some change was 'accidental' and unintended for good and ill. Of course, where there is change, there are those who benefit and those who lose, those who embrace it and those who resist. The story of global industrialization is therefore a story of winners and losers. It is also a history of *unifying* and *diverging* forces.[28] On the one hand, the century witnessed the establishment of common ways of organizing communities and countries, of developing rules and political values to regulate the relationship within and between those countries and even of setting common 'bodily practices' (how to dress, eat, live and think). On the other hand, the increasing interaction between cultures and communities during the nineteenth century heightened the sense of difference between them, at times fuelling conflict and aggressive assertions of identity and rights.

As an example, by the year 1900, the political idea of *nationalism* came to dominate how people thought about their identity and political loyalties. Nationalism was both a unifying ideal (enabling individuals from different socio-economic backgrounds to claim a common identity) and a provocative and divisive concept that pitted nations and ethnic groups against one another or against the wider empire in which they often subsisted. Nationalism was the most important political ideal to come out of the nineteenth century. It would also determine the trajectories of global power in the twentieth century.

But nationalism was not the only important political concept to develop during the nineteenth century. In addition to contesting imperial ideals, it was often considered alongside the idea of *internationalism*. Internationalism was a fluid concept with numerous variations: there were liberal internationalists, Marxist and socialist internationalists, Fabian internationalists, religious internationalists and so forth. What all proponents of internationalism had in common was their focus on the interconnections between different people and the assertion of a common humanity beyond the nation (and empire). Like nationalism, internationalism also shaped the contours of the twentieth-century world, including advancing the equally important global principles of *humanitarianism* and *human rights*. Nationalism and internationalism were largely interdependent concepts, both were products of the increasingly globalized world forged in the 1800s.

The rest of this book is organized around a number of key premises. Each chapter focuses on a central theme that helps to explain the global contours of the industrializing processes of the nineteenth century. Chapter 2 begins with the central importance of geopolitics to understanding the rise of Anglo-European power in the global sphere after 1815. Chapter 3 connects these geopolitical developments to economics and shows how the stabilization of Anglo-European diplomacy opened up the seas and enabled industrializers to expand rapidly and globally. In so doing, the chapter describes nineteenth-century imperialism as an industrial process and shows how the empires that successfully industrialized came to dominate the international environment, economically, diplomatically and militarily.

Chapter 4 addresses the growth of a global infrastructure enabling a relatively open and easy flow of money, goods, people and ideas. The chapter includes both changes to the physical environment (such as the building of railway lines, the laying of telegraph cables and the digging of interoceanic canals) and conceptual ones (including the standardization of time, money and scientific values, as well as international rules to regulate the conduct of states and companies). It highlights the importance of rising literacy, written documents, newspapers and the development of government bureaucracies to track people, their wealth and their ideas. It also shows how overwhelming Anglo-European standards were to dominating the physical and conceptual infrastructure of globalization.

Chapter 5 turns to the human face of globalization, charting the massive flows of human migration across the planet during the nineteenth century. It links these to the expansion of both *formal* and *informal* webs of empire. Globalization and imperialism were also built on a great amount of violence and destruction. Chapter 6 looks at the environmental impacts of industrial globalization which threatened species with extinction, damaged the habitat and ecosystems of flora and fauna in many parts of the world and contaminated and often undermined the stability of many societies. Chapter 7 addresses the role of warfare in the nineteenth century and focuses particularly on the military campaigns conducted within, by and between the industrializing empires. These wars highlight not only how significant industrialization was to giving these powers a military and technological advantage over their rivals but also how important diplomatic restraint and war avoidance was to helping these industrial rivals focus on their imperial and globalizing missions.

Chapter 8 focuses on the spectrum of ideas that globalized during the nineteenth century and highlights the most important of these and the ways they impacted how contemporaries considered themselves and their place in the world. It emphasizes the significance of industrialization, global interconnectedness and the global capitalist environment to advancing concepts of ethnic nationalism, socialism, Marxism, liberalism, anarchism, anti-colonialism, racial differentiation, class consciousness, internationalism, social conservatism, democracy, women's rights and so forth. It brings out both the ideas that helped to stabilize the power of the industrial empires and those that challenged, critiqued and undermined that power. In so doing, it emphasizes just how important the creation of the 'international' as a sociopolitical arena was as a feature of the nineteenth century and brings out the new challenges at play in the geopolitical sphere by the early twentieth century, many of which helped to bring about the First World War.

The global origins of that war are considered in Chapter 9, which describes the breakdown of the system of diplomatic restraint that had dominated global relations since 1815. The European powers who had set up the system and had benefited most from it were also the ones who brought that system to a decisive and calamitous close between 1914 and 1918. Chapter 10, then, describes the contours of the First World War as a global total war which reshaped the geostrategic and geopolitical balance of power, ending the conflict-ridden 'first age of industrial globalization' and bringing the next conflict-ridden century into being.

By no means do we consider this book a complete history of the nineteenth century. We do hope, however, that it offers a useful starting point for readers to consider the contours of this key century which did so much to shape the world we inhabit today.

Study questions

1. What is industrialization? Why does it matter as a force (or process) of historical change?

2. Why can the period 1815–1918 be defined as an age of 'industrial globalization'? What were its component parts?

3. Though powerful changes occurred throughout the nineteenth century, what continuities endured alongside these changes?

4. How do international historians differ from socio-economic and cultural historians in their approaches to the past? How do these differences matter in explaining the history of the nineteenth-century world?

Recommended readings

C. A. Bayly, *The Birth of the Modern World 1780–1914: Global Connections and Comparisons*. Blackwell, 2004: 'Introduction', pp. 1–21.

Paul James, Manfred B. Steger, 'A genealogy of "globalization": The career of a concept', *Globalizations* 11, 4, 2014, pp. 417–34.

Marilyn Lake, Henry Reynolds, *Drawing the Global Colour Line: White Man's Countries and the International Challenge of Racial Equality*. Cambridge UP, 2012: 'Introduction', pp. 1–12.

J. M. Roberts, *The New Penguin History of the World*. Penguin, 2002: Chapter 5 'The European world hegemony', pp. 789–812.

Peter N. Stearns, *The Industrial Revolution in World History*. Fourth edition, Westview Press, 2013: Introduction 'Defining the industrial revolution', pp. 1–18.

Peter N. Stearns, *The Industrial Turn in World History*. Routledge, 2017: Preface 'Why do we need another look at industrial society?', pp. vii–xiii.

Theodore H. von Laue, *The World Revolution of Westernization: The Twentieth Century in Global Perspective*. Oxford UP, 1987: 'Introduction', pp. xi–xx.

2

Of concerts and restraints: The international diplomatic system, 1815–56

When setting time periods around their arguments, historians rarely feel encumbered by calendar years. The nineteenth century for them is almost never dated from 1800 to 1900.[1] Where they start and finish their periodization depends in large part on what relevance they give to key events and developments. The periodization of this book is no exception. We begin the 'long' nineteenth century in 1815, while other scholars often use 1789 (the French revolution) or even 1776 (the American Declaration of Independence) as its starting point.[2] Certainly, both these dates witnessed a major break with the past and brought new dynamics into play that were powerful catalysts of nineteenth-century industrialization and globalization. But our emphasis is on 1815, the year that the Napoleonic Wars, which were an outcome of the French revolution, came to a decisive end; and the year that the War of 1812, fought between the United States and Great Britain over who controlled the trade that crossed the Atlantic Ocean, petered out. In 1815, the upheavals of almost three decades of interstate conflict that crossed the world wound down. The early modern period, at least as Europeans considered it, also concluded with these wars. Europe, Great Britain and the United States now looked to reconfigure their security at home and abroad.

The wars fought in and by Europeans and Americans in the period 1775 and 1815 were decisive. In successfully establishing the United States of America, the American War of Independence (1775–83) fought against the British crown helped to legitimize the promise of republican idealism and revolutionary action around the world.[3] It certainly inspired French revolutionaries in 1789 to effect the overthrow of the French monarchy (and cost the French king and queen their heads), establishing a French republic and triggering a series of wars between the citizen armies of France and the other European monarchies (who looked to restore the Bourbon family to the French crown and prevent revolution in their own lands). In 1799, the French general Napoleon Bonaparte installed himself as Consul of France after returning from a series of successful battles in northern Africa and the Middle East. In 1804, Napoleon declared himself Emperor. By this stage, Napoleonic France ruled much of the European continent. In 1806, it caused the collapse of the centuries-old Holy Roman Empire. But after Napoleon's disastrous military campaign in Russia in 1812 and a series of further defeats in Europe, a coalition of European armies invaded France and captured Paris in 1814. Napoleon abdicated and was forcibly exiled to the Mediterranean island of Elba.

The wars that were waged in the aftermath of the French revolution of 1789 were global affairs. Between 1792 and 1814, military campaigns were conducted in Europe, in India, in the Americas, in northern Africa, South East Asia and the Middle East and on the Atlantic Ocean. Revolutionary wars of independence also raged across the Caribbean and South American continent. Altogether, these conflagrations cost more than 4 million people their lives. Britain's naval campaigns against the French resulted in a protracted economic war between the two rivals, which resulted in major disruptions to overseas trade getting to continental European ports after the naval battle of Trafalgar in 1805.[4] These campaigns devastated the European economy and had a decisive impact on the triangular trade system of the Atlantic world. They also disrupted the economic affairs of the fledgling nation of the United States. In 1812, that country declared war on Great Britain in response to Britain's restrictive wartime trade policies, its seizure of goods from American merchant vessels, the impressment of American sailors into service on British ships and the raids onto American soil by First Nations' people from British-controlled Canada. The war came to an unsatisfactory end in February 1815, after both sides recognized that neither could win.

Altogether, the wars of the 1792–1815 period devastated the European economy, seriously impacted on American economic security and turned the Atlantic Ocean and Mediterranean Sea into war zones.[5] For Europeans and many in the Americas, it represented a devastating age of warfare. China, on the other hand, only profited from these distant military conflicts. During the eighteenth century, China benefitted from the able rule of two long-lived emperors ensuring political stability. Its economy dominated the region and many of its goods were in demand worldwide. The great Russian General Alexander Suvorov even wore Chinese silk when he rode into battle against the French army. When tremors of these distant wars came close to the Chinese coast, as they did when British vessels intercepted American ships in their war of 1812, the Qing ruler noted the 'petty quarrel' between these 'small nations' and warned that China would destroy foreign warships and curtail trade if such annoyances continued.[6] Though change was on the horizon, in 1815 China was the world's richest empire in part because it was not wrecked by warfare and revolution.

Still, after 1815, the Qing dynasty was unable to sustain its commercial pre-eminence. Within two decades, it would be surpassed by the rise of a new breed of industrial 'blue water' empires, of which Great Britain was the strongest, largest, wealthiest and most influential. By aiming at peaceful relations between themselves, the European powers and the United States enabled the rise of their collective industrial, economic, military and imperial power, at the expense of almost all other societies, China's included. Through the course of the nineteenth century, these Western states profited from the condition of an international diplomatic peace in ways that the Chinese (and other empires like the Mughals) did not.

In 1814, then, the representatives of Europe's many monarchies, princedoms and independent cities met for a grand diplomatic spectacle in Vienna, the capital of the Austrian Habsburg empire. The Habsburg Emperor, Francis I, almost bankrupted himself in wining, dining and entertaining his illustrious guests.[7] The key concern of these diplomats and leaders was how to reconstruct the European order to provide stability for them all. The collapse of Napoleonic France had unravelled the social, economic and diplomatic fabric of most European countries and the surviving aristocrats of the pre-1789 era quickly laid claim to their traditional lands. How the map of Europe would be reconfigured was effectively up for grabs.

Still, the men and women who negotiated the Vienna settlement in 1814 and 1815 were also aware that they could not conduct their dynastic affairs as if the American and French revolutions had not occurred. The only way to prevent the onset of another anti-monarchical revolutionary movement was to mediate their competing dynastic claims and join forces against domestic upheaval. Compromise rather than hegemony was the order of the day. The importance of this great power cooperation was heightened when on 20 March 1815 Napoleon returned from exile to reinstall himself as emperor of France. The European monarchs scrambled their forces to defeat Napoleon's armies at the battle of Waterloo, ending Napoleon's hundred-day reign.[8] After Waterloo, the ongoing peace of Europe became a pressing priority: no new Napoleon should be allowed to come to power and rule Europe. Furthermore, the revolutionary impulses that might stem from below (from the people) and challenge the 'right to rule' of the re-established monarchies and empires needed to be quelled.

The Treaty of Vienna signed in 1815, then, was a decidedly conservative one. It aimed at restoring power to the old order (which is the reason some historians describe the period 1815–48 as an 'age of restoration'). But the leaders who composed the Vienna treaty looked both backwards and forwards. They aimed to preserve their right to rule against popular revolutionary forces *and* sought to achieve that end by aligning that priority with the other monarchies (which was something new). In the context of the revolutionary changes and movements in play, it made complete sense that the best way to protect their stability was to establish principles of collective security that would avoid a war breaking out between them. They understood all too well that given an opportunity the people were dangerous (which is the reason many historians call the period 1815–48 an ongoing 'age of revolution').

The historian Paul Schroeder describes the Congress of Vienna as the most successful peace treaty of all time in large part because the principles established in Vienna in 1815 shaped the contours of the international diplomatic system for the ensuing century and ensured that no general war developed between the great powers until the outbreak of the First World War.[9] While the terms of the Vienna treaty were contested at various times between 1815 and 1914, the general principles established at Vienna had a remarkable longevity.

What then were these principles? First, the Treaty of Vienna aimed at restoring monarchical power to Europe. This meant that after 1815, most European countries were ruled by a monarch or aristocratic family, including in France, where Louis XVIII (the brother of the beheaded Louis XVI) came to power. Second, the map of Europe was reconfigured to restore traditional lands back to the aristocratic families. Even France was returned almost to its pre-revolution borders. There was, however, a limitation: where ownership of lands was contested between the monarchs or where land ownership would favour one power too greatly in relationship to its neighbours, compromise solutions were usually embraced. Thus, the third and perhaps most important foundation of the Vienna treaty was that no one country could dominate the continent like Napoleonic France had done. The monarchs agreed that an equilibrium of power should exist between them and agreed on a series of principles to balance that power relatively equally. The diplomatic system that evolved in the wake of the Vienna treaty was invariably labelled the 'concert of Europe' or the 'congress system'. It aimed at compromise, negotiation and collective solutions rather than unilateral or bilateral decision-making.

The congress system worked because the compromises developed by the European powers were effective ones. They depended on the willingness of the European governments (and particularly the great powers of Russia, Britain, Austria, Prussia and France) to negotiate solutions to international crises. The historian Hedley Bull described this willingness to compromise a 'custodial duty': a recognition that if the great powers collectively managed each and every diplomatic crisis, however small, then wars could be avoided, revolutions could be prevented and stability could be sustained.[10] Restoration largely depended on the avoidance of revolutions and wars: revolutions because the people could overthrow the monarchies, and wars because they created insecurities that might lead the people to revolt.

The Congress of Vienna treaty then established key principles to avoid war between rival European nations. In the first place, it did so by setting up buffer states and independent cities. The Holy Roman Empire, for example, was not re-established. It was replaced by the Austrian Habsburg empire, the Kingdom of Prussia, and 37 other independent German territories, each with their own ruler (see Figure 2.1). All these German lands (but not the Habsburg empire's non-German lands) were loosely brought together in a 'German Confederation', which had no sovereign power (it could not go to war), but its representatives met regularly to discuss common policies and goals, particularly economic ones. In effect, the 37 smaller German states balanced out the rivalry between Prussia and Austria. At the same time, they acted as an effective geostrategic buffer between Prussia and France.[11] In eastern Europe too, the creation of the independent city of Cracow aimed at balancing the rival claims of the Russians, Prussian and Austrian Habsburgs to the city. Because they all wanted it and could not abide one of their rivals holding on to it, they all agreed to Cracow's independence.

To further aid the balancing of power, key buffer territories were also neutralized.[12] This meant that these territories were considered unassailable. No one could attack a neutralized state without the other powers coming to the aid of the neutral. Switzerland was neutralized in 1815 for that reason. Situated in the heart of Europe, the numerous Swiss cantons had competing cultural and historical allegiances to the various European monarchies: a recipe for potential strife. To avoid war breaking out over who controlled the cantons, the Federation of Switzerland came into being, which brought the cantons together and prevented anyone from going to war with the Swiss. In turn, the Swiss could not go to war with another European country. In a similar fashion the city of Cracow was also neutralized to protect it from the ambitions of its powerful neighbours.

The dual purpose of the Congress of Vienna then was to keep Europe's monarchies from going to war with one another and to establish principles that would help them to keep the peace in Europe. Multilateral negotiations, in the form of congresses and ambassadorial meetings, became the norm after 1815, particularly in moments of high diplomatic tension (e.g. when war threatened between two European states). Neutrality and neutralization too featured prominently in European diplomatic affairs after 1815. Thus after 1815, while the European governments always had the option to go to war, they often chose not to do so, opting for diplomatic solutions instead. Furthermore, when warfare did occur in Europe (which it did on and off throughout the

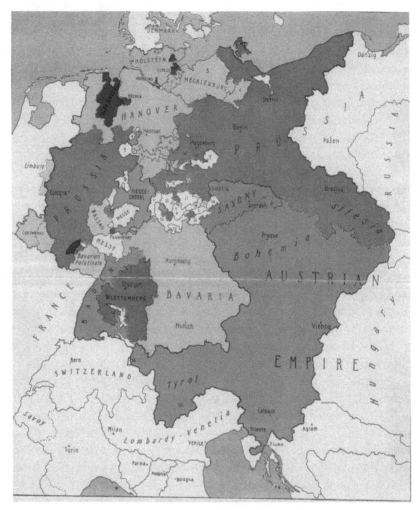

FIGURE 2.1 *The German Confederation, 1814–66. The Confederation of German states was a product of the Congress of Vienna and encapsulated its principles really well. The confederation was a loose association of independent states (both countries and cities), all ruled by their own monarch or aristocratic family. Prussia and Austria were the most important and powerful states in the confederation, but it was in their collective configuration that compromise and power was balanced between them. As Paul Schroeder shows, the thirty seven smaller German states managed the political equilibrium within the confederation (including between Prussia and Austria) and within Europe, acting as geostrategic and diplomatic counterweights to manage the great power dynamics of the great powers (France, Prussia, Austria, Russia and Great Britain). Much like, Switzerland (also pictured), which was established as a permanently neutralized federation of cantons at Vienna in 1815, the smaller German states were essential intermediaries in managing the European concert system.*
Source: Getty Images, 464784927.

century), most other European countries declared their neutrality rather than join in. As a result, *neutrality* (the choice not to go to war) and *neutralization* (the long-term neutrality of a state) were key mechanisms for protecting the principles of the congress system.

But it was not only the European powers who committed to a foreign policy of war avoidance, neutrality and collective security. In the aftermath of 1815, the United States government too decided that it would adopt a long-term position of neutrality when it came to European affairs. Instead, it would focus on its own 'sphere of influence', which in 1823 was defined by American president James Monroe as the continents of North and South America and their surrounding waters, including the Caribbean Sea. Monroe feared interference from Europe in the Americas and hoped his assertion of rights would protect the United States' security.[13] The Monroe Doctrine effectively kept the United States from going to war with a European great power until 1917 (when it declared war on Germany and Austria-Hungary during the First World War), although it fought the Spanish in Cuba and the Philippines in 1898 and undertook wars against the Mexicans in Texas in the 1840s.

With the United States' return to neutrality in 1815 (it had originally declared itself neutral in 1793), the Atlantic Ocean also returned to a peaceful condition. Europeans and Americans could now focus on imperial ventures that crossed continents and seas, enabling industrial processes and the expansion of their economic power alongside (see Chapter 3). The general peace in Europe and across the Atlantic world effectively underwrote the ascendancy of their collective global power during the nineteenth century. In other words, while the principles of the Congress of Vienna were decidedly Eurocentric, they had numerous global ramifications.

The Congress of Vienna not only rejigged the respective borders of Europe, it also confirmed a recalibration of the imperial holdings of the European powers. Great Britain was the biggest winner in these imperial stakes, acquiring Malta, Mauritius, the Caribbean islands of St Lucia, Guyana, Trinidad and Tobago and the Cape Colony in southern Africa as well as extending its authority over the island of Ceylon (Sri Lanka). Given its naval supremacy, the ingredients for British nineteenth-century super-power status were firmly in place by 1815. Still, from the perspective of many Britons, these new imperial acquisitions did not make up for the loss of the United States in 1783.

For many contemporaries, the age of European empires seemed to be over in 1815. The Latin American colonies (most of which were ruled by Portugal or Spain) had conducted protracted military and political campaigns during the Napoleonic era and were on the brink of declaring their own independence, much as the United States had done in 1776. After years of violent resistance, mainly by rebellious African slaves, France recognized Haiti as an independent state in 1804. Brazil acquired independence from Portugal in 1825. Argentina finally broke free from Spain in 1816. Venezuela and Mexico did so in 1821, Ecuador in 1822, Bolivia in 1824 and Uruguay in 1828.[14] The fact that the European great powers did little to help the French, Spanish or Portuguese in their wars to repress these anti-imperial movements signaled how focused they were on the stability of the European continent first and foremost. In 1815, overseas empires seemed a burdensome and dangerous endeavour that drained military and economic resources.

Yet, as Chapter 3 shows, a new age of empire would evolve after 1815 as the seas reopened, which allowed for the relatively easy movement of people (settlers, soldiers, sailors, missionaries and colonial officials), money, goods and ideas across the world. That access was enabled by the relative peace of Europe and the principles of the congress system: diplomatic restraint, neutrality and war avoidance among the great powers. During the nineteenth century, the industrializing powers in Europe (followed later in the century by the United States and Japan) thrived in large part because they were able to project their economic, military and cultural power outwards: acquiring new territories, claiming sovereignty over other communities and expanding trade and investment networks globally. Because they felt relatively safe 'at home', they could focus on supporting these global economic and imperial pursuits.

Thus, the nineteenth century became a century of Anglo-European expansionism and witnessed the phenomenal growth of industrial empires in Europe, North America and abroad. Furthermore, because the chance of interstate warfare in Europe declined after 1815, smaller weaker European states also felt safe enough to present themselves as long-term neutrals, allowing them to focus on industrialization and even the expansion of their own 'blue water' empires. As a result, a vast interdependent international economy evolved out of Europe and the United States, which was supported by the relative security of the world's oceans. That international economic system was dominated by the industrializing states. Their economic power also underwrote the great powers' military and diplomatic strength, which continued to dominate the international system. Across the nineteenth century, the powers that industrialized early or fastest were the winners. Almost everyone else lost out.

This is not, of course, to say that the concert system always worked or that Europe was actually a politically stable or peaceful place. The fact that many historians call the period 1815–48 an 'age of revolution' highlights just how precarious the political power was of the various European monarchies both within and outside the continent.[15] The 'restoration' principles of the Congress of Vienna came under repeated attack 'from below' after 1815.[16] For all their careful planning, restoring the European monarchies to full power, let alone maintaining their control over their empires, was even more difficult than the

Vienna diplomats had imagined. Still, throughout the crises of the 'age of restoration', the overarching success of the congress system lay in the ability of the European powers to avoid general warfare. Even during the tumultuous revolutions of 1848, the European monarchies acknowledged their mutual dependency on the principles of the concert system: diplomatic restraint, war avoidance, neutrality and the prevention of hegemonic power in Europe. These same principles ensured that even the 1853–6 Crimean War, pitting Russia against a coalition of France, Britain, Sardinia and the Ottoman empire, remained militarily and economically localized (see below).

It is also important to recognize that the compromise peace established at Vienna was precarious, not least because the monarchies of Europe did not have a long tradition of working together. Despite acknowledging a common cause in 1815 (to prevent revolution and the rise of another Napoleon), the pre-existing rivalries between Europe's monarchies were well-entrenched. Some were linked to long-held religious enmities, others to economic and geostrategic rivalries, yet others to different systems of rulership. Britons, on the whole, prided themselves on their parliamentary system of politics which, even though it only gave a tiny proportion of land-owning men the vote, also made them unwilling to support the autocratic rule of the Russian tsar, Austrian emperor, Prussian king or Ottoman sultan. The British model of parliamentary politics explains in part why Britain did not join the 'Holy Alliance' set up by Tsar Alexander I at Vienna in 1815, which linked the Russian, Prussian and Austrian monarchies together. This 'Holy Alliance' of Christian kings (albeit Orthodox, Lutheran and Catholic monarchs) promoted their shared duty to protect the peace they had helped to create in Europe. Given that two of these powers (Austria and Russia) were multi-ethnic empires that bordered the multi-ethnic empire ruled by the Islamic Ottoman sultanate, this show of unity was particularly useful when ethnic nationalist challenges arose, as these were often infused with religious dimensions.

Still, the Vienna treaty and its underlying principles seemed to work. In its immediate aftermath, the powers solved key issues by holding more congresses: the congress at Aix-la-Chapelle in 1818 aimed at integrating France fully into the restored European order; the conference at Troppau in 1820 looked to suppress a liberal revolution in Naples; the one at Laibach in 1821 aimed at supporting Habsburg intervention in suppressing a revolution in the Two Sicilies; while the Verona congress of 1822 met without Britain and allowed France the right to invade Spain to repress a liberal rebellion against the Spanish throne (once the French forces succeeded, they left Spain).[17] At the time of the Verona congress, the powers also realized that meeting in congress each time a crisis hit was not necessarily the most efficient or useful way to come up with acceptable solutions, not least because it also exposed their rivalries. The British government certainly had become more entrenched in its position of non-interference in domestic European affairs and refused to partake in anti-revolutionary actions outside its own empire. Rather than spell the end of the concert system, however, as some historians claim, from the 1820s on these same powers resorted to less overt politics of compromise. Yet they continued to micromanage global crises and aimed at protecting the systemic balance of power and their own place within it.

The effectiveness of this diplomacy of compromise is well illustrated by the manner in which the great powers dealt with the Greek nationalist uprising in the 1820s.[18] For centuries, the Ottoman sultans had ruled over a vast empire that stretched across the Middle East, south-west Europe and northern Africa. The empire survived the Napoleonic Wars but in 1815 Sultan Mehmed II also recognized that his empire faced numerous internal threats, not least because a number of ethnic groups looked to break away as independent states. The Ottomans ruled their state as a decentralized structure, empowering local administrators to make decisions, impose taxes and organize their regions with considerable autonomy. While this system of governance helped to prevent conflict arising between the various communities within the empire, it also made it easier for particular groups to vie for autonomy. The Greeks were one such group.

The viability of the Ottoman empire was of grave concern to the European great powers. They all recognized that as long as the Ottoman empire remained intact, it would prevent the rest of them competing for the geostrategic opportunities the region proffered. The Middle East was essential to them all, but for Britain it was particularly critical due to the proximity of its prized imperial position in India. Similarly, the Russians saw the region as an important outlet from the Black Sea to the Mediterranean and Red Seas. To prevent competition between them and to keep to the principles of the concert system, the European monarchies recognized that the Ottoman empire was best kept intact. Any serious crisis within the Ottoman empire, then, was recognized as a crisis of the European concert system.

Thus, when the Greeks rebelled against the Ottoman authorities in the early 1820s, the European great powers were placed on high alert. The conflict between the Greeks and their allies (including Romanian mercenaries) and the Ottoman armies was brutal, involving militia bands and the slaughter of civilians. More than a third of the Turkish inhabitants of the Peloponnese were killed off by Greek revolutionaries in April 1821. In reprisal, nearly seventy thousand Greeks out of a population of one hundred thousand on the island of Chios were either killed or forced into slavery by soldiers loyal to the empire.[19] In January 1822, the Greeks used the language of revolution made famous in the United States and France in the 1770s and 1780s to declare their independence from Ottoman rule.

The Greek situation inspired widespread support throughout Europe and the United States, where the path to independence by a Christian people over a Muslim overlord was hailed as inspirational by many co-religionists and liberal revolutionaries.[20] It also gravely concerned the great power governments, who feared the collapse of Ottoman power. So, while many Britons happily raised money and offered loans to fund the Greek rebels, the British government felt compelled to find ways to end the war. The Russians too were deeply concerned.[21] On the one hand, they were incensed at the Ottomans for killing fellow Orthodox Christians (the Greeks); on the other, they were worried about the impact of the Greek rebellion for destabilizing the Ottoman regime and inflaming anti-imperial revolutions elsewhere in Europe and in their own empire.

Amidst many diplomatic power plays, in the end, the Russian, British and French governments cooperated to force a solution on the Ottoman regime. In 1827, they signed the Treaty of London which asked the Ottomans to recognize nominal Greek independence (in return the Greeks would pay a vassals' fee to the Ottomans). When Mehmed II rejected the treaty, rallied his troops and obtained military support from the Egyptian leader, Mehmet Ali, Britain, France and Russia combined their naval forces and successfully defeated the Ottoman and Egyptian navies at the Battle of Navarino. It was only after the Russians sent a force of one hundred thousand troops into the Danubian principalities (starting the Russo-Turkish War of 1828–9) and came to within marching distance of the Ottoman capital of Constantinople however, that Mehmed II sued for peace.

The resulting Treaty of Adrianople (1830) highlights just how willing the Russian Tsar Nicholas I was to enforce the general principles of the congress system. While his troops were within reach of Constantinople and occupied the Danubian principalities, Nicholas I did not press for major concessions. He did not insist on access to the Dardanelles Straits (which connected the Black Sea to the Mediterranean), for example, although Russia did obtain sovereignty over the mouth of the Danube river. In order to protect the existence of the Ottoman empire and not upset the European balance of power, Nicholas I accepted the need to return the terms of the 1827 Treaty of London.[22] While the Greeks demanded full independence, they too were made to accede to the 1827 agreement: Greece would not become a republic but instead was governed as an absolutist monarchy ruled by the Bavarian prince Otto von Wittelsbach, whose position was created and protected by the great powers. The size of his territory was smaller than most Greeks desired, housing about a third of all Greeks who resided in the Balkan region, but the Greeks now had their own state.

The Greek road to independence in the 1820s highlights a number of essential attributes of congress system and one of its ongoing concerns.

Though the British, French and Russians had different state interests, all three were drawn into the domestic crisis of the Ottoman empire and, in the end, worked together to address and limit the course of Greek nationalism and moderate its impact on the Ottoman empire. Although the 'concert of Europe' intervened to protect a revolt against a legitimate power, the intervention was nevertheless intended to contain revolution and maintain a viable Ottoman empire. It also confirmed the principle of monarchical rule that sat at the heart of the concert system. The management of the Greek situation demonstrates how fundamental differences between the European great powers (for example between Britain and Russia) could coexist with a desire and willingness to work together to maintain a general peace.

The Greek example also highlights two ongoing concerns for the stability of Europe's multi-ethnic empires, that of *self-determination* (the desire for self-rule by an ethnic group) and *irredentism* (the desire to recover lost people and lands of a newly created nation-state). While the Greek revolt provided inspiration to many other Christian peoples in Ottoman lands over the coming century, in all cases, the great powers felt obliged to shape, moderate and restrain the aspirations of these nationalists. This was true in the 1870s when other Balkan peoples achieved their independence, again in the 1880s when the Bulgarians tried to act without great power consent against the Ottomans, and in the Balkan wars of 1912–13, when the Balkan states found that the terms of their treaties would not stand when the great powers met to rewrite them. All the great powers feared the power vacuum that precipitous action against a weakened Ottoman empire might provoke and, while they could not prevent nationalist challenges to the empire in the Balkans, they repeatedly sought to contain its systemic impact and did so with success until the summer of 1914.

At a global level, the Greek revolt also presented a powerful example of successful revolutionary and anti-imperial action. Much like the successful independence movements in Latin America, Greece inspired all manner of groups to revolt against monarchical and imperial rule or to establish new forms of political organization. The period 1815 to 1848 featured numerous desperate attempts to provoke political change, many of which did not succeed, some of which did. Such revolts were not isolated to Europe.[23] In 1824, the Chumash tribes in California rebelled against the Spanish and Mexican authorities in part because they were not being treated as equal citizens, which the recent Mexican constitution (1821) guaranteed and for which liberal revolutionaries in Spain also argued.[24] Although the Chumash rebellion was suppressed, it spoke both to the existence of the grievances of indigenous communities and to the global currency of revolutionary political ideas, including the concept of statehood and the framing of political rights for citizens and subjects (for more, see Chapter 8). The Cherokee peoples engaged in similar debates, designing their own constitution for a Cherokee nation in 1827, including executive, legislature and judicial branches of government, before becoming embroiled in a civil war and succumbing to repeated military attacks by the United States government, which decimated Cherokee society and forced their people's displacement across the American continent.[25]

Another powerful example of the global currency of such ideas was the 1835 declaration of independence made by a number of Maori tribes in the south Pacific islands of Aotearoa New Zealand. The declaration aimed both at combatting lawlessness among European individuals residing in New Zealand and at preventing a declaration of sovereignty by the French over the islands and peoples.[26] The declaration established a confederation of tribes, which operated much like the German Confederation in Europe, to assert territorial sovereignty, establish common laws and enable full participation of Maori in the global economy. The United Tribes of New Zealand even adopted a flag, which they used to commission ships to ply trade across the Asia-Pacific region. Both the 1835 declaration and the subsequent Treaty of Waitangi, signed by Maori chiefs and the British crown in 1840, spoke to the importance of treaty law, claims to sovereignty and statehood and to the power of people and communities to determine their own future in a world ruled by powerful empires.

The military campaigns conducted by the Dutch in their East Indian (now Indonesian) archipelago after 1815 also bring out the imperial applications of the European congress system. When the Javanese prince Dipo Negoro incited an armed rebellion against the Dutch colonial authorities on the island of Java in 1825, he did so with an eye to ending the increasingly invasive interference of the Dutch in what he considered local dynastic affairs.[27] His rebellion was also underwritten by global ideas, not least the spread of Islam into the region by missionaries straight from Mecca (in the Ottoman empire). The ensuing war, which lasted until 1830, was as much a 'holy war' as it was an anti-imperial conflict. Fought largely by guerrilla tactics and met with repressive counter attacks by forces loyal to the Dutch, it cost more than 200,000 Javanese their lives. The war halted in 1830, when the Dutch captured Dipo Negoro using the ruse of a negotiated peace. The military repression of resistance among the local peoples across the archipelago would be an ongoing feature of Dutch imperialism for the next century.[28]

Like the Maori, the Chumash and many other societies, the Indonesian peoples were not pliant imperial subjects. Their agency sat as much at the heart of the 'age of revolution' as any other community.[29] They actively and repeatedly resisted Dutch imperialism and economic exploitation. For its part, the Dutch kingdom suppressed these imperial rebellions because its wealth, industrial growth and international status were dependent on these imperial holdings. Like Britain, the Netherlands was able to sustain and expand its authority over the south-east Asian archipelago in part because its security was not threatened in Europe.[30] Its long-term policy of neutrality and the ongoing European balance of power ensured that an invasion by a European neighbour was highly unlikely.

The Belgian revolt in the 1830s also confirmed to the Dutch monarchy that its imperial possessions were vital. The Dutch needed the wealth of Indonesia to fund its military campaigns against the Belgian revolutionaries. The revolt, a costly affair which began in 1830 and lasted until 1839, also highlights how the 'restoration' principles of the Vienna treaty were repeatedly contested by the subjects of the European monarchies. The 'age of restoration' was very much an 'age of revolution' and an 'age of empire'. On the one hand, the Belgian revolt was a challenge to the domestic authority of the Kingdom of the Netherlands, which had been established in 1813 and confirmed at Vienna in 1815 to include lands and people who had not previously been part of the United Provinces (as the country was called in the eighteenth century). In 1830, inspired by revolts in Paris, the Catholic communities in the southern Netherlands rebelled against the Protestant Dutch king, calling for their own independence. King Willem I asked for support from Europe's other monarchs to suppress the revolution in the spirit of the concert system.

The resulting Treaty of London (1830), however, augured a surprise. Rather than send their troops to the Netherlands, the great powers reconsidered the Vienna agreements. The political stability of the region and all of Europe was at stake since France, Prussia and Great Britain all had geostrategic interests in the region. Instead of supporting the Dutch monarch, they decided that greater stability would be won by the creation of a new state, the Kingdom of Belgium, with a German aristocrat, Leopold of Saxe-Coburg, acclaimed as its first monarch. The Dutch king did not agree and sent his troops into Belgium to fight a war which the Dutch eventually lost. At its end in 1839, a revised Treaty of London not only recognized Belgium's independence, but it also imposed permanent neutrality on the new monarchy. Like Switzerland, Belgium's neutrality was guaranteed by great power agreement. If it came under military attack, all the signatories to the London treaty (including the Netherlands) were required to come to its defence. In so doing, the powers hoped to keep north-west Europe safe from war. They all recognized that the region was too important for it to be ruled by one of the major powers alone. Most remarkably, the principle that Belgium should be kept free from hegemonic rule was protected by these powers until 1914, even though it came under threat at various key junctures.[31] Belgian independence and its permanent neutralization was one of the success stories of the concert system.[32]

The greatest threat to the concert of Europe came with the revolutions of 1848, which developed all over the continent as locals took up arms and

FIGURE 2.2 *The 1848 revolutions. This Berlin scene, captured by a contemporary artist in February 1848, shows a massive crowd waving revolutionary flags (advocating for German unification and the establishment of a federal constitution) in honour of their compatriots who had died during the revolutionary violence. A mountain of coffins is arraigned on the celebratory stage. The Prussian king, Frederick Wilhelm IV, briefly toyed with the idea of supporting the revolutionaries' demands, but in the end sent troops in to repress the rebellions and re-establish the primacy of his monarchical rule. Scenes like this occurred all over Europe in 1847 and 1848, including in the German Confederation, Russia, France, Switzerland, Austria, the Italian states, the Danubian principalities and Spain. While Britain remained relatively immune to similar revolutionary movements, an attempted nationalist uprising in Ireland in 1848 was brutally repressed by the British authorities.*
Source: *Johann Jakob Kirchoff, drawing 22 March 1848, Getty Images, 515417256.*

rose up against their monarchical leaders, demanding meaningful political, constitutional and economic change. The revolutions were interconnected and looked a lot like the anti-imperial revolts occurring around the world: some stemmed from extreme disaffection with the ways in which the local aristocracy ruled over the people, some erupted in response to economic impoverishment (a product of the industrial revolution) and political alienation, much of it from the failure of various states to respond effectively to a series of devastating harvest failures and the resulting catastrophic misery. The revolts were bloody and intense and brought to the fore the power of a range of competing political ideas ranging from liberalism, republicanism, anti-imperialism, nationalism, socialism and democracy. Karl Marx and Friedrich Engels composed their seminal *Communist Manifesto* in response to the revolutions, which (like the other ideas) would define the international political environment through the late nineteenth and twentieth centuries. All of these political ideas challenged the notion that the landed aristocracy had a natural right to rule (see Chapter 8).

Still, the 1848 revolutions failed to remove the European monarchs from their thrones. Only in Switzerland did the revolutions lead to the confirmation of a federal state system. For their part, the French returned a Bonaparte to power, establishing a short-lived Republic. In 1852 this Louis-Napoleon Bonaparte, the nephew of the first Napoleon, declared himself emperor. A primary reason for the failure of most of Europe's revolutions 'from below' was due to the willingness and ability of the European monarchs to combine their efforts to repress them. The Russian Tsar Nicholas I sent a force of 200,000 troops into Hungary, for example, to contain the rebellions there in support of the Austrian monarchy and to keep such dangers from spreading to Poland.[33] The willingness of Europe's ruling elite to not allow the revolutions to turn into wars between the monarchs highlights the success of the 'restoration' principles of the congress system.

Yet the other prime reason why the revolutions failed in overthrowing the monarchical order was because the monarchies showed a willingness to adapt their domestic laws and even their constitutions to offer more power to the people. In that sense, the 1848 revolutions were a success. After 1848, many European states adopted systems of representative governance: sometimes establishing forms of parliamentary rule, often adopting liberal constitutions and addressing the idea that at least some of the people should have a say in the ways their society was run. In many respects, then, by adapting their monarchies to accept principles of nationalism and representative politics, Europe's elite survived the 'age of revolution' with their sovereign power largely intact. That enabled them to continue to look outwards. Increasingly, they co-opted their citizens in recognizing the advantages of peace at home to protect the expansion of influence, power and imperial wealth outwards. This expansion of Western power across the world was supported by the widespread acceptance among Europeans that they had a 'right to rule' an overseas empire based on the premise that they alone were 'civilized' and could bring the premise of 'civilization' to the rest of the world and that they were doing a 'good' by imposing their ways of thinking, behaving and living on others.

Thus, where the period up to and including the revolutions of 1848 was an 'age of revolution', we might describe the period after 1848 and leading to the outbreak of the First World War in 1914 as an 'age of industrial expansion and imperial consolidation', a period in which the principles of the concert system enabled exponential industrial growth in Europe, then in the United States and Japan, and in the spread of their industrial empires globally. How fundamental the concert principles were to the economic and imperial growth of these powers is well illustrated by the conduct of the only war of the era that involved more than three major powers, namely the Crimean War (1853–6), fought between the Russian empire on the one hand, and an alliance of the Ottomans, French, British and Sardinians (in northern Italy) on the other.

The Crimean War began over issues of religion: a contestation about which Christian monarch would act as protector of Christianity's holy sites in the Ottoman-controlled city of Jerusalem. When, after much prompting from France, the Ottoman Sultan Abdulmejid transferred protector rights from the Russian-backed Christian Orthodox Church to the Roman Catholic Church it incensed the Russian Tsar Nicholas I who mounted a series of fierce diplomatic protests to restore Orthodox rights. Historians now acknowledge the important role played by the French emperor Napoleon III in orchestrating the war, which he hoped would upset the concert system and offer France more power and influence in Europe and the wider world.[34] In the end, however, the war failed to achieve any substantial geostrategic advantage for France. It certainly did not upset the diplomatic principles that underpinned the concert system, although it destabilized the Russian empire considerably. Russia lost the war after suffering a series of military defeats on the Crimean Peninsula (in the Black Sea) and in the Caucasus. At the Treaty of Paris of 1856, it was made to accept a stringent peace deal, including the neutralization of the Black Sea, which prevented Russia from moving any naval battleships on these waters.

Above all, however, the Paris treaty of 1856 highlights how essential the principles of diplomatic restraint were to how the great powers conducted themselves even in time of great power warfare.[35] While the Crimean War could easily have evolved into a general war, bringing in all the European powers and militarizing the world's seas, it did not. From the outset, the military conduct of the war was localized to the Baltic, Crimean and Caucasus regions (with a few campaigns fought in the Pacific as well). While Britain and France could have conducted an intensive naval war against Russian trade, they did not, preferring to keep the seas open for their own and everyone's trade and passenger shipping. Only a few Russian ports were blockaded. All the major belligerents looked to protect their economic and imperial interests, particularly in the Asia-Pacific region.[36]

As a result, the belligerent powers overturned many of the economic warfare practices that they had utilized in past wars and issued new international rules of war to support this development. Their aim was to ensure that the war did not interrupt the flow of trade across the world's seas and oceans: they wished to separate the military conduct of the war from the global economy. In effect, the Crimean War showed how little any of the belligerents were interested in interfering with the global economy to aid their warring ventures. They all worried that if they did so, their own wealth would be affected, but also that any international advantages they held (including in the acquisition of empire) might transfer to a non-warring state. In other words, the Crimean War highlighted the systemic advantage of localizing a conflict. Even the belligerent governments realized that protecting the principles of neutrality would allow them to reap the economic benefits of their own future neutrality when others went to war.[37] It is most significant then that they asserted these new rules of economic warfare in the Declaration of Paris of 1856. After 1856, privateering was deemed illegal by international agreement.[38] Blockades in time of war had to be effective to be considered binding and a neutral's right to trade and access the open seas was guaranteed. These principles spoke to the idea that military warfare could be separated from an economic peace.[39]

The next chapter highlights just how essential these principles of keeping the seas open were to sustaining the global industrial and imperial power of the European and American states. For while the Crimean War raged, industrial imperialism advanced apace. More European settlers came to the islands of New Zealand in the 1850s, for example, than ever before. Their ships were not attacked by the Russian navy. Meanwhile, the gold rushes that had begun in California in 1849 spread to Australasia in the 1850s heightening the movement of people in all directions across the Pacific Ocean and the movement of gold deposits across the world. Furthermore, the outbreak of the Crimean War in 1853 coincided with a successful mission by Commodore Perry of the United States to Japan, initiating a new era of trans-Pacific economic and diplomatic relationships that within a generation would see Japan openly and actively industrializing.

Study questions

1. What was the Congress of Vienna? What do historians mean by the 'concert of Europe' or 'congress system'? Why does the European concert system matter so much to explaining the onset of industrial globalization in the nineteenth century?

2. Why do different historians describe the period 1815–48 alternatively as an 'age of restoration' or 'age of revolution'? Why are they more reluctant to call the same period an 'age of empire'?

3. What was the Monroe Doctrine? Compare its functions in the international environment to the principles of the European concert system.

4. What role did neutrality and neutralization play in the concert system?

5. In what ways might the European concert system be deemed a success? In what ways might it be deemed a failure?

6. What importance should historians attach to the Crimean War (1853–6) in explaining the history of industrial globalization?

Recommended readings

Maartje Abbenhuis, *An Age of Neutrals: Great Power Politics 1815–1914*. Cambridge UP, 2014: Chapter 3 'The neutrals' war: Britain and the global implications of the Crimean War, 1853–1856', pp. 66–95.

Maartje Abbenhuis, 'A most useful tool for diplomacy and statecraft: Neutrality and Europe in the "long" nineteenth century 1815–1914', *International History Review* 35, 1, 2013, pp. 1–22.

Rafe Blaufarb, 'The western question: The geopolitics of Latin American independence', *American Historical Review* 112, 3, 2007, pp. 742–63.

Kathleen Burk, *Old World, New World: Great Britain and America from the Beginning*. Atlantic Monthly Press, 2008: Chapter 3 'War and rumours of war 1783–1872', pp. 189–276.

Robert Gildea, *Barricades and Borders: Europe 1800–1914*. Oxford UP, 1996: Chapter 4 'The revolutions of 1848', pp. 83–104.

F. H. Hinsley, *Power and the Pursuit of Peace: Theory and Practice in the History of Relations Between States* Cambridge UP, 1985: Chapter 10 'The Concert of Europe', pp. 213–37.

Jonathan Israel, *The Expanding Blaze: How the American Revolution Ignited the World 1775–1848*. Princeton UP, 2017: Especially Chapter 17 'Reaction, radicalism and *Américanisme* under "the Restoration"', Chapter 18 'The Greek Revolution', Chapter 19 'The Freedom-Fighters of the 1830s' and Chapter 20 'The revolutions of 1848: Democratic republicanism versus socialism', pp. 456–567.

Mark Mazower, *Governing the World: The History of an Idea*. Penguin, 2012: Prologue 'The Concert of Europe 1815–1914', pp. 3–12.

Paul Schroeder, 'The lost intermediaries: The impact of 1870 on the European system', *International History Review* 6, 1, 1984, pp. 1–27.

Bo Stråth, *Europe's Utopias of Peace 1815, 1919, 1951*. Bloomsbury, 2016: Chapter 1 'The Vienna peace utopia and the world of trade', pp. 23–91.

3

Industrializing empires and global capitalism after 1815

When Commodore Matthew Perry sailed his steam-powered gunboats into Tokyo Bay in 1853, he did so with the express purpose of opening up the isolationist Japanese empire to American trade and diplomatic relations. Perry's mission was authorized by the United States president Millard Fillmore and sought to expand and consolidate American economic (and some would argue imperial) interests in the Asia-Pacific, by force if need be. Perry's was not the first such American venture. The Treaty of Wangxia, signed between the Chinese and United States governments in 1844, began the process of forging trans-Pacific links. The American gunboat mission to the Korean peninsula in 1871 – resulting in a short battle during which two hundred Koreans were killed – extended the trans-Pacific mission, although the Joseon dynasty did not enter into a formal diplomatic relationship with the United States until 1882.[1] The formal acquisition by the United States of the islands of Hawai'i, American Samoa and the Philippines in the late 1890s signaled just how effective American economic and military imperialism across the Pacific ocean had become by the end of the century.[2]

From the perspective of the Japanese, Perry's expedition ended the Tokugawa empire's self-imposed diplomatic and economic isolationism.[3] From 1853 on, the Japanese government had no choice but to looked outwards as more and more foreigners were arriving on its shores looking for opportunities to extend their wealth. In response, it sent its own diplomats into the world: in 1860 to the United States and in 1862 into China and Europe.[4] After years of internal strife, the 'reform and renewal' movement in Japan inspired a political revolution in 1867. After 1868, under the guidance of the emperor Meiji, the government sought to modernize Japanese society and invest and expand its industrialization aiming to compete fully as equals in the global sphere.

From the perspective of the American and Japanese governing elite, the industrialization of the United States and Japan were nineteenth-century 'success stories'. Both states industrialized rapidly and efficiently and expanded their geopolitical power alongside. In so doing, they joined an exclusive club of other successful industrializing empires, all of which were concentrated in western Europe, including Great Britain, France and Prussia/Germany.[5] What all these great powers had in common was effectual industrialization at home and the expansion of their economic, military and imperial power abroad.

Industrialization is the most important development to affect global humanity since the invention of agriculture. Industrialization brought modernity into being, creating a world increasingly defined by technological and scientific discoveries and innovations and by the expectation of change. Historians have expended much ink in explaining its contours, its impacts and its agents. Their histories show just how complex the dynamics of modernization and industrialization were (and remain).[6] Such histories highlight that there was not one path to modernity, nor one way to industrialize. This chapter cannot do justice to all these historiographical approaches or even attempt to summarize the complexity of the scholarship. The purpose of this chapter then is not to explain industrialization as it impacted and was shaped by humanity writ large (we have provided some useful readings at the end of the chapter to help with that context). Instead, the chapter focuses on the geopolitical importance of industrialization in the nineteenth-century context and highlights how industrialization helped to grow the global power of a handful of states, including Japan and the United States, and reduced the relative power of many others, including the Ottoman, Qing and Mughal empires.

The geopolitical principles established at the Congress of Vienna offer a useful starting point: the relatively peaceful relationship between the European great powers and the relatively peaceful condition of the world's seas and oceans enabled industrializers in these countries to take their economic endeavours outwards into the world. In so doing, the diplomatic principles of the concert system helped to spur industrial capitalism as a global phenomenon, upending the principles of the pre-existing mercantilist economic system that had dominated the Atlantic world in the early modern period. After 1815, the states that successfully industrialized tended to flourish, while those that failed to develop them effectively tended to flounder. The growth of global industrial capitalism, then, is a story of the opportunities and risks taken by individuals and states. It is also a story of the violence, destruction and immense and intense changes they exacted in the process.

'The sea is open, trade lives again!' These were the celebratory words of the Dutch statesman, Gijsbert Karel van Hogendorp, as the long years of the Napoleonic Wars gave way to a comprehensive European peace.[7] His proclamation reflected the reality that economic warfare no longer strangled the European ports and that with the peace, the 'blue-water' world of trade and commerce reopened for Europeans. Hogendorp's sentiments spoke not only to the interests of the newly-formed Kingdom of the Netherlands in 1813. At the end of the Napoleonic Wars, much of Europe struggled with economic depression and popular unrest, which the European leaders feared might lead to further revolutions. The statesmen and women at the Congress of Vienna in 1815 certainly recognized that economic recovery was essential to sustaining the political and diplomatic stability of their newly created European order.[8] What they were less cognizant of was the powerful impetus the concert system provided for economic and industrial expansionism. In combination, the relatively peaceful circumstances of the post-1815 European world and the relatively peaceful condition of the world's seas and oceans (protected in part by the powerful British Royal Navy) proved a fertile environment for the dual forces of industrialization and global migration (for which see Chapter 5) to take off.

Van Hogendorp was one voice among many economic advisers and thinkers that played a key role in shaping European governmental decision-making in the decades after 1815.[9] He was a champion of the economic theory called *free trade liberalism* and was influenced by such well-known advocates as Adam Smith. Smith's *Wealth of Nations* (1776) offered a searching critique of the global economic order known as *mercantilism* that dominated the Atlantic world in the eighteenth century. In the mercantilist era, the European blue-water empires (consisting mainly of Spain, Portugal, Britain, France and the Netherlands) expanded their colonial holdings across the Atlantic and into South East Asia. These empires were largely extractive ones: their agents seized control of local resources such as silver and gold, or brought goods and spices from distant lands (including from the economic powerhouses of China and Mughal India) back to Europe. In some instances, they established settler colonies and some of these, most notably in the Americas, relied heavily on slave and indentured labour (brought there from around the world) to work on sugar and cotton plantations.

The source of these mercantilist empires' wealth and global power was often concentrated in monopolistic chartered enterprises (somewhat akin to multinational corporations today) that invested in ships, goods and people to explore the world, acquired sources of wealth and transported slave labour from Africa to the plantations of the 'new world'. The British East India Company (BEIC) and the Dutch East India Company are two well-known examples of highly successful mercantilist companies. They were fully supported by the Dutch and British governments who imposed tariffs, designed labour policies and manipulated access to ports and waters to protect the wealth generated by these companies from outside competition. Imperial navies were critical to the success of these ventures: they protected the company's ships from pirates and privateers and assisted in the seizure of territories for the establishment of colonies and plantations (for the extraction of resources and wealth for the company's coffers).

The overall economic principal that defined mercantilism was that the world's wealth consisted of a finite array of treasures. The goal of any mercantilist empire, then, was to get the maximum share of this largely static pie of wealth and exclude competitors. The battle for the wealth of the world was in their eyes a zero-sum game: one empire's gain was a loss for another. According to the mercantilist model, economic growth was only really possible by taking wealth from others. As a result, mercantilism inspired a wide range of violence, both in the acquisition of wealth, goods and labour and in the maintenance of exclusive economic zones where only the agents of the mercantilist empire (or company) in question could trade. The eighteenth century, then, witnessed a long slew of wars between the European states as they fought to protect and expand their own wealth and overseas holdings.

The American War of Independence (1775–1883) and the wars that developed in the aftermath of the French revolution (1789) presented some fundamental challenges to these mercantilist principles, not least because the wars conducted at sea had a decisive impact on the ability of the mercantilist empires to keep exclusive control over their trade monopolies. In the context of global war, the growth in revolutionary thinking and the development of new industrial inventions, free trade liberal theories like those posited by Adam Smith gained traction. Smith advocated for ending the closed-off economic principles of mercantilism, curtailing the monopolies of the imperial companies and opening up the global economy to competition. Industrialization would spur the appeal of these ideas along further.

In 1815, there were many who thought that a return to normalcy and an end to economic warfare in Europe and across the Atlantic Ocean would mean a return to mercantilist practices. In Vienna in 1815, the British government certainly refused to discuss whether there should be collective restraints imposed on economic warfare. It also refused to negotiate neutral economic rights with the Americans at the end of the War of 1812.[10] From the British government's perspective at least, might made right, and as its navy now dominated the world's oceans, it felt safest by protecting its continued right to use its naval power in unrestricted ways. In 1815, the British government certainly did not foresee what the impact of industrialization would be on its own global power.

Yet very quickly, it became apparent that there was little chance of 'going back'. The imperial companies still existed (BEIC would not lose its sovereignty over India until the late 1850s, for example), but the economic dynamism of the post-1815 period which grew out of the industrialization processes that first stirred in Britain in the middle of the eighteenth century were now well underway. These new systems of production gained in intensity in western Europe and the United States before globalizing in the middle of the nineteenth century.[11] By 1850, the mercantilist age was truly over. While governments still controlled the flow of goods into and out of their sovereign territory (primarily by setting tariffs and regulating ports and borders), they also recognized the potential for economic growth when markets opened up for their traders and citizen investors to access. This was particularly true for Great Britain.[12] During the Crimean War (1853–6), the British government acknowledged how fundamentally its position in the global economic environment had shifted. It now recognized that it had much more to gain from protecting access to the 'open seas' and advancing free trade principles around the world. The 'first age of industrial globalization' evolved as a concomitant of the growth of a global capitalist economy.

In its simplest form, industrialization was the process by which manual labour was replaced by mechanical labour (mainly in the form of fuel-powered machines), speeding up manufacturing processes, increasing the quantity of output and decreasing its cost to produce. The process was so radical and revolutionary because it reconfigured existing economic and social structures. In most pre-industrial societies, wealth and well-being were intimately tied to the produce derived from the land or sea. In nineteenth-century industrializing societies, wealth and well-being were increasingly tied to the flow of money: to wages (for workers) and investment capital (for those elites who invested in technological innovation, industrial production and its trade and exchange). Industrial societies thus also depended on reliable banking systems, exchange rates, taxation regimes and the like. Governments were key partners in industrialization. Above all, effective industrialization relied on the sourcing of (cheap) raw materials, developing reliable networks of transportation and communication, encouraging the growth of consumer markets (increasing the number of people with money to buy the influx of available manufactured goods) and creating wage-labour economies (where labour was rewarded with money, as opposed to goods in kind, so that wages could be spent on the purchase of manufactured goods). As we shall see, industrialization was a globalizing phenomenon, which only accelerated during the century as technological inventions enabled speedier communications by railway, steamship or telegraph cable (for which see Chapter 4).

Like many successful revolutions, once begun, industrialization gained a momentum of its own. At first, much of this momentum was pushed by the opportunism of a new class of economic elites namely the entrepreneurs, bankers, industrialists, lawyers and other professionals who derived their wealth and status from investing in industrial processes, in seeking out new sources of raw materials, in establishing and extending communication networks, in opening up new markets and in maximizing access to the open seas. Initially, these elites all came from the heartlands of the early industrializers in Great Britain, the United States and western Europe. They demanded support from their governments, not only in providing them with political power to affect economic policy-making at home (in the metropole) but also to underwrite and protect their global endeavours. In this respect, the nineteenth-century age of industrial globalization was clearly an age of industrial imperialism.[13] For where the money went, so the governments followed. With the seas open for business, as van Hogendorp described it, the world after 1815 was also opened for business.

As the historian Jürgen Osterhammel reminds us, industrialization was not a singular or uniform process. Its tentacles reached far and wide and had numerous ramifications and drivers, some of which came 'from below' and others 'from above'.[14] In terms of geopolitics, however, there are two important things to say about nineteenth-century industrialization. The first is that industrialization transformed global power, global economics and global politics. The second is that the wealthiest and most powerful empires (the 'winners' as the historian Eric Hobsbawm describes them)[15] in 1900 were those that had industrialized quickly and well and who maximized access to the world's trade networks and its natural and human resources. In 1900, these 'winners' included most west European countries, the United States and the late industrializers Russia and Japan. Collectively, these powers claimed formal dominion over more than 84 percent of the world's land mass and people and drew the rest of the world into their *informal* orbits of capitalist concentration. The historians Erick D. Langer and John Tutino accurately describe the shift from the 'polycentric world economy' of the early modern period to the interconnected industrial capitalist economy of the late nineteenth century as follows: by 1900, the 'Latin American republics and African, Islamic and Asian[-Pacific] imperial subjects became essential peripheries in the world of concentrated industrial capitalism'.[16]

Of these 'winners', Great Britain was by far the most successful. Not only did it industrialize first, but until the 1870s was unrivalled in its industrial and economic strength. Britain's industrial pre-eminence was dependent in part on key agricultural reforms that occurred in the eighteenth century and in part because in 1815 it already had a global empire to exploit (including its long-time economic and social ties to the United States).[17] British industrialization was also aided by a strong banking system able to underwrite investors and proffer insurance, a sizeable merchant marine to enable transportation, a navy to protect trade routes against pirates and to enforce compliance on other states and communities and a ready supply of locally mined coal to fuel its factories. That Britain had a relatively stable and centralized political system was also in its industrializers' favour.

Britain's industrialization processes were peerless and pioneering. They offered a 'how to industrialize' model for other governments and entrepreneurs to follow, which many attempted in emulation. Yet Britain's industrialization (like its imperialism) was entirely chaotic, unplanned and sweeping.[18] It effected radical and profound changes at home and abroad, some of which were replicated as industrialization went global, others which were unique to this island nation and global empire. In the 1960s, Eric Hobsbawm wrote an influential book about the central importance of Great Britain in explaining the 'fundamental transformation of human life' that occurred as a result of industrialization. In it he argues that 'an entire world economy was ... built on, or rather around, Britain' and that 'this country ... temporarily rose to a position of global influence power unparalleled by any state of its relative size before or since'.[19] Historians today rarely explain industrialization as a singularly British phenomenon. Yet Hobsbawm's focus on the global and imperial power occasioned by British industrialization remains appropriate. For he was not wrong. By 1914, Britain controlled the largest empire the world had ever seen, covering 24 percent of the world's land mass and including 446 million subjects.[20] Forty percent of the world's merchant marine flew the British flag and the Royal Navy purported that its strength was equal to the power of two of its nearest rivals combined.

The impact of industrialization on British society, politics and even its landscapes was all too obvious to contemporaries. In demographic terms alone, the period after 1815 witnessed a population explosion, a shift away from agricultural settings to urban centres and the exponential growth of industrial cities.[21] These cities grew around factory districts, railway hubs and seaports. All aimed at maximizing manufacturing capacity and access to the global economy by sea (see Figure 3.1). In 1850, Britain was the world's first society to have 50 percent of its population living in cities over one hundred thousand people.[22] By this time, only one in four British workers earned their keep as agricultural labourers.[23] The speed at which pre-industrial British social forms and norms were being eclipsed also astounded contemporaries.

In 1838, Britain's prime minister Benjamin Disraeli described the country as the 'workshop of the world': drawing on raw materials sourced from around its empire and further afield to manufacture goods, which were then redistributed at considerable profit back into the world economy.[24] Britain was, of course, not the only industrial workshop of its time and many rivals soon appeared, but in 1850 it still produced as much as two-thirds of the world's coal, half its pig iron and about half of its commercially produced cotton-cloth (see Table 3.3).[25] By 1870, its production capacity had grown exponentially again, producing

FIGURE 3.1 *The industrial port of Hull, 1900. This advertising poster for the North Eastern Railway, which operated from the industrial port city of Hull (on the north-eastern coast of England) illustrates the key importance of Britain as a hub of industrial trade and exchange. Note the railway lines leading to the various in-land towns and cities, many of which were major industrial manufacturing centres, and the steamships leading away from the railway heads out into the North Sea and the wider world. As the world's 'largest dock-owning railway company', the poster aimed at persuading investors, merchants and traders to use Hull as their base of operations in Great Britain and the North Eastern Railways as their preferred mode of transportation. During the 'first age of industrial globalization', Hull's population multiplied tenfold. It developed its own cotton manufacturing industry and was one of Britain's principal trading ports.*

Source: Percy Home (artist), c.1900, Getty Images, 90735368.

five times the amount of coal and pig iron as it had in 1830 and importing six times the amount of raw cotton to repurpose as cloth. Across the same time, the average productivity per industrial worker increased by 100 percent due to improvements made in manufacturing processes and machinery.[26] As a result, British exports expanded equally quickly, flooding the world with its manufactures. British wealth, global power and prestige grew alongside, which its citizens reinvested into growing manufacturing capacity, sourcing materials and labour, building infrastructure support and accessing markets and seaports. Where in 1860, Britons held 370 million pounds in foreign assets (which translates to around 33 billion pounds in real price terms today), by 1913 they had grown their foreign investments more than eleven times to 3.9 billion pounds (approximately 365 billion pounds in today's terms).[27] No other single investor society came even close to matching these figures.[28] By 1900, Britons were omnipresent in the global economy.

Of course, the evident success of factory production in Britain was not a secret and many individuals and states sought to emulate Britain's example. Immediate neighbours such as the Belgians, the French, the Dutch and Germans, copied (and sometimes stole) factory and machine designs. Some of them even invited British entrepreneurs and their workers to help establish factories in their countries. So too did the Americans.[29] Their successes were enabled by a whole range of factors. Other states were not as fortunate. The Egyptian leader Mohammed Ali, for example, sought to import virtually all the elements needed for the launch of industrial production in the 1830s, including sending Egyptian students to study these processes in Britain and bringing in large numbers of British factory workers to lift the Egyptian economy to new heights of efficiency. These Egyptian ambitions faltered as a result of local resistance to rapid change and the prohibitive importation costs of raw materials, particularly of coal. That British agents used diplomatic negotiation, military threats and monopolistic tactics to force Egypt's neighbours to purchase British manufactures above Egyptian wares only augmented Egypt's industrialization woes. Until it could compete with the rate of production and cheaper cost of British producers, Egyptian industrialization could not take off. When the costs of sustaining a naval war with the Ottomans against Greece also became prohibitive (see Chapter 2), the Egyptian industrial experiment effectively failed.[30]

That successful industrial empires, like the British, could mobilize their existing economic and industrial dominance to keep nascent industrial competition at bay was an essential feature of their nineteenth-century industrial and imperial 'success' story. The rapid growth of their wealth and investment capacity also enabled them to invest in industrial projects across the world (often at the expense of local initiatives like the one described here in Egypt) and in so doing not only reap the material benefits of the investment but also gain greater political control over the region in which the investment was made. The expansion of Britain's industrial imperial power, then, was enabled by the fact it industrialized first and already ruled a large colonial empire. These two 'advantages' enabled Britain to expand its realm of dominance over others economically, diplomatically and militarily.

Importantly, it is really no surprise that the places where industrialization quickly took off and succeeded after 1815 were also party to the principles of the 'concert of Europe'. After all, Britain could not dominate its American and European rival states in quite the same way as it did other governments and communities. By 1830, much of western Europe was industrializing and advancing its own industrial initiatives: laying down railways, developing areas of strength in metallurgy, contributing to advances in the textile industry (particularly in France), and in the decades that followed, developing new fields in the chemical and electrical industry (particularly in Germany). Massive increases in coal mining were seen all across the region alongside state investment in heavy industry. Industrial cities grew across Europe too. While the British continued to lead in the industrialization stakes, they were by no means without serious competitors. By 1870, these British and European industrializers also faced heightened competition from out of the United States. By 1910, Germany and the United States outproduced Britain in terms of pig iron, raw steel and chemical production (see Table 3.3).

In geopolitical and geostrategic terms these industrial developments were all important. Not only could the industrializers monopolize the global economy by outproducing and undercutting any competitors who did not enjoy their advantages in manufacturing size and scale, but their wealth also grew as their investments spurred further investment. Technological innovation followed technological innovation while scientific discovery stimulated further scientific discovery. Where industrializing states were successful, success generally reaped further success. Where they were not, they tended to succumb to the investment and domination of one of the 'successful' empires.

The coming chapters highlight the substantive human, material and environmental costs inaugurated by the nineteenth-century's industrial turn on a global scale. For industrial capitalism thrived on exploitation, acquisition and expansionism. All the successful industrial states noted above were able exploiters, acquirers and imperialists. Successful industrialization in this respect resulted in the expansion of both formal and informal empires. Governments 'followed the money' and aimed at protecting the global interests of their enterprising citizens, who opened up markets, established banking and financial operations, invested in local industry, ships and communication networks, sourced and extracted vast amounts of raw materials, established (or invested in) plantations and mines to source even more primary resources, monopolized human labour and demanded security for their investments and profits. Much of the wealth and global advantages experienced by the 'first world' today can be traced back to these nineteenth-century industrialization processes and the concentration of global wealth in the heartlands of nineteenth-century industry. Those heartlands thrived in large part because the states that protected them rarely needed to worry about the potential of invasive warfare by a major industrial competitor: the congress system gave them that advantage. Instead, they could focus on protecting and advancing their own economic and imperial interests abroad, if need be by violent means.

There were then clear 'winners' and 'losers' in the nineteenth-century industrialization sweepstakes. In terms of states, the winners were those countries that could adopt and adapt industrial changes and engage readily and easily in the global economy. The states and societies that struggled to do so had a clear and immediate disadvantage and became likely targets of the 'successful' industrializers' economic ambitions, investments and imperial opportunism. In the 'first age of industrial globalization' this meant that only a very few states won big.

As an example, consider how the much the 'age of industrialization' cost the Chinese Qing dynasty and Indian Mughal empire in geopolitical terms. The former lost is position of economic pre-eminence, the latter disappeared completely. In 1815, the Qing empire was more than the equal of any individual European state in terms of wealth, manufacturing output, regional power and relative political stability. The artisanal crafts of China were widely sought after around the world and its well-organized trading systems brought much of the world's silver and gold into the coffers of its merchants and the Qing's royal treasury. China was the dominant military and economic power in the region and leveraged this strength into strong tributary and trading relationships with Siam (Thailand) and most of Indo-China. The one Eurasian great power that China worked consistently with across the eighteenth century was that of Tsarist Russia and here the Qings and the Romanovs engaged in a stable and carefully managed system of trade that maintained the peace along their lengthy shared border.

There were disquieting signs, clearly visible to the Qing emperors, that the status quo might not last. After 1750, particularly, increasing numbers of Europeans were settling in the South and South East Asian region and the various European trading companies operating there aimed at accessing China's internal economy. The Qings took steps to manage these developments. They established what was known as the 'Canton system' that operated out of the port of Guangzhou (Canton). Foreign traders could only come into the port for six months of the year and needed an operating licence to trade with local merchants.[31] Taxes, licensing fees and duties grew the wealth of the Chinese merchants and the Chinese state, especially as the demand for Chinese teas, spices and luxury goods grew in Europe and the United States. It was in this

TABLE 3.1 Relative share of world manufacturing output, 1800–1900

	1800	1830	1860	1880	1900
Europe (as a whole)	28.1	34.2	53.2	61.3	62.0
Great Britain	4.3	9.5	19.9	22.9	18.5
Austrian empire	3.2	3.2	4.2	4.4	4.7
Germany	3.5	3.5	4.9	8.5	13.2
Russia	5.6	5.6	7.0	7.6	8.8
United States	0.8	2.4	7.2	14.7	23.6
Japan	3.5	2.8	2.6	2.4	2.4
China	33.3	29.8	19.7	12.5	6.2
India	19.7	17.6	8.6	2.8	1.7

Source: Paul Kennedy, *The Rise and Fall of the Great Powers: Economic Change and Military Conflict from 1500 to 2000.* Vintage Books, 1987, p. 149.

TABLE 3.2 Per capita levels of industrialization, 1800–1900

Relative to Great Britain in 1900 (= 100)

	1800	1830	1860	1880	1900
Europe (as a whole)	8	11	16	24	35
Great Britain	16	25	64	87	100
Austrian empire	7	8	11	15	23
Germany	8	9	15	25	52
Russia	6	7	8	10	15
United States	9	14	21	38	69
Japan	7	7	7	9	12
China	6	6	4	4	3
India	6	6	3	2	1

Source: Paul Kennedy, *The Rise and Fall of the Great Powers: Economic Change and Military Conflict from 1500 to 2000.* Vintage Books, 1987, p. 149.

TABLE 3.3 Production of coal, pig iron and raw steel, 1830–1910

In millions of metric tons

	Great Britain	Germany	United States
Coal			
1830	22.8	1.8	0.8
1870	112.0	26.4	36.3
1910	269.0	152 and 70 (lignite)	473.0
Pig iron			
1830	0.69	0.11	0.17
1870	6.06	1.26	1.69
1910	10.57	13.17	27.10
Raw steel			
1830	0.33	0.13	0.77
1870	3.64	2.10	4.34
1910	6.48	13.10	25.71

Source: Charles S. Maier, 'Leviathan 2.0' in Emily Rosenberg, ed., *A World Connecting, 1870–1945*. Harvard UP, 2012, p. 100.

context that the confidence of the last great Qing emperor of the eighteenth century, Qianlong, was on display when, in 1793, he made the rare decision to allow a British delegation led by George Macartney to bypass normal court rituals and practices and meet him. Qianlong assumed, wrongly as it turned out, that the delegation came to pay tribute. Instead his court was treated to an ill-conceived demonstration of astronomical instruments and an impolitic request for a permanent British presence in Beijing and a reduction in the Chinese restrictions on British trade. Qianlong's honour was impugned and he felt no compunction in expelling Macartney and his entourage out of his empire.[32]

Despite such increasing foreign pressures, during the Napoleonic wars China's wealth grew immensely as tons of foreign silver flowed into Chinese coffers in exchange for Chinese products.[33] But after 1815, China's fortunes turned. First, the BEIC challenged the workings of the Canton system by demanding that China accept British goods as payment in kind for Chinese products (as opposed to payment in silver or gold). The decision was decisive. It opened up China to foreign manufactures, undermining the sale of local manufactures of similar goods (which were more expensive to produce) and decreasing the tax take of the Chinese state. The new arrangement also offered a powerful justification for British merchants to smuggle opium into China, a trade that expanded eightfold between 1815 and the 1830s.[34] Unsurprisingly, the Qings outlawed the sale of opium, fully aware of the injurious social and economic impacts of the drug and of the deleterious impact its importation had on China's balance of trade. In response, the British smugglers, many of whom were formally connected to the BEIC, demanded that the trade be legitimized.

The impact of British opium trading in the opening decades of the nineteenth century highlights some key elements about the 'successes' of British industrialization on a global scale. First, the trade aimed not only at exacting great profit for particular individuals but also at expanding the overall wealth and power of the British empire. Second, the trade sat at the heart of expanding British economic and imperial power globally. Much of the opium traded by the British merchants in China came from South Asia, a region where British imperial power was expanding, but which in 1815 had a thriving manufacturing economy (operated by manual labour) and a vast regional economic influence. Like China, Mughal India was an economic powerhouse, operating one-fifth of the global economy.[35]

By investing in Indian opium, the British merchants helped to undermine these Indian advantages. The British not only incentivized the spread of opium plantations but also expanded the potential export gains from the produce. As the British colonial administrator John Crawfurd explained in 1837, the export of opium from out of India was larger than the 'sum paid by foreign nations for all the wines exported from France, Spain and Italy'.[36] British oversight of the sale of the opium in China (and elsewhere, including in Britain itself) not only grew British wealth but it also allowed India, as Crawfurd also argued, 'to increase ten-fold its consumption of British Manufactures', in the process undermining local artisanal industries.[37] For in India too, British manufactured goods, as opposed to expensive gold and silver, were increasingly used as trade commodities. In this way, both India and China became economically dependent on Britain.[38] In the case of South Asia, that dependence helped to expand British formal dominion over the sub-Indian continent, which was completed in 1858 when the Mughal empire collapsed and symbolically heightened when Queen Victoria declared herself 'Empress of India' in 1876. Chinese dependence on British manufactures helped to undermine the ability of the Qing dynasty to sustain its own sovereign and regional power.

The story of opium and its impact on expanding Britain's formal and informal empire is a telling example of the costs and benefits of nineteenth-century industrial imperialism. As the following chapters will explain in more detail, 'winning' in this age of industry came with much violence and destruction. It also occasioned considerable resistance. The Qings, for one, did not let the British attack their sovereignty unopposed. Thus, when the governor of Canton dumped several shiploads of British opium into his harbour in 1839, war ensued. Britain fought two wars with China (the first between 1839 and 1842, the second from 1856 to 1858; see Figure 3.2). Both aimed at forcing the Qings to accept British opium sales and expanding British trading power in China.[39] China lost these wars in large part because of the clear technological advantages enjoyed by Britain's naval ships and the weapons employed by British troops. The Qings were left to sign two treaties opening up five Chinese ports to British trade and conceding Hong Kong as a permanent base for British operations in the region.

The Opium Wars set the stage for the rapid decline of the Qing empire in terms of global power. Not only did the Qings concede trading rights to a growing number of other foreign powers – all of them industrializing empires, including France, Germany, Russia, Japan and the United States – they also conceded extra-territorial rights to a number of their seaports. By 1911, fifty Chinese ports were bound by some kind of extra-territoriality clause providing exclusive access to a foreign state.[40] Similar kinds of concession agreements were wrestled by these same industrial powers in Vietnam, Siam (Thailand), Korea and Japan (the Japanese ports were returned to the Meiji in 1889). These 'unequal treaties' were a manifestation of the asymmetries evolving out of the advantages enjoyed by the industrializing powers.

The treaties also reflected the fact that the Qings failed to industrialize at the rate and efficiency of these other powers. There were numerous reasons for that failure, some of which were related to the choices made by China's ruling elites, some of which were a result of the growing political instability within China (which heightened during the devastating Taiping rebellion, a civil war that raged from 1850 to 1864 and cost more than 20 million Chinese their lives) and some were a result of the problems encountered by a dynasty ruling a vast landed empire steeped in centuries of tradition and struggling to adapt to the rapid rate of change confronting it. From the 1860s on, the Qing government needed the collective diplomatic support of all the industrializing empires to sustain their own dynastic power and to keep the empire from disintegrating.[41] From the perspectives of the other empires, neutralizing China (so that no one power enjoyed an exclusive economic or diplomatic advantage over it) was akin to sustaining the concert system in Europe or protecting the Monroe Doctrine in the Americas. These industrial powers

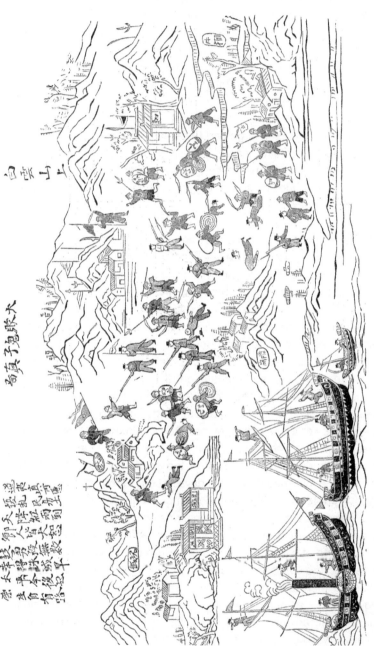

FIGURE 3.2 *The Second Opium War, 1856–8. This Chinese depiction of the campaign fought between Chinese and British forces at the battle for Fatsham Creek on the Canton river brings out the technological differences between the opposing forces: the British had steamships and rifles, the Chinese operated junks, swords and shields. While the British certainly had invested in more modern military equipment by the 1850s, they did not have the manufacturing capacity to modernize in the way the British were able to at the time.*
Source: *Wood engraving, c.1856, Getty Images, 88890336.*

could all share in the opportunities offered to them by accessing the Chinese economy without endangering the balance of power between them.

This is not to say that the Chinese were pliant victims of these industrial empires. The Qings also looked to adapt, reform and change in the face of the economic, military and political pressures of the industrial age. One of their strategies was to wage commercial warfare in Korea. Wary that any seizure of territory in the Korean peninsula might provoke the European great powers or Japan, the Qings instead used its merchants as a vanguard of intervention and imposed their own unequal commercial treaties upon the Hermit Kingdom. Though deeply resentful of the impact of such agreements in its own treaty ports, the Qings saw their value when imposing them on others.[42] Like China itself, Korea would become the target of economic and military imperialism from many directions (including by China, Russia and Japan) and, in the end, was formally incorporated into the Japanese empire after the Russo-Japanese War of 1904–5. More generally, however, when modern industrialization did begin to take off in China it was located in the foreign settlement areas that sprung up in the concession ports. By 1900, for example, the concession port of Shanghai was a modern metropolis with a well-functioning industrial core. Its economic growth depended both on its connection to the world economy and on a combination of foreign and Chinese investment in new industry.[43]

In contrast, where the Qings and Mughals failed to adapt effectively to the 'age of industrialization', the recently independent United States thrived as an industrial power in the nineteenth century. In 1815, the United States was not considered a great power let alone a global power. By 1900, it was both of these things. Its rise to geopolitical significance was dependent on effective industrialization (aided initially by British investment), geographic expansion across the north American continent and a massive swelling of migrants who brought their wealth, ideas and labour potential with them (for which see Chapter 5). American expansionism across the century involved direct military conflict with Mexico, the remnants of the Spanish empire and with the many indigenous peoples who lived in the region or were driven west by this white power where slaves were still owned until 1865. The civil war between the Union forces and the Confederacy ended in that year and provided further military strength for the United States government to consolidate its claims across the sweeping north American plains. Settlers, miners, the transcontinental railways and telegraph lines, Chinese labourers, white man's law and governance all flowed across the continent drawing on the tools and systems of the industrial global age (for which see Chapter 4). After 1870, the United States rivalled the other industrial powers in terms of production and innovation. It also grew its own global connections, including across the Pacific Ocean. It utilized easy access to the Latin American states for primary products and raw materials that helped to both expand and cement its industrial advantages. In turn and much like China and Mughal India, these Latin American states struggled to break free from the economic yokes imposed on them by the United States and the European industrial powers.[44]

There were, then, clear advantages to be enjoyed by those states that industrialized early and fast. When circumstances permitted, however, late industrializers could catch up. The example of the Russian Romanov dynasty is a case in point. In 1815, and like the Qings and Ottomans, the Romanov dynasty was a powerful landed empire steeped in tradition and age-old economic practices. It controlled more than 10 percent of the world's landmass and its tsar played a major role in determining the contours of the concert of Europe established at Vienna in 1815. After Russia's defeat in the Crimean War (1853–6), a war that cost the Russian serf-based economy dearly,[45] Tsar Alexander II embarked on a modernization campaign aiming both to industrialize the Russian empire and protect Russian geopolitical and economic power in so doing. Serfdom was abolished in Russia in 1861 (see Figure 3.3) before slavery was abolished in the United States (1865). Emancipating more than 23 million people from economic servitude was a monumental development and massive step towards industrializing the vast Russian empire. The Romanov regime of the 'Tsar Liberator', as Alexander II came to be known, passed further agricultural, educational, legal, military and administrative reforms in the 1860s and 1870s.

Despite Alexander II's intent and in contrast to that of the United States or the west European countries, Russia's industrialization process was slow and encountered formidable obstacles that were broadly present in the peasant economies of other landed empires as well (like those of the Austrian Habsburgs, Qings or the Ottomans). Some of these obstacles related to the relative lack of capital, education and opportunity the vast proportion of former serfs and agricultural labourers struggled with after emancipation. Like the Habsburgs, Qings and Ottomans, Russia's elite also debated what they considered to be the costs and benefits of adopting Westernization practices and worried about their impact on native traditions and customs. In the face of rising foreign investment in the Russian economy (not least by the French, British and Germans), the concern was pressing.[46] This caution was one of the reasons why Russia retained the peasant commune (*mir* or *obshchina*) within the structure of the post-emancipation peasant village. It was hoped that this traditional Slavic institution could buffer the shock of change and give some social stability to the agricultural economy that was now open to the full force of market capitalism. By 1900, Russia was starting to compete with its great power rivals. Over the course of the 1890s, the number of factories in Russia doubled and the rate of economic growth reached 8 percent per annum, which matched that of the United States. Over the next fourteen

FIGURE 3.3 *The emancipation of Russia's serfs, 1861. A crowd of people in the Russian city of Moscow greet the news of Tsar Alexander II's emancipation declaration with celebration. The emancipation of Russia's serfs in 1861 brought 23 million people out of economic servitude and aimed at modernizing the Romanov empire so that it could start to compete effectively with its successfully industrializing imperial rivals.*
Source: Photograph of Moscow gathering, 1861, Getty Images, 625141398.

years, Russia established itself as a leading producer in cotton textiles, iron and petroleum.[47]

Like the other industrializing great powers, Russia also looked to expand its economic and imperial global reach and looked for them particularly along its southern and far-eastern Pacific borderlands.[48] The Trans-Caspian railway begun in 1880 brought Russian power more effectively into the borderlands of the Persian empire (present-day Iran) and in the 1890s, further lines provided better access to Afghanistan. All these developments increased tensions with the British who were particularly concerned about Russian encroachments into India.[49] Similar efforts brought increased Russian pressure on the struggling Chinese empire and the Manchurian peninsula where Japan would soon have rival interests.[50] These Asian ventures accelerated in the 1880s and 1890s (also souring Russia's relationship with Germany while improving those with France). The building of a large railway system to connect the European part of Russia with its long-held but underutilized Siberian and Asian regions, was one of the principal instruments of Russia's industrialization process. Extending the trans-Siberian rail system east and south into the Manchurian region of the Qings brought Russian productive capacity into one of the great hubs of the Asian marketplace and was one factor in the 1890s that drew extensive Chinese migration from Hebei and Shandong north into the region.[51] Russia's industrial-driven drive to the Pacific effectively connected the European world directly with the Asian world over the longest railway line on the globe.

These Russian developments occurred at about the same time as the Japanese, under their revitalized Meiji imperial order, embarked on a similar effort to redeploy their considerable energies and talents to the needs of the industrializing global age. Like Russia, the Japanese had to overcome serious obstacles, albeit obstacles of a different kind. Until the 1850s they had limited contact with foreigners other than the Dutch and were lacking in the fossil fuels needed to power industrial production. This meant that the Japanese had to import a great many elements, just as the Egyptians had tried unsuccessfully to do in the 1820s. Fortunately for the Japanese, their domestic manufacturers were open to change, they had a relatively high rate of literacy and a culture that was open to Western science and adaptation.[52] Japanese reformers in the 1860s and 1870s encouraged changes in education that soon were coupled with the goals of the resurgent imperial regime and invited collaboration with the existing economic and military powers. Meiji elite aimed to distinguish Japan from the rest of Asia (and especially China) as it sought to 'enter the West' by demonstrating its 'civilization' and 'enlightenment' (bunmei kaika). In particular, it imposed a strong anti-narcotic regime that highlighted its difference from China, which continued to struggle with the British-led opium trade.[53] By the 1890s, Japan was a powerful state able to compete with all the other industrial empires in the region. It used warfare and economic strategies to expand its influence, not least over Korea, the Manchurian peninsula and into China. Japan's victory in the Russo-Japanese War (1904–5) signaled to the world that it was a significant industrial power.[54]

Two other important empires, namely the Austrian Habsburg and Ottoman empires, played significant roles in the nineteenth-century international system and were also late industrializers. Both empires struggled with industrialization not least because they were preoccupied with maintaining their own domestic order in this era of massive economic and political change. Austria (later Austria-Hungary)[55] possessed some important industrial advantages, not least the Skoda metallurgy and munitions works (established in 1859). The imperial capital, Vienna, boasted the wealth of numerous financial houses that were also active in the global market places of industrial capitalism. The Hungarians were also very active in the later part of the century leveraging a strong agricultural base with new industrial production in food processing and manufacturing. By the late decades of the century industrial growth rates across the empire were approaching 4 percent per annum, a rate that was certainly competitive with most of Europe.[56]

Having said all this however, it is critical to understand that unlike the Russian and Japanese examples, there was no real 'imperial' consensus in place to develop the empire as a whole and much of the industrial dynamism was localized and regionalized. Thus, as the historian Dominic Lieven argues, Austria-Hungary might well have become a real player in an era where economics, rather than social-political cohesion dominated, but the immediate concerns of the imperial government were never left to rest on economics. In the Habsburg empire, divisive politics consumed the attention of the governing elite to a degree rivalled only by that of the Ottoman empire.[57] As nationalist movements developed in the Balkans and produced nation-states such as Serbia, Romania and Bulgaria, the borderlands of Austria-Hungary were inevitably inflamed. All of this meant that Austria-Hungary remained an important power in Europe and especially in the changing landscape of the Balkans, but it lacked the imperial strength and will to look much beyond its changing borderlands. As a state, it could not play a major part in the spread of global industrial capitalism.

The Ottoman empire, like the Russian and Austro-Hungarian empires, was also a multi-ethnic state with a large peasant population. It played a key role in the sustenance of the concert of Europe system as the Middle East was too geostrategically important for any one European power to dominate and thus they preferred it to rest in Ottoman hands. For much of the century, the empire also relied on foreign investment for its economic growth. Traditional Muslim elites were even more wary than Russian elites of introducing new and foreign systems into their society, so where there was growth Ottoman Christians and Europeans dominated. The Turkish carpet industry, for example, did modernize but it was controlled by six British companies. All the commercial banking houses and stock brokerages in Istanbul were run by Christians. Greeks comprised at least one-third of the Chambers of Commerce in the empire.[58] The Ottomans recognized the need to modernize transportation and communication networks and railways and telegraph lines expanded after 1860, albeit slowly. Some in the empire, like those who made up the Young Turk movement in particular, looked at the Japanese example as a potential model for Ottoman modernization with Turkish nationalism as a possible unifying identity but the deep religious and ethnic divisions made any sort of imperial strategy problematic.[59]

All of this meant that while the Ottoman empire laid across many of the most important corridors of global economic trade in the eastern Mediterranean, by the late nineteenth century it had become a target of foreign investment rather than one of the chief architects of globalization. Given more time it may have developed an economic strategy to strengthen the empire politically but this required more time and ongoing peace to be maintained. Given the ethnic and religious differences within the empire and the potency of anti-imperialist nationalism that had already successfully produced an independent Greece and the rise of a number of Balkan nation states in the 1870s, the challenges only increased. Like Austria-Hungary, the Ottoman sultanate looked to diffuse its own domestic concerns first and foremost. As long as the great powers worked in concert to help them to manage these issues peacefully, the Ottoman empire had some chance of survival. When war came again to the Balkans in 1912, 1913 and especially 1914, the empire was in peril.

Study questions

1. What were the defining features of the mercantilist system? How did they differ from the economic principles of nineteenth-century industrial capitalism?

2. Why was the shift from manual to mechanical labour so revolutionary?

3. In what way is the British opium trade to China after 1815 indicative of the geopolitical costs and benefits attached to 'successful' industrial imperial expansion?

4. In geopolitical terms, which empires thrived in the nineteenth century? Which struggled? What role did industrialization play in these struggles?

Recommended readings

Michael Adas, *Machines as the Measure of Men: Science, Technology and the Ideologies of Western Dominance*. Cornell UP, 1989: Chapter 3 'Global hegemony and the rise of technology as the main measure of human achievement', pp. 133–98.

Marie-Claire Bergère, *Shanghai: China's Gateway to Modernity*. Stanford UP, 2009: Chapter 3 'The birth of Shanghai capitalism (1860–1911)', pp. 50–83.

Hans Derks, *History of the Opium Problem: The Assault on the East c. 1600–1950*. Brill, 2012: Chapter 6 'Tea for opium vice versa', pp. 49–86.

Trevor Getz, *The Long Nineteenth Century, 1750–1914: Crucible of Modernity*. Bloomsbury, 2018: Chapter 4 'Industrialization', pp. 111–42.

Paul Kennedy, *The Rise and Fall of the Great Powers: Economic Change and Military Conflict from 1500 to 2000*. Vintage Books, 1987: Chapter 4 'Industrialization and the shifting global balances 1815–1885', pp. 143–93 (especially pp. 143–69).

E. D. Langer, J. Tutino, 'Epilogue: Consolidating divergence: The Americas and the world after 1850' in J. Tutino, ed., *New Countries: Capitalism, Revolutions, and Nations in the Americas 1750–1870*. Duke UP, 2016, pp. 376–85.

Dominic Lieven, *Empire: The Russian Empire and Its Rivals*. Yale Nota Bene, 2000: Chapter 8 'Tsarist empire: Power, strategy, decline', pp. 262–87.

Jürgen Osterhammel, *The Transformation of the World: A Global History of the Nineteenth Century*. Princeton UP, 2014: Chapter 12 'Energy and industry', pp. 637–72.

Carroll W. Pursell Jr, *Machine in America: A Social History of Technology*. Johns Hopkins UP, 2007: Chapter 4 'The expansion of American manufactures', pp. 87–107.

Peter N. Stearns, *The Industrial Revolution in World History*. Fourth edition, Westview Press, 2013: particularly Chapter 1 'Britain's revolution', pp. 21–40, Chapter 3 'The industrial revolution in western society', pp. 53–69 and Chapter 5 'The industrial revolution outside the west', pp. 89–108.

Steven C. Topik, Allen Wells, 'Commodity chains in a global economy' in Emily Rosenberg, ed., *A World Connecting 1870–1945*. Belknap Press, 2012, pp. 685–812.

4

Building globalization's infrastructure after 1850

Nineteenth-century imperialism was the product of industrial expansionism and capitalism. It relied on private enterprise and the active promotion of imperial endeavours by governments and states alike. By the late 1870s, formal and informal imperial ambitions were firmly embedded in the foreign policy objectives of most industrializing states. But nineteenth-century globalization and industrialization processes were also enabled by the investment made by businesses and governments in vast infrastructure projects, which augmented the growing interconnectedness of people, places, goods, money and ideas.

This chapter focuses on the processes and projects that helped to spur globalization during the second half of the century, manifested both as physical developments (like the building of railway lines, canals, serviceable roads, telegraph and telephone lines, public electricity supply and sanitation systems) and as conceptual ones (such as the assertion of sovereignty and property rights, the development of banking, insurance and legal systems and the rise of intergovernmental treaties and agreements). Global interconnectivity was the product of technological achievement and cerebral endeavour, of violence and cooperation, of private enterprise and public power. It depended on economic drivers, political will and physical exertion.

These nineteenth-century global infrastructure projects and their potential also excited the imagination of many contemporaries. As an example, consider French author Jules Verne's fictional account, *Around the World in 80 Days*, which was published as a newspaper serial for the first time in 1872. In the story, the protagonist Phileas Fogg took up the challenge to circumnavigate the globe in 80 days, the minimum time needed as estimated by the British newspaper the *Daily Telegraph*. The challenge, issued during a game of cards, saw Fogg leave London that very evening, travel via the Suez Canal to India, across the Great Indian Peninsula Railway, by steamer to Hong Kong and on to Yokohama, across the Pacific Ocean to San Francisco, aboard the American Transcontinental Railway towards New York and then by steamship cross the Atlantic Ocean back to London. Amidst numerous exotic adventures, the fictional Fogg made it home just before the deadline passed.

The novel was a huge success, particularly in the English-reading world. Unlike most of Verne's other work, which was more representative of science fiction (a literary genre invented in the nineteenth century to reflect on futuristic worlds based on imagined advances in science and technology), *Around the World in 80 Days* was founded on achievable goals. The journalist Elizabeth Cochran (who was also known as Nellie Bly) circumnavigated the planet in 1889 in the space of seventy-two days, reporting on her endeavours every step of the way by telegraph transmission. She even met up with Verne in Amiens.[1] But in 1872, Verne's fictional journey could also have been realized: the Suez Canal and American Transcontinental Railway were completed in 1869, followed by the Great Indian Peninsula Railway a year later. These incredible feats of engineering ensured that the world, as Verne described it, 'has grown smaller: since a man can now go around it ten times more quickly than a hundred years ago'.[2]

Of course, few nineteenth-century men or women could actually do what the fictional Phileas Fogg and the adventurous Nelly Bly did. The world was more accessible to some than others. Race, class, gender and wealth all played key roles in determining the prospects afforded to individuals in the nineteenth century. While industrial globalization opened up opportunities for some, it impeded, restricted and restrained others. The Polish sailor Konrad Korzeniowski, for example, penned a bleak novel about the impact of industrial imperialism in 1899 using his anglophile name Joseph Conrad. Conrad's *Heart of Darkness* reflected on the venal nature of global capitalism and the degenerate impact of greed and corruption operating at the edges of the industrial empires, in this case in the African region of the Congo. Conrad's derision of globalization was based on his own experiences travelling the world, including to the Congo, where he witnessed the unfettered exploitation of the land, wildlife and people first-hand.[3] Thus, where Verne celebrated the novelty afforded by the opening up the world to travel and enjoyment by those with wealth or opportunity, Conrad quailed at global capitalism's human and environmental toll.

The building of the Suez Canal, American Transcontinental Railway and Great Indian Peninsula Railway were all industrial and imperial projects aimed at improving the speed of travel, the movement of people and goods and at obtaining sizeable profits for the individuals and governments who invested in them. These were clearly also capitalist endeavours, products of the coming together of enterprising ideas with investment, government buy-in and the labour of thousands. The Suez Canal, for example, was initiated by the French diplomat Ferdinand de Lesseps in the 1850s, but it involved monetary investment from around the world. It took ten years to construct, involving tens of thousands of labourers from Egypt and elsewhere, many of whom worked on it under circumstances of duress, some of whom died in the process.[4] It was, like so many nineteenth-century industrial projects, the product of an immense well of blood, sweat and tears and a great deal of capital.

But the Suez Canal was also revolutionary. On opening in 1869, it cut a ship's journey from the Mediterranean to the Red Sea by 7,000 kilometres and changed the ways in which ships and people travelled across the world. The canal effectively linked Asia, Oceania, the Middle East and Eastern Africa, and with it the Indian Ocean economy, more directly to that of Europe. In so doing, it facilitated global trade, global migration and global capitalism and as Valeska Huber's work shows heightened global and regional interconnectivity in a multitude of ways.[5] Perhaps more than any other nineteenth-century enterprise, the Suez Canal symbolized the dynamism of a globally connected world (see the illustration on the book cover). Port Said, at the canal's Mediterranean opening, also grew into a bustling service town, proffering coal, victuals and entertainment to the steamships, passengers and crews that made the journey up or down the canal. The town quickly came to represent the Janus-face of nineteenth-century globalization. On the one hand it reflected the 'respectability' of a thriving industrial port city, filled with a cosmopolitan array of merchants, bankers, sailors, diplomats and migratory individuals: a microcosm of the world. On the other hand, Port Said was also a seedy town of drinkers, gamblers and prostitutes, a place of competing jurisdictions and racially defined neighbourhoods: a city where law and order were hard to sustain and where criminality thrived.[6]

Where the Suez Canal represented the globality of nineteenth-century infrastructure, the completion of the transcontinental railway system in the United States reflected the violent forces of nineteenth-century American nation-building. As Figure 4.1 highlights, the railway and the telegraph line connected the American frontier to the governing hub of the country on the east coast. It too was an imperial project involving tens of thousands of workers, costing many lives and providing even more impetus for settlers to eradicate the indigenous communities whose lands were carved up to accommodate this new form of 'progress'. Once completed, east coast met west, greatly shortening what had been a lengthy and dangerous journey by ship around Tierra del Fuego at the southern tip of South America or by wagon across the vast continental hinterland. Sizeable cities, like Chicago and St Louis, grew at the junction points of the ever-growing American railway net. The United States as a nation consisting of fifty individual states was very

FIGURE 4.1 *Manifest destiny. This 1870s rendering of the nineteenth-century American concept of 'manifest destiny' depicted the United States as an allegorical white woman (à la the Statue of Liberty) crossing the north American continent with settlers, farmers, telegraph and railway lines in tow, driving First Nations' communities, the buffalo and other wildlife out. It offers an excellent perspective of some of the human and environmental costs and benefits associated with the growth of the United States as an industrial empire during the nineteenth century.*
Source: *Chromolithograph, c.1873, Getty Images, 113491955.*

much the product of the age of industrialization. Once the Panama Canal was constructed across the Panama isthmus in 1914 – another American project with considerable international input and local agency – the Atlantic and Pacific Oceans were even more easily linked, forming a truly interconnected oceanic space and opening up the United States' rise to great power status over the ensuing century.

Meanwhile, the Great Indian Peninsula Railway connected up the interior of the Indian subcontinent to the global trade ports dotted along its lengthy coastline. It solidified Bombay's (known today as Mumbai) essential place as the economic gateway city to the region, not least because it was so easily accessible from the Suez Canal.[7] Throughout the nineteenth century, Bombay's population boomed. In 1833 it sat around 230,000, by 1891 it was more than 800,000.[8] India modernized on the back of its railway network, which by 1900 accounted for 5.3 percent of the world's total railway mileage. By 1910, India had the fourth largest rail network in the world, ranking only after Russia, Germany and the United States.[9] Still, the Indian railways were also colonial capitalist projects. They were built by the hard labour of locals but at the behest of the British colonial authorities for the profit of British investors. They also decimated the local environment. Of the 271 million pounds sterling invested by Britons in South Asia between 1845 and 1873, 200 million was spent on the railways.[10] The reasons were related to profit and imperial control, the promise of a growing market economy and hope of more easily and successfully ruling and exploiting the vast Indian subcontinent's human and material resources.

All of these infrastructure enterprises would not have been built without the convergence of a number of key developments, not least of which was the willingness of investors to spend a vast amount of money on the ventures. From their perspective, reducing the risks involved was paramount. Consider the range of associated questions: Is territorial sovereignty clearly demarcated across the physical space of the route? Is there a reliable (and cheap) workforce and a steady (and cheap) supply of steel, wood and other resources to build the route? Can a steady supply of reliable (and cheap) coal be secured to utilize the route? Is the territory safe from sabotage or attack? Do local laws and policing mechanisms allow for the safe collection of transportation fees? Are the taxes collected on profits by the local authorities reasonable? Is there a reliable banking system in place to handle the financial transactions? Is there a reliable monetary system operating in the region? Do local communities operate under a standard system of time? How easily can local and foreign businesses and merchants access the facilities? How will information about the movement of trains and ships be communicated locally and globally? What happens if the venture fails? Can I acquire insurance for my investment? What happens to the investment in time of war, popular unrest or strife?

Transnational infrastructure investments like railway lines, telegraph cabling and international canals needed guarantees of their long-term security. Achieving security depended on buy-in and support from local communities (or at the very least from local authorities) and from higher-level government officials. International treaties that aimed at mitigating risk and maximizing profit were often an integral part of the construction process. The building of the Suez Canal, for example, not only required a long-term lease from the Egyptian government (who owned the territory through which the canal passed) but also witnessed an international treaty effectively neutralizing the canal so that regardless of which state owned the Suez Canal company and the lease, all countries could send their merchant and naval ships through on payment of a fee to the company. They could do so regardless of a situation of warfare. During the Spanish–American War of 1898, for example, the Spanish government paid the Suez Canal Company £12,000 to enable its naval fleet to pass through.[11] The Panama Canal involved a similar treaty. These interoceanic canals were deemed too important for the functioning of the global economy (and the well-being of all industrial states) to be controlled by any one sovereign power alone.

For similar reasons (namely, maximizing access to markets and profits as well as improving the cohesion and interconnectedness of their empire or country), the industrializing states invested heavily in their own internal transportation and communications infrastructure. They also issued contracts and concessions to private companies to improve roads, build railway tracks, open up canal systems and establish telegraph and telephone lines and public electricity supplies. They centralized postal services and regulated banking systems. They expanded police and judicial systems in part to increase security, police labour unrest and enforce contracts. They designed laws to legitimate the seizure of land. In no way were these endeavours benign: they aimed at profit, surveillance and growth. They enforced a particular version of 'law and order' on citizens and subjects alike. The most successful infrastructure projects adapted to local conditions and engaged local support to make them work.[12] Successful infrastructure, much like successful empires, depended on the workability of the relationship between individuals on the ground, local communities, business interests, governments and the international environment.

In the second half of the nineteenth century, the number of global infrastructure projects supported by the industrializing states expanded exponentially. For example, where in 1868 the world supported 135,378 miles of telegraph cabling and counted 25.5 million telegraph messages sent that year, in 1905 it supported 786,340 miles of cables transmitting 392 million messages.[13] Across the same period, the available tonnage on steamships plying global waters grew from 2,700,000 tonnes (in 1870) to 26,200,000 tonnes (in 1910).[14] The world's rail network increased from 5,500 miles (mostly built in Britain, Europe and the Americas) in 1840 to 6,404,000 miles by 1910 (built in all continents, barring Antarctica).[15] Enterprising private investors and agents, both local and foreign, made their fortunes on the back of these developments.

The net result of this frantic infrastructure building boom was a more globally connected planet, one in which it did not take many months for a person of means to circumnavigate the globe, but rather a matter of weeks. Once the trans-Pacific telegraph cable was completed in 1902, a message could make the same journey in a matter of minutes. Nineteenth-century globalization was thus clearly a product of the industrial revolution, the offspring of the marriage between technological innovation and capitalist investment. As shown in the previous chapters, while industrialization began as a private enterprise (where entrepreneurs invested in new endeavours), it thrived when governments at an imperial and local level enabled and supported its growth. Globalization was thus also an imperial and capitalist development. It drew the world into its web, or as the historian Stephen Kern metaphorically describes in his book *The Culture of Time and Space*: globalization expanded as a 'stranglehold of iron tentacles' sucking all into the 'mainstream of national and international markets' and uniting 'the land masses to sea lanes in a single commercial unit'.[16]

Of course, the infrastructure that sustained the rise in global power of the industrializing empires was built on more than transportation and communication networks. It also needed a viable and stable international economy in which to function and a stable and reliable international political system in which to grow. The success of industrialization depended, substantial to a degree, on ensuring a stable, predictable and reliable international environment for the movement and exchange of goods, ideas and people. It needed military and policing power to back it up. As Jared Diamond explains, Western power was also built with *Guns, Germs and Steel*.[17] It was enabled by ready access to the world's seas and oceans. It also depended on the development and acceptance of a set of uniform concepts to regulate and regularize international relationships (be they economic, diplomatic, legal, social or scientific). The second half of the nineteenth century saw the proliferation of a range of new institutions to systematize these international relationships. The rest of this chapter focuses on some of the most important of these.

Unsurprisingly, given that the leading industrializing powers were largely Anglo-European, it was according to Anglo-European standards and values that many of these international concepts evolved. Furthermore, the acquisition of overseas empires by the industrial powers enabled the speedier imposition of standardized rules and ways of behaving on colonized communities. The conceptual framing of global interaction – be it an economic transaction, the scheduling of a passenger ship's timetable or the movement of a posted letter – helped to organize the world according to Western principles of law and order. Western concepts as much as people and materials colonized the world. This did not mean that local cultures ended nor that cultural appropriation was a one-way process. Globalization made the movement and exchange of ideas and people (where-ever their point of origin) easier and more frequent. But it did mean that Western norms dominated the global environment and that all communities encountered those norms and had to engage with them.

The rest of this chapter explains how key conceptual infrastructure projects, namely the imposition of universal time keeping, the growth of a global banking and insurance system and the advance of international treaty law, helped to underwrite the growth of global capitalism and the rising power of the industrializing empires. It shows how contemporaries attempted to regulate and regularize global interactions by means of international agreements and the creation of international institutions. It highlights two fundamental impacts of the growth in international interconnectedness: the development of a global media environment and the rise of cosmopolitan spaces where people, ideas, money and influences from around the world interacted. Chapter 5 augments these arguments by highlighting how the movement of people affected these developments, while Chapter 6 describes the massive environmental costs involved. Chapters 7 and 8 analyse their impact on international stability, the waging of warfare and the policing of unrest and on the advance of a range of global and local political ideologies.

In an agricultural world, time tended to be kept by the movement of the sun and the changing of the seasons. In an industrial world, time tended to be kept by clocks and watches. Wages could be calculated by the hour. A fundamental outcome of the industrial revolution, then, was the widespread adoption of mechanical timekeeping and eventually the invention and adoption of universal time (Greenwich Mean Time (GMT)), which divided the globe into time bands and aimed at the adoption of the new time system by governments. In 1880, the Great Britain adopted GMT for all public timekeeping purposes, Japan did so in 1888, Belgium and the Netherlands in 1892, Germany, Austria-Hungary and Italy in 1893.[18] One driving force behind the adoption of universal timekeeping was improving the predictability of global trade and the simultaneous functioning of telegraph and telephone operations. Shipping timetables became common place in ports, so much so that they were published in most major newspapers. Passengers and traders could rely on these connections to get themselves and their goods to their desired destinations. Railway timetables were equally well organized and widely distributed.

For states to maximize profits from global interaction required careful tracking of imports, exports, duties and taxation. Industrialization was accompanied by a huge amount of paperwork, bureaucracy and rule-making, especially at a country's borders. But it also relied on a high degree of transnational cooperation. Diplomacy was carried out by an increasing number of individuals, both formal representatives of governments and representatives of commercial enterprises and the like.[19] Unsurprisingly, the nineteenth century witnessed the growth of diplomatic services and the opening up of embassies and consulates as entrepôts of commercial and diplomatic exchange in almost every global seaport and trade hub. The century also witnessed an increase in the professionalization and expansion of government services at home, ranging from tax collection to building educational facilities to the management of roads and health care.[20] In this industrializing age, the state came to play an increasingly prominent role in the lives of citizens and subjects alike.

Consider, for example, the expansion and centralization of postal services under government control. With the spread of railways and the timetabling of shipping connections, regularizing the movement of letters, parcels and printed materials also became possible. Enterprising governments realized that they could not only make money on facilitating a safe and reliable user-pays postal service but that they could also keep a closer check on the movement of goods while doing so. Standardized post became the norm in the wake of the invention of machine-produced envelopes and postage stamps around 1840. The first pre-printed postcards also date from this time. Many steamship companies made considerable profits from obtaining mail contracts from local authorities as agreements to carry the post from one city to another.[21]

But to enable such postal systems to truly function internationally, namely to guarantee a user that their item would reach a foreign destination, also required agreements between governments. In 1874, the Universal Postal Union was established in Switzerland at the behest of the industrializing states.[22] They agreed to guarantee delivery on each other's post, so that a parcel originating in New Delhi would reach its destination in São Paolo, even if it had to be carried and handled by a range of postal companies and shipping services along the way. With similar ends in mind, the International Telegraphic Union was established in 1865 to enable a speedy and effective international communication network, even when it passed through a number of different sovereign territories and telegraphic companies. In 1906, the Union was augmented to include a wireless telegraphy convention as well.[23] Integrating private enterprise with government agreements was an essential component of the growth of these services.

Equally important to growing the infrastructure of global industrialization was the standardization of the world's monetary systems. Not only did the expansion of global trade require greater security for the exchange and protection of funds, it also relied on improvements in international banking systems. By 1880, the global economy was increasingly integrated in part because global banking was a reality and because the gold standard was accepted as the global marker for the exchange rates of local currencies.[24] London sat at the heart of the global banking system.[25] Banks, like governments, had representatives in almost all outposts of the global trade network, be it Port Said, Hong Kong or the Samoan town of Apia.

The growth in insurance schemes also marked the expansion of global trade and the development of a global economy. Such schemes aimed at offering merchants and shipowners guarantees for any potential losses, where-ever they might occur along the global supply chain. For banks and insurance brokers, stability in diplomatic affairs and the protection of the stable functioning of the world's communications and transportation networks was essential. They looked to the governments of the industrializing empires to manage those elements of global interaction for them.

Governments also had a lot to gain by understanding who and what passed into their jurisdiction. They had to weigh up the potential benefits and dangers of setting import and export duties and other taxes on the wealth generated within their sovereign borders. Whether they advocated for free-trade policies (as the British generally did) or greater protectionism (as many other governments did, particularly during the global recession of the 1870s and 1880s),[26] monitoring domestic and foreign trade was a paramount responsibility of all states. So was the surveillance of the movement of people within and across territorial boundaries.[27]

A remarkable feature of the nineteenth-century global communications network, however, was that it offered relative ease of movement. While passports had existed for centuries, and their use fluctuated during the nineteenth century, by the 1860s citizens from European countries and the United States required little formal documentation to move around the world. Their governments looked to protect their citizens' right to travel. The same could not be said for the rest of the world's population. While migration was a common feature of the century (see Chapter 5), aided by the expansion of the number of passenger vessels traversing the world's seas and oceans, the destination of migrants came increasingly under scrutiny within and between the industrializing empires. By the latter decades of the century, most industrial states formally identified 'desirable' migrants and foreign visitors from 'undesirable' or potentially dangerous ones. Race, class, gender and place of origin all played a key hand in deciding who needed a passport and who had a legal right to enter a country and settle there.[28]

The ships that carried migrants also carried geographers, scientists and tourists, who travelled the world seeking out novel experiences. For these individuals, at least, access to the world could be 'bought' and 'consumed' through the purchase of a travel ticket, or as the French poet Valéry Larbaud proclaimed in 1908, 'The entire surface of the planet is ours when we want!'[29] Tourism thrived as a consumer product in all industrializing communities by the latter decades of the nineteenth century. The British tourism agency, Thomas Cook, set up shop in the 1840s, initially organizing local trips. By the 1860s, Cook was renowned for his tours of Europe and offered round-the-world trips à la Jules Verne by the 1890s. He also published popular destination guides, helping his travellers make the most of their foreign visits. The German Baedeker family also began printing guides to popular European destinations from 1827 on. During the 1870s, the company expanded its guides to include a number of non-European places, including the United States, Syria, Egypt and India. Until the outbreak of the First World War, the Baedeker was the most trusted tourist almanac available, published in German, French and English, richly illustrated with maps and local advice. Global tourism, then, was a commonplace phenomenon by 1900, dominated by wealthy white Westerners.[30]

As international economic, diplomatic, social and cultural interaction intensified across the century, so too did the attempts at creating viable international organizations to standardize and universalize essential international values. Alongside the Universal Postal Union and International Telegraphic Union, international organizations and institutions popped up in their dozens, offering mechanisms to make international communication and cooperation work.[31] They were well supported by the industrializing governments as essential tools for managing a complex range of international issues. Some of these, like the International Union of Railway Freight Transportation (set up in 1878) or the Automobile Conference of 1909 aimed at standardizing international transportation connections, including things like what side of the road one should drive on, the size of railway gauges and the steady supply of fuels.[32] Others, like the International Union of Weights and Measures (1875) and the International Union of Customs and Tariffs (1890) looked to establish workable norms for the movement, measurement and taxation of goods. The Union for the Protection of Industrial Property (1883) meanwhile regulated patents and the Hague Union for the Protection of Art and Literature (1886) established copyright rules that could be enforced across borders.[33]

Yet others aimed at combatting common public health concerns, including the improvement of sanitation systems and the control of communicable diseases in people and animals (like tuberculosis, cholera and mad cow disease).[34] The cooperation between governments on health issues was particularly important. The Bombay plague of the 1880s, for example, not only decimated the city's population but also threatened the health of the entire Indian Ocean region (and potentially further afield) because Bombay was such a globally connected industrial centre. Controlling the movement of people and goods across state borders was considered an essential part of growing a responsibly globally connected world.[35] Even the restriction of the sale and trade in addictive substances, including alcohol and drugs, came under the purview of international organization and policing by the latter stages of the century.[36] Britain's unrestricted opium-selling days were numbered.

The existence of the multitude of international organizations speaks volumes about the globalization and internationalization of everyday life.[37] It also speaks to the power of number-crunching, record-keeping and data collection. The International Statistics Congress of 1860, for example, argued that data collection was a government's most valuable tool enabling it to discover problems and improve people's lives. According to these statisticians, if you could measure it, you could improve it and thus statisticians aimed to use numbers to advance the 'universal happiness of mankind'.[38] If knowledge was power, then statistics and data became valuable currency for governments, banks and companies alike.[39] Well before the invention of twenty-first-century social media and 'big data', the measuring of human activity was a common feature of the industrializing state. So was keeping track of the internationalization processes in play, so much so, that plans for improving international affairs more logically and consistently also heightened during the latter stages of the century. By 1900, a Central Office of International Institutions was set up in Brussels and plans for centralizing these institutions in a single 'world city' proliferated.[40]

Many of these institutions were formally recognized by governments, part and parcel of the growth in international treaties and friendly agreements.[41] Others were private endeavours with widespread international application, including geographic and cartographic societies that aimed at mapping the topography of the world, and in so doing provide information to individuals and states alike to claim ownership, define borders and facilitate building projects. The British Royal Geographic Society was established in 1830 and began publishing its popular *National Geographic* magazine in 1888. Chinese geographers invested in mapping the globe for similar reasons, wanting to define 'their' space in the world.[42]

In their book, *A Rage for Order*, the historians Lisa Ford and Lauren Benton explain how the desire of British settlers in the early nineteenth century to impose law and order on colonized communities aimed at managing what they perceived as the 'chaos' of foreign places and foreign cultures to the colonizers' advantage. Ford and Benton argue that the origins of modern international law can be found in the desire of these colonists to establish predictable and sustainable police and legal powers in the formal and informal outposts of empire (i.e. both in 'formal' British colonies and settler communities and in 'informal' markets and places where British commercial interests grew).[43] Such laws enforced individual property rights, enabled commercial exploitation of the local community and standardized commercial transactions in line with these Westerners' expectations of what these standards should be. They also imposed a Western model of *sovereignty* (the concept that determines who has the right to make and enforce laws in a defined territory) on much of the world, supplanting the many pre-existing and alternate models of governance, property ownership and rule-making authority.

Certainly, nineteenth-century industrialization and imperial expansion were made possible by enforcing the industrializing states' rules and values onto their imperial outposts. But nineteenth-century industrial imperialism was also enabled by the signing of agreements and treaties between governments, between international companies and between international stake-holders.

Contracts, treaties, laws and lawyers all played key roles in the growth of industrial globalization, so much so that after the 1850s, governments increasingly employed international lawyers to help them to manage their imperial and foreign policies. This was a particularly urgent development as the growth of international commerce and the expansion of international business treaties also heightened the potential of disagreements, conflicts, fraud and breaches of contract. How to manage infringements or to enforce compliance had the potential to draw governments into complex and dangerous diplomatic situations, including the possibility of war.

As an example, consider how the European 'Scramble for Africa' in the 1870s and 1880s was conducted by means of both paper battles and forceful acquisition. In his book, *Rogue Empires*, the historian Steven Press shows how fraudulent treaty-making by a large number of enterprising (and 'ethically flexible') Europeans handed over large swathes of African territory to private companies, who ruthlessly exploited and ruled the land and its people as their private fiefdoms.[44] The Treaty of Berlin of 1885 (for more, see Chapter 5) presents one example of how the great powers attempted to regain the imperial momentum in Africa by formal means. By neutralizing the Congo, these powers ensured equal access to the territory's commercial, communications and transportation routes. By establishing a private company to administer the region, which was led by the King Leopold I from Belgium (a European neutral power), the Berlin treaty also aimed at minimizing the potential for a war developing in Africa between the rival empires (and companies). Above all, the 1885 Treaty spoke to the urgency all the industrializing governments felt that they needed to reclaim the 'right to rule' in the international environment.[45] While the Treaty failed to end the exploitation of Africa and Africans (Conrad's *Heart of Darkness*, shows up just how exploitative 'the unseen presence of victorious corruption' in Europe's conquest of Africa actually was),[46] it did frame the terms of formal governance in Africa as being determined by the great powers and in accordance with Western models of statehood, sovereignty and law-making, even if in effect many private companies still called the shots.

In many ways, the growth of international law in the nineteenth century and the development of a range of international conflict resolution processes were a logical by-product of the concert of Europe.[47] In a diplomatic environment that aimed at avoiding unwinnable or expensive wars between rival states, agreeing on rules and regulations that improved and standardized international relations and enabled international business made sense. It is not surprising then to see the industrializing states enter into a range of international agreements in the second half of the nineteenth century that aimed at standardizing the international law of neutrality (to protect non-belligerent commerce in time of war) and at improving international conflict resolution mechanisms, such as *arbitration* (resolving a conflict by having a neutral party adjudicate) and *mediation* (resolving a conflict by having a neutral negotiate a settlement between the affected parties).

It is also unsurprising to see that international law professionalized in the second half of the century, in line with the professionalization of state bureaucracies and diplomatic corps more widely.[48] International law became a recognized subject at universities from the middle of the century on, as a distinct field from domestic legal practice. The non-European states and empires, including those in Latin America, China, Japan and even Korea, invested heavily in training their own international lawyers, who were well-read in Western legal principles and concepts.[49] These states were all too cognizant of the fact that the international environment was increasingly determined by Western legal traditions and Western conceptions of statehood. Whether they liked it or not, they had to align their practices with these traditions in order to sustain their own sovereign existence and protect their interests within the global diplomatic and economic framework.

Like so much else associated with nineteenth-century globalization and imperial processes, international legal practices were also products of the Western world's racial and cultural biases. Even more importantly, these treaties, rules and international laws framed the right to claim sovereignty and power – 'the right to rule' – in racialized ways. In other words, the laws not only reflected but also enforced the white world's racial priorities by identifying those who claimed the right to rule as *citizens* of a 'civilized' state or empire and those who were to be ruled as *subjects*, a legal category that offered fewer rights and privileges. In Anglo-European empires, citizens tended to be white; subjects, non-white. Within this *Zeitgeist*, the claim to racial superiority also came to be directly connected with the technological and scientific progress made in (and the capitalist profits enjoyed by) the citizens of the industrializing states. As we will see in Chapter 7, this formulation of the concept of 'civilization' also allowed and enabled a sea of violence by Anglo-Europeans against non-European peoples.

In the nineteenth century, many white Christian Anglo-Europeans considered that 'civilization' was not a matter of opinion or perspective, or even of race *per se*. Rather, they considered 'civilization' a quantifiable quality, something that the century's statisticians could measure and describe. Accordingly, for a state or empire to be considered 'civilized' it needed to have clearly defined territorial borders, to be ruled by a sovereign law-making authority who protected private property rights, accepted the concepts of Western international law and be engaged as an equal in the international diplomatic sphere.[50] To become a member of the 'family of civilized nations' required a ruler to accept these principles and behave accordingly. Any community that did not abide by them was not considered 'civilized' but 'barbaric' (or, at best, 'semi-civilized'). As a result, such a society was a ready target for 'civilizing', which could involve the acquisition of a territory and its people by an already 'civilized' state. Paternalistic claims that their imperial wars and activities fulfilled a 'civilizing mission' and aimed at educating so-called 'lesser' people in 'superior' ways of behaving, underwrote and validated many Anglo-European self-assessments of their global activities in the nineteenth century. Of course, many of the non-European peoples who were being colonized and exploited considered these same activities invasive and derogatory and, as we shall see in Chapters 7 and 8, expended considerable energy in resisting them.[51]

The growth and spread of nineteenth-century international law then was an inherently colonizing development that aided the rise of international industrial capitalism and the political and cultural domination of the Anglo-European world over the rest.[52] Even Japan, an Asian country which managed to modernize quickly and efficiently after 1870, operated within the international legal, diplomatic, military and economic systems established by the Western industrializing states. Meiji Japan succeeded in large part because its government accepted the requirement to working within the international system developed by the West. The Japanese too advanced arguments of their own citizens' racial superiority in part because of their effective and efficient industrialization and growth in military power.[53]

Still, the globalization processes of the nineteenth century did much more than implement a racially defined international power structure, although it did that very well. As with so many of the nineteenth century's developments, globalization was infused with juxtapositions and paradoxes. Where on the one hand, the industrial globalization processes firmly embedded a racialized power structure – a 'global colour line' – onto global relations,[54] on the other, it opened up numerous cosmopolitan spaces and places where cultures and ideas intermingled.[55] It also heightened contemporary understandings of 'belonging' and 'difference' (see Chapter 8). Modernity grew as much in these interactive cosmopolitan spaces as it did in the global power system.

The very awareness of living in a globally connected world was carried by the infrastructure of globalization: on trains, ships, telegraph lines, in letters, newspapers, telephone conversations, in the exchange of money and in the sale of goods. Where people mingled and goods and ideas were exchanged, cultures connected. Even the plantation economies in Africa, the Caribbean and Latin America relied on the importation of European and American manufactures after all. *Globality* (the awareness of being connected to other people around the world) grew as the infrastructure of globalization expanded and as people moved around the world. It was particularly strong in the numerous cities that evolved as hubs of global commerce and migration, like London, Liverpool, Bombay, Singapore, Shanghai, Chicago, Port Said and

Los Angeles.[56] But even outside these globally connected urban spaces, unexpectedly cosmopolitan communities evolved.

Consider the nineteenth-century history of Aotearoa New Zealand for example. By the early 1800s, the Maori settlement at Kororareka (present-day Russell) expanded to include a multi-ethnic array of whalers, sailors, missionaries, bar tenders and prostitutes. Local Maori utilized their connections with these strangers to gain their own foothold in the international economic system. They expanded their farm lands, invested in shipping and sold their produce at markets in Port Jackson (Sydney), Pape'ete and Norfolk Island. Maori chiefs travelled to these markets and on to Europe, returning home with new crops, tools, weapons and animals and looked to maximize their opportunities.[57] Other Maori took jobs on board whaling and trading ships and travelled the world.

From 1815 on, the number of foreigners making their way to New Zealand also increased, so much so that the French and British governments competed to gain formal control of these South Pacific islands. After the Maori Declaration of Independence failed (see Chapter 2), the signing of the Treaty of Waitangi (from 1840 on) formally turned New Zealand into an outpost of the British empire, with predictably disastrous results for the indigenous population. Not only did even more foreigners and migrants arrive in New Zealand, but the British imperial authorities imposed their legal norms on all inhabitants, seized Maori-owned lands and ignored many Treaty terms. Maori hapu (tribes) in the centre of the North Island even went to war with the British to contest these incursions.[58]

Still, the foreigners kept coming. The port city of Auckland was a hub of international visitors, ship and fishing crews, signaling just how globalized the Pacific Ocean had also become by the 1850s.[59] By the time of the New Zealand gold rushes of the 1860s, even some of the remotest parts of the country had turned into multicultural spaces. The West Coast town of Hokitika with its inhospitable beach head, for example, had a population of six thousand in 1867 (it was the sixth largest municipality in the country at the time) and boasted more than one hundred hotels and numerous brothels. It also counted as the country's richest and busiest port.[60] When gold was discovered on the reefs of the Southern Alps in 1870, another new town appeared, Reefton. Within two years, its population numbered three thousand, including many individuals from China, the Americas, Australia and Europe. By 1888, Reefton was the first town in the southern hemisphere to acquire a public supply of electricity. Like so many other communities around the globalizing world, Reefton also boasted its own newspaper, the *Inangahua Herald*.[61]

Meanwhile, the geothermal region around the Rotorua lakes, including the springs at Te Aroha and the picturesque Otukapuarangi (Pink Terraces) and Te Tarata (White Terraces) became famous tourist destinations, bringing other

FIGURE 4.2 *New Zealand's pink and white terraces, c.1880. This photograph was taken around 1880 of the magnificent Pink and White Terraces (Te Otukapuarangi and Te Tarata) on Lake Rotomahana near the popular tourist town of Rotorua in Aotearoa New Zealand. Considered one of the 'wonders of the world' at the time, the terraces were a major reason why tourists flocked to New Zealand in the late nineteenth century. When the Mount Tarawera volcano erupted in June 1886, causing widespread damage, bombarding several villages with debris and killing 150 people, the terraces were also destroyed. Despite the massive change in the local landscape, foreign tourists continued to flock to New Zealand and Rotorua's geothermal region.*
Source: *Photograph at Lake Rotomohana, c.1880, Hulton Archive, Getty Images, 73101914.*

kinds of foreigners to New Zealand, including well-known authors Anthony Trollope and Mark Twain (see Figure 4.2).[62] These wealthy and largely white visitors came mostly from Britain, Australia and the United States. They reveled in the scenery and made the most of the 'exoticism' of local Maori culture. For locals there was substantial money to be made from the tourist industry. The New Zealand government also recognized the value of promoting the country as an exciting tourist destination. It purchased land from the Te Arawa people in Rotorua to set up European-style health spas and established a dedicated Department of Tourist and Health Resorts in 1901, the first of its kind in the world.[63] It also aimed at building a nationwide rail network. By 1900, more than six hundred thousand excursions were made on New Zealand's railway routes, a phenomenal number given the country's population was little more than eight hundred thousand.[64]

In making their way to New Zealand, these tourists also visited a range of other global entrepôts, such as Port Said, Bombay, Sydney, San Francisco and Singapore or the smaller Pacific ports of Pape'ete (Tahiti), Apia (Samoa) and Honolulu (Hawai'i), whose deepwater harbours proved to be excellent coaling stations.[65] These same locations proved essential telegraphic way-stations as well. It is really no surprise that the United States formally acquired the islands of Hawai'i in 1898 (its fiftieth state) to protect American access to this essential geostrategic location in the middle of the Pacific Ocean.[66] The struggle over which industrial empire would control the harbour of Apia also heightened tensions among the Samoan people, resulting in warfare and ongoing strife from the 1840s. In an extraordinary 'concert of Europe' style twist, a neutralized municipal zone was established in Apia in 1879, signed by the American, German, British authorities and local Samoan chiefs. It effectively sustained open access to the commercial heart of Apia beach, aiming to protect the ships, goods and people that utilized the port from around the world.[67] While the municipal experiment only had limited success (the first Samoan Civil War broke out in 1886, the second in 1898, and governance of the islands was split between the German and American empires in 1899), Apia is a clear example of how fully Pacific Island communities were part of the nineteenth-century globalizing world.

But even in less globally connected spaces, understanding that there was a world 'out there' heightened. Much of that awareness advanced with the rise in literacy and the spread of global news in newspapers. The invention of the linotype printing press in the 1890s in particular was revolutionary, making it possible to quickly and cheaply produce newspaper editions in vast numbers, which in combination with the expanding telegraph network ensured that a global media space evolved. By 1900 then, news not only passed along the global telegraph network, it also spread as physical newspapers circulated around the world's ports and railway hubs. Almost every town and community produced its own paper. According to the International Institute of Bibliography (itself set up in 1895),[68] there were 52,000 newspapers in circulation globally in 1898. By 1908, there were 71,000, a number that included several thousand newspapers in Asia, more than 300 in Africa and an astounding 1,175 in the sparsely populated Pacific region (including Australia and New Zealand).[69]

Most importantly, these journals not only commented on local issues, promoted local business and advertised rail and shipping timetables; they also reported and commented upon global news, garnered from international news agencies like Reuters, Wolff, Havas and the Associated Press, which circulated daily updates across the world's telegraph network.[70] As a result, no newspaper was without a reliable source of global information, which they diligently republished. Journalism also professionalized. Some of the larger newspapers took their responsibility to truth and accuracy very seriously indeed. They employed 'special correspondents' who travelled to or resided in far-off places and relayed news about major global events first-hand. We can mark the rise of newspaper reporting as the 'fourth estate' – a forum to keep governing authorities in check and give the public a voice in decision-making – with these developments in international newspaper circulation in the late nineteenth century. But newspapers were also capitalist ventures aimed at sales. As such, they were forums for gossip, political and ideological bias and the spread of popular ideas. Needless to say, governments recognized the growing importance of the public voice as expressed in the global press as well and aimed at directing it to meet their needs as much as possible.

Certainly, the evolution of a global media space ensured that, as the Chinese scholar Liang Qichao explained in 1900, by reading newspapers, 'One could stay at home and reach the world.'[71] Globality grew in direct relationship to the advance of global communications, global news, global capitalism, global migration and global infrastructure. Altogether, as the next chapters explain, that knowledge both heightened a sense of interconnectivity and a perception of simultaneity *and* brought with it human and environmental costs, new challenges, heightened competition and increased the potential for warfare and conflict.

Study questions

1. In what ways did nineteenth-century globalization rely on infrastructure construction?

2. What role did governments and treaties play in developing global infrastructure during the nineteenth century? What about private investment and local enterprise?

3. Make a case for the relevance of the principles of 'reliability' and 'predictability' in expanding global infrastructure.

4. Pick one of the nineteenth-century projects listed below and describe its role in nineteenth-century industrial globalization

   a. Suez Canal
   b. Panama Canal
   c. American Transcontinental Railway
   d. Trans-Pacific Telegraph Cable
   e. Great Indian Peninsula Railway

f. Linotype printing press

g. Greenwich Mean Time

5. Identify one impact of nineteenth-century industrial globalization and describe the long- and short-term costs and benefits of that development.

Recommended readings

Tony Ballantyne, Antoinette Burton, 'Empires and the reach of the global' in Emily S. Rosenberg, *A World Connecting, 1870–1945*. Harvard UP, 2012: Chapter 2 'Remaking the world', pp. 348–89.

Jonathan Daly, *The Rise of Western Power: A Comparative History of Western Civilization*. Bloomsbury, 2014: Chapter 12 'Technological revolution', pp. 299–328.

Pallavi V. Das, *Colonialism, Development and the Environment: Railways and Deforestation in British India 1860–1884*. Palgrave MacMillan, 2015: Chapter 1 'Railways and development in colonial India', pp. 17–47.

Daniel R. Headrick, *The Tools of Empire: Technology and European Imperialism in the Nineteenth Century*. Oxford UP, 1981: Chapter 12 'Global Thalassocracies', pp. 165–79.

Valeska Huber, 'Multiple mobilities, multiple sovereignties, multiple speeds: exploring maritime connections in the age of empire', *International Journal of Middle East Studies* 48, 2016, pp. 763–6.

Maya Jasanoff, *The Dawn Watch: Joseph Conrad in a Global World*. William Collins, 2017: especially 'Prologue: One of us', pp. 1–16.

Charles King, *The Black Sea: A History*. Oxford UP, 2004: Chapter 6 'Black Sea 1860–1990', pp. 189–215.

Marilyn Lake, 'Lowe Kong Meng appeals to international law: Transnational lives caught between empire and nation' in Desley Deacon, Penny Russell, Angela Woollacott, eds, *Transnational Lives: Biographies of Global Modernity, 1700-Present*. Palgrave MacMillan, 2010, pp. 223–37.

Mark Mazower, *Governing the World: The History of an Idea*. Penguin, 2012: Chapter 3 'The empire of law', pp. 65–93.

Simone M. Müller, Heidi Tworek, 'The telegraph and the bank: On the interdependence of global communications and capitalism, 1866–1914' *Journal of Global History* 10, 2015, pp. 269–83, doi:10.1017/S1740022815000066.

Lincoln Paine, *The Sea and Civilization: A Maritime History of the World*. Vintage, 2013: Chapter 18 'Annihilation of space and time', pp. 508–45.

Michael Pearson, *The Indian Ocean*. Routledge, 2003: Chapter 7 'Britain and the ocean', pp. 190–248.

Steven Press, *Rogue Empires: Contracts and Conmen in Europe's Scramble for Africa*. Harvard UP, 2017: 'Introduction', pp. 1–10.

Carroll Pursell, 'Herbert Hoover and the transnational lives of engineers' in Desley Deacon, Penny Russell, Angela Woollacott, eds, *Transnational*

Lives: Biographies of Global Modernity, 1700-Present. Palgrave MacMillan, 2010, pp. 109–20.

Steven C. Topik, Allen Wells, 'Commodity chains in a global economy' in Emily S. Roseberg, ed., *A World Connecting, 1870–1945*. Harvard UP, 2012: Chapter 2 'The sinews of trade', pp. 628–84.

5

Migration and the spread of formal and informal empires

Much of the focus of the previous three chapters was on the individuals and states that gained the most from their involvement in the globalization processes of the 'long' nineteenth century. The endeavours of what Hobsbawm would call 'winners' helps to explain much about the global dynamism of the 1815–1914 period. But, as we have repeatedly emphasized, globalization was not only the product of planning and intent. It also evolved out of a chaotic web of human initiatives, some of them anticipated, others altogether chaotic and uncontrolled. One of the most important of the elements that characterized the nineteenth-century age of industrial globalization was that of global migration: the movement of people and communities aiming to settle in a new place often at a vast distance from their place of origin.

In a seminal journal article published in 2004, the historian Adam McKeown charts the astonishing range of transoceanic and transcontinental migrations that occurred in the nineteenth century.[1] He shows that global migrations surged after 1848. He accounts for more than 55 million people entering the Americas before 1940, most of them migrants from across the Atlantic Ocean, but a sizeable minority (2.5 million no less) coming from India, China, Japan and Africa. Across the same period, another 50 million or so people moved across the vast Indian and South Pacific oceanic worlds (including 4 million or so from further away), while anywhere up to another 50 million moved across the Central Asian continent as well as into and out of Japan.[2] Not all of these migrations occurred before 1914, but a sizeable proportion of them did.

While Liang Qichao may have been content to 'stay at home' in China and 'reach the world' by reading his newspaper in 1900,[3] McKeown's figures suggest that the dynamism of the nineteenth-century age of industrial globalization was also created by the phenomenal numbers of people who moved themselves across the planet. These migrations were caused and enabled by a number of factors, including the opening of the seas to relatively safe travel after 1815, the expansion of shipping and transportation routes and the demographic 'push and pull' dynamics of the global industrial economy. At the heart of each and every one of these millions of migrations was also a story of an individual or family who chose (or was forced to choose) to move themselves away from all that was familiar to make a new life in what they would have considered a 'new world'. Some of them, like gold diggers or railway workers, migrated across long distances more than once in their lives.

Migration was clearly not a European phenomenon alone. Still, historians have long used migration patterns to explain the rise of Western global dominance in the nineteenth century. In his book *Replenishing the Earth*, for example, the historian James Belich argues that an 'explosion' of settlers from the English-speaking core in Britain and the United States spread their colonies across the globe after 1815 and that, in so doing, they established the basis for the political and cultural domination of the Anglophone world over the rest.[4] While Belich suggests that this settler explosion was not dependent on industrialization for its initial impetus (as much of the migration occurred before the prevalence of steamships but after the 1815 Congress of Vienna), it nevertheless expanded exponentially as industrial cities boomed in the outposts of the British empire (such as Sydney, Singapore, Hong Kong and Bombay) and in the United States (in places like Los Angeles, San Francisco, St Louis, Chicago and New York). There is much to be said for Belich's argument. Over half of all migrants to the United States before 1870 were from the British Isles, after all.[5] But as industrialization globalized and affected more and more communities after the 1850s, migration patterns also expanded.

Industrialization played a key hand in these developments, in large part because industrialization affected the socio-economic foundations of most communities. On the one hand, industrialization offered the means and opportunity to move (we might consider these 'pull factors' and count the rise of industrial cities as places for finding work and to enjoy the 'delights' of modernization as an example). On the other hand, industrialization also created social conditions that made the desire to move greater for many (these would be 'push factors', pushing individuals away from their known life into an unknown future). Consider, for example, the societal impact of the industrial revolution in the heartlands of nineteenth-century industry. From the outset, industrialization caused fundamental changes to social structures as the uneven and unequal results of industrial capitalism overturned the lives of traditional craftsmen, labourers and landed elites and brought harsh working and living conditions to the working classes of the industrial cities. Great wealth was created for the industrial middle classes to enjoy, cheaper consumer goods were produced for all to purchase and the genius of invention was widely celebrated. But all this change came at a high cost and at a rate of change that confronted many and impoverished many more.

Some of those most immediately affected by industrialization were skilled artisans and their guilds, whose labour and political value ended as their jobs and their crafts were replaced by low-cost labourers and machines. Such developments resulted in considerable resistance. Luddite craftsmen in the midlands of England, for example, unleashed their anger by destroying cotton and wool mills in the opening decades of the 1800s. Silesian weavers in the German lands were equally destructive as they protested the flood of cheap manufactures in the 1840s. In India, too, Bengali artisans chopped of their own thumbs to protest against the importation of cheap British manufactures of their highly skilled handmade craft.[6] In some places in Europe, the 1848 revolutions were inspired by the revolt of artisanal communities against industrialization's impact on their livelihoods and traditional values. Over and over, this grim story was repeated as the industrializing world turned its mechanized advantages against those of skilled manual workers who found their livelihoods threatened as the advance of the machine, the factory, the unskilled (or certainly less-skilled) industrial worker and the growing wealth of the new industrial middle classes marched on.

Even those who might be thought to have gained from the success of industrial capitalism – namely the industrial workers – increasingly considered themselves the victims of industrialization's success. When Karl Marx and Friedrich Engel's 1848 *Communist Manifesto* argued that the workers of the world had nothing to lose but their chains, their critique of the raw capitalist system pointed to the very serious inequalities experienced by the *proletariat* (the industrial working class) in every metropole.[7] Still, as the number of jobs and overall importance of the industrial economy grew, agricultural labourers left the countryside to try their luck earning wages in the cities. These cities exploded in size as a result. But the lives of most proletariat who lived in them was miserable. Theirs was a world of bleakness so poignantly described by Charles Dickens's *Hard Times* (1854), Elizabeth Gaskell's *North and South* (1855) and Victor Hugo's *Les Misérables* (1862) (see also Figure 5.1).

Consider, for example, how in 1850 more than a third of Britain's population were industrial workers, residing in one of an ever-growing number of industrial cities. These workers had a life expectancy of about thirty-six years as compared to the middle-class average of about fifty years. The difference was the result of massive wealth differentials. Where the British middle classes (who made their wealth from the profits of the global industrial capitalist economy) could afford the best food, accommodation and health care available. The industrial working classes (who mined the fuel and manufactured the goods that made industrialization work) lived in the most abject of conditions, often in slums

FIGURE 5.1 *Labour and capital. This cartoon, published in the British satirical journal* Punch *in 1843, responded critically to the findings of a report commissioned by the British parliament into the conditions of child employment in Britain. The report reflected on the extreme conditions of industrial labourers in mines and factories across the country and especially brought out their impact on children, some as young as three, who worked in them. The cartoon brings out how the toiling working classes (some of whom worked 'like dogs' on their hands and knees for more than twelve hours a day) produced the wealth for Britain's upper classes to enjoy. Note not only how the cartoonist depicts the wealth of the mine overseer (sitting on his bags of gold) and the comforts afforded to the upper- and middle-class families (with their servants and exotic goods) but also how this wealth creation and working-class misery relied on the peace of the seas (the anchor flanked by the angel of peace and lady fortune).*
Source: 'Capital and Labour', cartoon, Punch *London, 1842, Getty Images, 815202910.*

without adequate provisions. Theirs was a world of poverty. The historian Richard Evans offers us some excellent statistics to bring out the distinctions further. As an example, he notes that the average height of a well-born officer cadet at Britain's Sandhurst military academy was a full 9 inches (23 centimetres) taller than that of a working-class boy of the same age attending the charity school of the Royal Navy's Marine Society. Infant mortality rates were equally definitive. In 1900, a baby born to middle-class parents had a 96 percent chance of surviving its infancy, a child born to working-class parents only had a 67 percent chance. Similar statistics hold true for the major French and German urban centres and especially in industrial cities where tuberculosis and cholera were even more fatal in their crowded and poorly ventilated slums.[8]

These inequities did not go unnoticed. They provide a key explanation for much of the revolutionary resistance, labour unrest, strikes and protests that occurred 'from below' in all nineteenth-century industrial societies. They also underwrote a range of globally relevant political ideas and ideologies (for which see Chapter 8). While such political activism resulted in the alleviation of some of this collective working-class misery, the industrial world of 'satanic mills' and the 'greed of capitalism' also had a major impact on the will of many people to flee their dank conditions and to risk overseas voyage, new lands and new people to begin a new life.

The social impact of industrialization thus had a fundamental impact on the decision to emigrate. Pre-existing cleavages of religion, ethnicity, political views and class were only aggravated by the urbanizing dynamics of industrial life. Some, like the Irish and other north Europeans who suffered the terrible potato famine of the 1840s and others who saw their liberal revolutions fail in 1848 looked abroad for new beginnings. After 1850, on average about 250,000 Germans left Europe annually forming 'German towns', business networks and communities in the 'new world'. They did so even before there was a formal German empire across the blue waters to speak of. In some instances these migrants forged German imperialism much like British migrants forged the British empire.[9] Between 1876 and 1914, as many as 14 million Italians, most of whom were agricultural workers, left the newly unified Italy for the hope of better lives in western Europe and the Americas. Twenty-two percent of them ended up in Argentina or Brazil.[10] In other contexts, changing government policies or actions related to religion and minorities prompted the decision to leave the metropole. In Russia, for example, pacifist Mennonites, who had long been exempt from military service in Tsarist Russia, were told in the 1870s they too would be asked to join the military ranks. Some left for Canada as a result, while others chose life in other parts of the Americas.

It is also important to remember that nineteenth-century industrial capitalism inspired cycles of economic boom and bust. In times of economic depression, few governments had the social welfare structures or financial instruments in place to cushion the blow of widespread unemployment and poverty. Some of these 'cushions' would be developed as a result of political agitation by the latter decades of the 1800s, but for much of the period 1815–1914, the experience of poverty presented plenty of reasons for workers to leave the metropole for a new life in an imperial outpost. Some of the largest emigrations out of Europe occurred during the long depression of the 1870s and 1880s, for example. During these two decades in Britain there was a 26 percent drop in grain production due to a substantial price decrease and a corresponding shift to grazing animals (as opposed to raising crops). The shift also caused massive rural unemployment: rearing animals required fewer workers after all. As a result, over a quarter of a million men left the agricultural sector in Britain. Many tried their luck as industrial workers, others left the country entirely.[11] For related reasons, millions of peasants in the Mediterranean region left for foreign destinations (some of them in Europe itself) as industrial employment opportunities were limited at home. Their migrations were also influenced by the fact that the produce from their agricultural communities could not compete effectively with the price, quality and quantity of specialized plantation crops growing in California, Florida, Australia, South Africa and Brazil, which were now entering the European market place.[12] A globalized industrial economy enabled wealthy countries to rely on cheap foreign imports for their basic food consumption needs. The impact was a fundamental shift in the way food was produced and consumed around the globe (for more, see Chapter 6).

As the historian E. H. Carr notes, numbers count in history.[13] Settler colonies had been created by empires for centuries, but the nineteenth-century movements of peoples occurred in such great numbers that the impacts were profound. To illustrate, consider the impact of immigration into Canada where in 1790 there were about 250,000 mostly French settlers and by 1860 there were over 3 million mostly English-speaking Irish, Scots and English. These would soon be joined by a wider range of Europeans fleeing poverty and political upheaval. Similar growth occurred in Australia where there were scarcely one thousand white inhabitants in 1790 but 1.25 million non-indigenous people by 1860. The largest of the expansions in what Belich calls 'the Anglo-world' occurred in the United States where the original thirteen colonies grew from 3.8 million to almost 16 million people by 1860.[14] Within another forty years, the population of the United States counted 76 million. Many of the newly arrived came from Ireland, the German-speaking parts of Europe and later from Italy, eastern Europe and the Baltic.

But permanent migrations were not only a distinctive feature of the industrializing metropoles. As noted at the outset of this chapter, equally impressive demographic shifts occurred across the Central Asian, Asia-Pacific and Indian Ocean regions. Many of these non-European migrations were also the product of the nineteenth-century age of global industrialization. Consider, for example, the push-and-pull factors associated with the growth of massive plantation economies, which supplied the manufacturing hubs of the industrial metropoles. The labour needs of these plantations, which existed all over the world, attracted free and unfree labourers from across the planet, as did the vast infrastructure projects that were built in the latter decades of the century. More than 2 million Chinese and Japanese labourers left for the United States after 1849, attracted to the Californian gold rushes and to the work opportunities offered by building the transcontinental railways. Many millions more Chinese migrated to Manchuria and Siberia to work on railway projects there. But even the plantation economies in the Caribbean, South Pacific, Africa and Asia counted thousands of Chinese and Indians among their labouring classes.[15] The emancipation of Russia's serfs in 1861 also set off a major Russian diaspora both into the Americas and eastwards into Asia. Meanwhile, the fast-expanding port cities of Shanghai, Singapore, Hong Kong and Bombay attracted migrants from around the world to its industrial opportunities.

Not all this migration was undertaken willingly. While the slave trade was abolished by international agreement at the Congress of Vienna in 1815, this really only applied to the Atlantic world. After 1815, that trade petered out, although slavery itself was not abolished in the United States until 1865 (it took a civil war to achieve that result). But slavery in one form or another continued to operate around the world and Africans continued to be procured as slaves and forced to work on plantations around the Indian Ocean region and in the Middle East.[16] It was only in 1838 that slavery, not just the slave trade, was formally abolished in British-held territories, followed by the French empire in 1848. Spain did not embrace abolitionism until the 1880s, following the Dutch who had done so only a decade earlier.[17] But despite these formal agreements, the industrial heartlands of Europe and the United States continued to profit from the labour of African slaves. For example, slavery continued to thrive in the clove plantations of Zanzibar and Pemba, the date plantations along the coast of eastern Africa and in the pearl-fishing centres of Ceylon (Sri Lanka). French-controlled Madagascar was also riven with slave labourers and in many parts of the Middle East, slavery did not let up either. Many of these slaves were sourced in eastern Africa by local raiders who also supplied the global demand for ivory by killing hundreds of thousands of elephants (for more, see Chapter 6).[18]

Another major source of plantation labour was supplied by indentured workers: individuals who agreed (or were forced to agree) to work several years 'for free' to pay for their passage to the 'new world'. Indentured labour existed in all manner of forms, much of it highly exploitative, some of it no different from slavery. For example, between 1834 and 1907, the island of Mauritius attracted 450,000 Indian indentured labourers. All of them were subjected to extremely harsh local laws and taxation rules that effectively forced them to re-indenture themselves repeatedly, their status reduced in effect to that of slaves.[19] For the Caribbean region, the formal end of slavery posed an economic conundrum for plantation owners: how might they ensure the long-term viability of their plantation economy, which required a large pool of cheap labourers to keep functioning? Between 1811 and 1916, as the historian Dirk Hoerder estimates, around 1.75 million free and unfree foreign workers arrived in the region to work on its sugar plantations, including 800,000 Africans, 550,000 Asian Indians and 270,000 Chinese.[20]

All these global migrations speak to the profound power of human diasporas to affect local environments. Where-ever people moved, they brought their cultures, world views and social expectations with them. In their new places of settlement, they built homes, community facilities, villages, suburbs and even whole towns according to familiar patterns and structures. They reshaped their new environment to remind them of 'home' and named things as if they were 'home' (see Figure 5.2). In the Anglophone world, for example, many place names began their spread across the globe with London, Paris, Berlin, Baden, Wellington, Wellesley, New Hamburg, New Dundee, Hamilton, Nelson, York, Waterloo, Stratford, Thames and hundreds of other city-names, battle sites and the names of famous persons appearing on distant continents, islands, peaks and water passages across the globe. As we saw in Chapter 4, the cosmopolitan nature of many of the world's super-cities were also the product of the diversity of the nineteenth-century's global migrations.

The human costs of all these nineteenth-century diasporas, then, were greatest for the indigenous communities whose lands were wrested from them by the industrial empires and by the arrival of so many foreign settlers.[21] It was one thing for indigenous peoples in Australia, New Zealand, Canada, the United States, much of Africa, some of Latin America, South and South East Asia and the Pacific to endure sailors, soldiers, traders, and even missionaries in the ports, rivers and coastal regions of their homeland. It was quite another to have shiploads of settlers arriving who wanted to recreate 'their home' in yours and duly set about to reshape 'their' new home accordingly. Indigenous social structures also had to accommodate the shift to plantation and extraction economies and to the imposition of foreign governance. Given the rapid rate and fundamental impact of these changes, it really was no wonder that there were many efforts 'from below' to resist not only industrialization but also the expansion of imperial power. Such resistance took many forms (for which see Chapters 7 and 8) and reminds us that from the point of view of many there was often little that was benign or kind-hearted about the processes of nineteenth-century industrial globalization or the growth of industrial empires.

The expansion of the nineteenth century's industrial empires, including the 'explosion of the Anglo-world' as James Belich posits, was in part the product of these global migrations. To this end, it is useful to identify the kinds of industrial-imperial holdings that appeared in the nineteenth century. Historians broadly agree that *formal empires* typically consisted of three types of colonies, each characterized by the kinds of people who lived and worked in them. *Settler colonies*, for example, attracted large numbers of migrants

FIGURE 5.2 *Indian indentured workers in Jamaica, c.1905. This photograph captured a group of Indian indentured workers on a Jamaican plantation in 1905 in the midst of a religious ceremony. Having travelled halfway across the world from the Indian subcontinent to the Caribbean for work, these migrants (like all migrants) brought their social customs and religious traditions with them and used them to recreate a sense of 'home' in their new place of residence. Because plantation economies like Jamaica attracted workers from across the globe, they evolved into remarkably cosmopolitan spaces of social interaction.*
Source: Adolphe Duperley, photograph in Picturesque Jamaica, *1905, Getty Images, 463971577.*

from out of the metropole, who aimed to live there more or less permanently. In contrast, *economic production colonies* did not typically attract large numbers of migrants from out of the metropole (although they might attract large numbers of non-indigenous workers). These imperial outposts housed large plantations, mines, trading ports or whaling fleet hubs. They were often administered by military or naval forces and a small number of civilian bureaucrats from the metropole. Similarly, *strategic outposts* such as ports and coastal possession served the needs of imperial navies, merchant marines, commercial networks and telegraph stations and did not usually attract large numbers of new settlers. Of course, the distinctions between the types of formal empire were never hard and fast. Where a place might begin as a strategic outpost it could easily become a settler colony if or when a sizeable number of migrants came. What made all these places outposts of 'formal' empire (as opposed to an extension of *informal empire* discussed below) was that there was a claim to sovereignty made by a state over the territory and that this claim was acknowledged as 'legitimate' by other states, if not by the indigenous people. Legitimacy was largely determined by international law and, increasingly, by treaties and contracts that laid out the terms of ownership and use (for more, see Chapter 4).

Let's consider the nature of formal empire building by looking at the British case. It is clear that Britain's success as an industrial power in the nineteenth century, powered as it was by the economic and political forces of the industrial revolution and its dominant position on the world's oceans, was also reinforced by the growth of its formal empire and the migration of its people across that empire. Britain's settler colonies, including the 'white' Dominions of Canada, Australia, New Zealand, Newfoundland and South Africa, presented the most obvious path for the replication of Anglo-European economic, social and political structures globally. Much of the settler population in these dominions came from Britain itself, but over the course of nineteenth and twentieth centuries, peoples from all over the world took advantage of the relative openness and opportunities access to these 'white' outposts of the British empire offered them.

But settler colonies existed in all manner of forms. Consider present-day Kenya, for example. Throughout much of the nineteenth century, the East African region formed an integral part of the global economy. At first, Kenya's African communities dealt with Portuguese traders and then with the colonization of their coastal regions by Omani Arabs. The Omani sultanate profited from fostering a friendly trade-based relationship with the European powers, and especially with Germany and Britain. That relationship helped to bring greater numbers of Europeans to East Africa after 1850 as explorers, traders and missionaries. At the same time, much of the slave raiding for the Zanzibar and Pemba plantations (which were also within Omani control) occurred from out of Kenya. The British government did not establish a formal protectorate over Kenya until 1895, after trading its sovereign claims over Tanganyika to Germany.[22] The declaration brought this region of East Africa into the formal dominion of the British empire and resulted in a sharp decline in slave raiding. Britain now had to attempt to rule the region without maintaining a large settler population. It did so by utilizing its existing links to the Omani Arab bureaucracy to establish administrative control over local African communities, who actively resisted the shift to British sovereignty.[23] The Kikuyu people, for example, feared what the move portended for their own future and felt betrayed as the terms of earlier treaties (such as the one signed between chief Waiyaka Wa Hinga and the Imperial British East India Company) were overturned.[24]

In almost all respects, British-controlled Kenya was both an *economic production colony* and a *strategic outpost* of the British empire. The building of the Ugandan railway, connecting Mombasa to Kisumu and then to Kingala, brought tens of thousands of Indian indentured labourers to East Africa and connected the region even more directly to the global economy. Still, Kenya also developed its own version of a tiny white *settler colony*, by attracting a small number of extremely well-to-do Europeans to live there. In 1901, there were a little over 500 Europeans residing in the Kenyan protectorate, as compared to 27,000 Indians and around 1.5 million Africans. These Europeans, most of them from Britain, were in large part drawn to the Kenyan countryside in the hopes of re-establishing an 'old world squirearchy', with land-holding privileges, servants and an elite culture based on 'old world' aristocratic values. Race hierarchy, the culture of 'gentlemen', retired and active military officers and civil service officers all helped to perpetuate a lifestyle that was being challenged by the advance of the *bourgeois* middle classes back in Britain itself. As Kenya offered big-game hunting, including of lions and elephants, it easily attracted the rich and famous, including British royalty and the American president Theodore Roosevelt (see Figure 5.3). As a result, this 'island of white', as the historian Dane Kennedy describes the protectorate, was much more of an expatriate community than any settler colony in Canada, New Zealand or Australia.[25] It was also a distinct product of the nineteenth-century age of industrial globalization.

Kenya's history reminds us too that the 'success' of British imperialism was closely linked to the success of its overseas economic assets. Of these, India, 'the jewel' in the British imperial crown, was the most important. The 'Raj' of formal British government control took over from the BEIC after the calamitous India mutiny of 1857 and extended over not only India but also the states we know today as Pakistan, Bangladesh and Burma. The British Raj ran India largely as an *economic production colony*. The actual British presence on the ground after 1858 remained small, counting no more than a few thousand government officials and less than seventy thousand British troops, who collectively governed 250 million local subjects. The key to British imperial control was the accommodation of local community structures and hierarchies to serve the economic and strategic needs of the British state. As a result, the British Raj educated and empowered thousands of local clerks, administrators and soldiers from existing warrior castes. These people became part of a mobile imperial cadre that moved around the British empire and helped it to function within and outside the South Asian region. Tens of thousands of Indians were sent to Africa to build the railways and

FIGURE 5.3 *President Roosevelt's Smithsonian expedition to Africa, 1909. At the end of his 1909 presidential term, Theodore Roosevelt took his son Kermit on a richly publicized hunting expedition to eastern Africa. Ostensibly pitched as a scientific journey aimed at bringing a 'complete representation' of African fauna back to the Smithsonian museum in Washington DC, the expedition killed an estimated eleven thousand animals. Funded by private donors who, according to Roosevelt's own published account of the expedition, 'appreciated the value of such a collection to the National Museum', the journey made Kenya a popular hunting and tourist destination for well-off Americans and Europeans. Pictured here, the President (in the middle) stands with his son (second from the left) at a buffalo-hunting camp at Kijabi. Three buffalo skulls sit in front of the hunters and the American flag flies proudly behind. According to Roosevelt's own account, the flag was on prominent display where-ever the hunting party went.*
Source: Theodore Roosevelt, African Game Trails. *Charles Scribner, 1909, p. 108.*

transportation hubs that sought to link British colonies from the Cape of Good Hope in South Africa to Cairo in Egypt. For example, between 1896 and 1901 over thirty thousand indentured Indian laborers from the north-west Pathan region of India built the Ugandan railway. These labourers worked alongside 2,600 Africans and were, at the insistence of the British Raj, hired for a three-year contract. About half of the Indians remained in Africa and during their stay many were stricken with malaria, jiggers, dysentery, scurvy, ulcers and liver disease. Indian government inspectors noted that those who returned home early due to illness were in a 'filthy condition'.[26]

Some Indians joined the ranks of the professionals, as was the case with the highly educated lawyer Mahatma Gandhi, who used his access to British education and mobility to advance social and political change at home and abroad. These Indians were part of a growing network of non-European, Western-educated professionals who worked in business and government around South and South East Asia and contributed to the intellectual dynamism of cities such as Bombay, Madras, Calcutta, Rangoon and Singapore.[27] Others joined in the wider global economy that connected India to the world. Importantly, the Indian army, both its white British regiments and the larger ranks of indigenous troops that included Indians and the Gurkhas from Nepal, served the empire as a type of global rapid reaction force where needed.[28] Force was a key element in the maintenance of empire but it was costly to send troops abroad and hence local troops were essential. Though never without challenges from below, the British Raj worked to harness the labour and talents of India's vast population, transforming much of India into a key primary product production zone supplying the British and global economy. This is not to say that there was no industry in India – cities like Bombay had a thriving textile industry with 136 industrial mills in operation by 1900 as well as chemical dye production and paper mills, for example –[29] but only that India's economic output existed first and foremost to augment the wealth and industrial productivity of the British empire.

Such examples from the British Raj indicate the diffuse and chaotic nature of much nineteenth-century imperialism. India may have been formally ruled by the British empire after 1858, but its 250 million people were not pliant subjects who meekly accepted the rule of the Raj. Many adapted to the circumstances of British imperialism where possible to advance their own wishes and desires. Their agency and activities were as important to determining the manifold global networks of people and information as any imposed by an empire 'from above'. Their activities also highlight how equally powerful the forces of *informal imperialism* were to affecting the course and impact of industrial globalization. As we have already seen, much of the impetus behind industrialization came from private enterprise: from individuals and companies maximizing the opportunities offered to them by technological advances, the open seas, capital investment, the building of infrastructure, trade and exchange. Formal empires (i.e. empires declared and shaped by governments and states) often followed in the wake of the enterprises of these private individuals, be they migrating to escape their 'old' world or looking expectantly to the opportunities opened up to them in the 'new world'.

The nature and forms taken by *informal imperialism* present a murkier area of historical debate. In essence, however, *informal imperialism* refers to the building of networks of economic, political and/or cultural power from out of a metropole that are not determined or officially authorized by the state. Formal empires often followed informal ones. Many nineteenth-century migrations from out of the industrial heartlands, for example, not only created informal webs of global connectivity but also offered incentives (and sometimes imperatives) for governments to subsequently declare 'formal' control over the territories in which their citizens settled. For example, the formal expansion of the United States and Canada across North America during the 1800s sometimes followed from the demands and interests of the thousands of settlers, railway companies, miners, timber companies and other opportunists who moved themselves into and across the continent. As they moved, they drove out and dispossessed the indigenous First Nations communities whose lands and ways of being were irreparably affected. Nevertheless, they behaved as colonizing masters with an imperative of the 'right to rule'.

From the perspective of the affected First Nations communities, the differentiation between 'formal' and 'informal' empire, thus, meant very little. Either way, the foreigners had come and were not leaving, no matter how much resistance they threw at them. As is discussed further in Chapters 6 and 7, violence (and, at times, genocidal violence) accompanied much of this settler expansion. The destruction of indigenous communities, lands and population proceeded in both formal and informal empires. More often than not, the declaration of sovereignty over a territory only enabled such violent practices to continue and sometimes to expand. Even when indigenous communities sought to protect themselves by signing treaties that set down boundaries and rights and privileges to the exchange of their sovereignty and land, more often than not these treaties favoured the new migrants and the foreign empire.

A common and highly exploitative nineteenth-century variant of informal empire was that of the *rogue empire*, as the historian Steven Press describes the phenomenon.[30] Rogue empires were particularly important in parts of South East Asia, the Pacific and Africa. At the centre of these 'rogue' entities were enterprising and not always honest individuals who negotiated treaties with local elites, chiefs and even sultans to claim economic and territorial rights. In many cases, these treaties claimed the rights of sovereignty usually restricted to governments and states. They did so most often in pursuit of personal gain. By international law, most of these treaties were not binding, but they nevertheless resulted in opportunities for formal empires to follow in their wake and caused considerable suffering among indigenous communities.

A case study of James Brooke provides an excellent example. Brooke's career as the self-proclaimed 'sovereign prince of Sarawak' provided the inspiration for Joseph Conrad's highly critical anti-imperial novel Lord Jim, first published in 1899. Brooke was a veteran of the BEIC's Bengal army, and was well acquainted with the Malay region. In 1840, the Sultan of Brunei asked Brooke for assistance in Sarawak, where the local population was giving him trouble. As Brooke had a ship with heavy guns and empowered with the deed from the Sultan to collect taxes in the region, he declared himself its vassal governor, effectively proclaiming his right to absolute rule. When this caused trouble both in Britain and Brunei, he moved to get his claim supported by the British government. When the British government recognized that by sustaining Brooke's position, it could extend informal control over Sarawak and do so at almost no cost (and against the claims of the Dutch and Americans who also had rising interests in the region), it agreed. In the face of British diplomatic and naval power, the Sultan had no choice but to accept Brooke's interpretation of his claims to Sarawak. Wealthy British investors soon erased Sarawak's debts and grew its plantation economy tenfold, including bringing Chinese migrant labourers to Sarawak shores. Though Brooke's rule of Sarawak was brought under government investigation in the 1850s and 1860s, he was formally recognized as the ruler of Sarawak by Britain and even given a knighthood in 1864. His family dynasty ruled the small protectorate until the Second World War.[31]

Brooke's story was by no means an isolated example of rogue practice aimed at extracting wealth and status for individuals or global companies.[32] The nineteenth century was beset with such enterprises. Small and large privately owned business interests, supported by increasingly sophisticated banking, legal, corporate, investment and insurance practices and professions, were equally eager to maximize their participation in the global economy. Many of these were family businesses that could combine multigenerational experience and capital in their ventures and use time-proven alliances of marriage to expand their operations.[33] Often these private initiatives worked with or alongside missionary organizations. Together they pulled the formal structures of empires out to the global hinterland in an effort to legitimize and regularize their activities, reduce the risk of their investments and increase their own safety.

In so doing, these private enterprises expanded the reach and impact of the increasingly globalized industrial economy. We might even label these enterprises, as the historian Robert Fitzgerald does, as nineteenth-century 'empires of business'.[34] Such enterprises existed even in countries that had no formal empire to speak of and did not have the means (or desire) to acquire or obtain one. The historian Bernard C. Schär shows, for example, how central the operations of Swiss family businesses were in the expansion of Dutch colonialism in the Indonesian archipelago.[35] Switzerland may not have had a formal empire, but tropical products, including cotton, sugar, tobacco, coffee and silk from Indonesia augmented the global power and wealth of several Swiss companies and the Swiss state. Switzerland's federal government even aided the interests of Swiss-owned enterprises in Brazil by refusing to ratify a new law in 1864 banning Swiss citizens from purchasing slaves while overseas. Switzerland then did as much as any formal empire in expanding and profiting from the globalizing industrial economy.

And so did the Hanseatic towns in northern Germany. Long before Germany was unified in 1871, Germans from the Hanseatic city states such as Hamburg, Bremen and Lübeck transformed their mercantilist networks into overseas ventures that often worked with or alongside British, Dutch, French, American and Chinese imperial networks. Before the final wars of German unification brought them into the Prussian-led German empire, these neutral German trading hubs posted their own trading consulates around the world and connected the global market place to the markets of dozens of German states. As an example, by 1860 the city state of Hamburg sustained 279 consulates, 69 in the colonies of other European powers and 66 in other foreign states. As small states, the Hanseatic cities could not compete directly with the larger imperial fleets in oceanic shipping but they took advantage of both their neutrality and the relative openness of free trade to occupy niche roles in coastal shipping and regional trade. In 1855, for example, 39 ships from Hamburg visited the Chinese port at Canton and by the 1860s Hamburg trade with China was exceeded only by that of Britain and the United States. Some of these Hanseatic businesses were even willing to play roles in higher risk regions such as equatorial Africa where formal European empires had a more limited presence until the 1880s.[36]

This kind of informal empire-building centred on maximizing the opportunities offered by exploiting the world's natural and human resources. It was as essential to shaping the contours of the nineteenth-century age of industrial globalization as the extension of the power and sovereignty of the formal industrial empires over foreign territory and peoples. Industrial imperialism then was as much about economics as it was about people. Still, no imperial networks, be they formal or informal, could form in places where its human agents could not physically go. As an example, consider how essential the invention of anti-malarial medicine was to enabling non-Africans to survive a trip into central Africa. Until the middle of the 1800s, in fact, most Europeans who attempted such journeys succumbed either to malaria or any other of a range of tropical diseases. In 1840, for example, a British military study showed how 97 percent of its soldiers who did so either died or were invalided by the experience.[37] By the 1850s, however, quinine-based medicines became more readily available. After the Dutch smuggled cinchona seeds, which were an excellent source of quinine, out of Bolivia in 1865 and started cultivating quinine crops on plantations in Java in the Dutch East Indies, Africa 'opened up' to European exploration and exploitation. In combination with increased understanding about the utility of filtering water and the management of sewage (which was particularly difficult in the rainy season), European missionaries, merchants, scientists, soldiers, settlers and other agents of industrial imperialism penetrated the African interior in increasing numbers after 1860.[38]

What followed was a mad 'scramble' for power and control over the African continent by these foreigners. Traditionally, historians tend to explain the European 'scramble for Africa' as an exercise in formal imperialism. They argue that an age of 'new imperialism' evolved in the 1870s and 1880s, where the industrial great powers competed with their industrial rivals in extending their sovereignty over the African continent. More recent studies, however, show how much of the impetus for the formal imperial control over Africa and its people also stemmed from informal and 'rogue' imperialism. In the 1870s and 1880s, hundreds of treaties of questionable legal validity were entered into between private European operators and local chieftains that granted ill-defined sovereignty and control over territories and resources to the foreigners. Unlike the example of Brooke in Sarawak, whose agreements were produced in two languages (Malay and English), many of these African treaties only existed in English or another European language and were signed by the illiterate chief with an 'X'.[39] In most cases, these treaties were not authorized by a sovereign government at all. Unsurprisingly, they resulted in a phenomenal amount of human suffering as these private companies then used the implied powers of the treaty (which they enforced by violent means) to exploit the local people and extract resources from the land. When these activities resulted in open conflict between rival enterprises – as also repeatedly happened – the potential for the scramble for Africa to affect the diplomatic balance of power between the industrial empires also heightened. As a result, Africa and Africans were drawn into the global industrial and imperial order in the most exploitative of ways.

One of the most important examples of this destructive 'scramble' involved the activities of the Belgian king Leopold II in the Congo. Even before he had succeeded his father to the throne in 1865, Leopold had watched with fascination at the success of Brooke's Sarawak project and for a time hoped Belgium might join its neighbour, the Netherlands, in the East Indies by getting British acceptance of a Belgian offer to buy Brooke's holdings in northern Borneo. British resistance to the idea prompted Leopold to enquire if Spain was willing to sell the Philippines to Belgium but this too was a non-starter. The interest of Belgian geographical societies in equatorial Africa then diverted Leopold's attention to the Congo River. By 1876, Leopold fastened on a scheme that combined his aspirations for a Belgian overseas empire with the various private business, Christian missionary and scientific community interests already operating in the Congo. They combined their interests under the auspices of a private company, the International African Association (AIA), for which Leopold 'bought' the full stakes in 1879.[40] The AIA company then built roads, established plantations and exacted taxes and fees from anyone wishing to cross the territory they had seized full control over by right of questionable 'treaties'. The imposition of despotic rule by the AIA's agents in the Congo resulted in an incredibly cruel and exploitative regime, which included imposing forced labour on the local population, summary executions, mutilations, torture and the burning down of villages.[41] Leopold II was the personal beneficiary of all these activities.

While international attention would eventually be given to these excesses (for which see Chapter 7), the initial problem for the rest of the world was not the AIA's cruelty but rather the legality of the AIA's actions. Did Leopold II and the AIA have sovereign and economic rights to the Congo? There were numerous competing claimants to such rights, including from Congo's king Mani Kongo, a number of lesser but powerful local chiefs, some Omani traders coming in from Africa's eastern coasts and from other Europeans.[42] Germany's chancellor Otto von Bismarck responded to these issues, fearing above all that the competing claims made by private companies and rival empires not only in the Congo, but also across the African continent, might lead to future warfare between the industrial powers. In true 'concert of Europe' style, he called for an international conference, which met in Berlin in 1885. It was publicized as a conference devoted to the task of ending African slavery, though critics such as Joseph Conrad referred to it as a conference for the 'Suppression of Savage Customs'.[43] In the end, however, the Berlin Conference set a precedent for extending sovereign rights to most of Africa for the industrial empires (as opposed to the private companies or the local people). The Congo was redefined as the Congo Free State and Leopold II and the AIA were granted sovereignty to do with it as they saw fit, as long as no restraints were imposed on the movement of goods and trade across the territory. In effect, the Congo was neutralized: it was opened up so all could access it as a vital trade route. Its people, however, were left to the mercy of the autocratic rule of the AIA.

The Berlin Conference of 1885 offers some essential insights into the dynamics of nineteenth-century industrial imperialism. For one, it registered a conscious move by Germany (and other imperial states) to exercise closer and more direct control over the private enterprises of their citizenry. In Germany's case, its chancellor Otto von Bismarck used the precedent set by the Berlin Conference to extend formal German state control over a range of private company initiatives that already existed in the Pacific (in Samoa and New Guinea) and across Africa (including in present-day Namibia, Cameroon, Burundi, Rwanda and Tanzania). Germany then acquired a 'formal empire' after 1885, some of it in Africa. Other empires followed suit. The results were disastrous for Africans, and not only for the people of the Congo who lost as much as half their population during the AIA's rule.[44] Where in 1880, the continent was ruled almost exclusively by Africans, by 1900 only 10 percent was formally left in African control. Unsurprisingly, wars of resistance flamed in almost every region of the continent as imperial powers sought to impose their view of order. Settlers were less common and certainly never but a small minority in any of these African outposts. For the most part, economic and strategic advantages were sought and extracted, transforming the economy and dramatically reducing the agency that the local African peoples retained in governing their own lives.

It is sometimes argued that the conquest of Africa in such a short space of time represented a 'new imperialism', quite unlike previous waves of empire-building. Certainly, Africa posed a range of 'new' challenges for the existing imperial powers. The 'scramble for Africa' also caused intense and immense change for African communities. But the drivers of this imperialism were not new as such. The foreigners who conquered Africa in the latter decades of the 1800s did so with the same ambitions as their predecessors in expanding their reach across other parts of the globe. What was so striking about the African situation, however, was the speed of change and the remarkable cooperation that existed between the industrial great powers in effecting the change. Their guns were not trained on each other but rather on their new 'subject' peoples. As we make clear in Chapter 7, globalization and empire used large amounts of violence to further Anglo-European power abroad.

Study questions

1. Why did millions of people migrate across the planet in the nineteenth century? How did these migrants contribute to the dynamism of nineteenth-century industrial globalization?

2. How do historians differentiate between *formal* and *informal* imperialism in the nineteenth century? How were they similar?

3. What does Steven Press mean by the term 'rogue empire'? What relevance did rogue empires have for the expansion of industrial empires in the nineteenth century?

4. What are 'empires of business'?

5. What does the Berlin Conference of 1885 suggest about how the industrializing great powers controlled and dominated the international environment?

Recommended readings

Edward A. Alpers, *The Indian Ocean in World History.* Oxford UP, 2014: Chapter 5 'The long nineteenth century', pp. 98–127.

James Belich, *Replenishing the Earth: The Settler Revolution and the Rise of the Anglo-World 1783–1939.* Oxford UP, 2009: 'Introduction' pp. 1–18 and Chapter 3 'Exploding wests', pp. 79–105.

Joseph Conrad, *Heart of Darkness.* Roads, 2013 [1899].

Richard Evans, *The Pursuit of Power. Europe 1815–1914.* Viking, 2016: Chapter 4 'The social revolution', pp. 274–354.

Robert Fitzgerald, *The Rise of the Global Company: Multinationals and the Making of the Modern World.* Cambridge UP, 2015: Chapter 2 'Empires of business, 1870–1914', pp. 24–155.

Robert Harms, 'Introduction' in Robert Harms, Bernard K. Freamon, David W. Blight, eds, *Indian Ocean Slavery in the Age of Abolition.* Yale UP, 2013, pp. 1–20.

Daniel Headrick, *Power over Peoples: Technology, Environments and Western Imperialism 1400 to the Present.* Princeton UP, 2010: Chapter 6 'Health, medicine and the new imperialism, 1830–1914', pp. 226–56.

Eric Hobsbawm, *Industry and Empire: From 1750 to the Present Day.* Penguin, 1968: Chapter 8 'Standards of Living, 1850–1914', pp. 154–71.

Dirk Hoerder, 'Migrations, free and bound' in Emily Rosenberg, ed., *A World Connecting 1870–1945.* Belknap Press, 2012, pp. 491–547.

Alan Lester, Zoë Laidlaw, 'Indigenous sites and mobilities: Connected struggles in the long nineteenth century' in Zoë Laidlaw, Alan Lester, eds, *Indigenous Communities and Settler Colonialism.* Palgrave MacMillan, 2015, pp. 1–23.

Adam McKeown, 'Global migration, 1846–1940', *Journal of World History* 15, 2, 2004, pp. 155–89.

Jürgen Osterhammel, *The Transformation of the World: A Global History of the Nineteenth Century.* Princeton UP, 2014: Chapter 4 'Mobilities', pp. 117–66.

John Anthony Pella, 'World society, international society and the colonization of Africa', *Cambridge Review of International Affairs* 28, 2, 2015, pp. 210–28.

Steven Press, *Rogue Empires: Contracts and Conmen in Europe's Scramble for Africa.* Harvard UP, 2017: Chapter 1 'The man who bought a country', pp. 11–51.

6

Global commodities and the environmental costs of industrial capitalism

As we have seen, the nineteenth-century age of industrial globalization occasioned fundamental changes to human communities around the world. But it also had a revolutionary impact on the world's ecosystems, the distribution and longevity of flora and fauna and the relationships that existed between human communities and the natural environment. Industrialization expanded the power of humanity to alter the environment in drastic ways, not least by extracting resources in escalating quantities. Where, on the one hand, the century witnessed the expansion of scientific knowledge and heightened understanding of how the natural world worked, on the other, new scientific and technological advances also damaged the planet's ecological diversity and threatened its long-term stability. For after 1815, more and more of the planet's natural resources were commodified to serve the expanding needs of a globally connected industrial and capitalist economy.

On its own, the 70 percent increase in the human population between 1815 and 1914 placed unprecedented strains on the planet's resources: all 1.8 billion individuals needed food, fuel and housing after all. But in combination with the growing demand for manufactured products, which relied on natural resources for fuel and primary materials, the strain on the planet's ecology only intensified. These environmental pressures deepened further as millions of humans also migrated across the globe during the nineteenth century; their railway lines stripped bare landscapes; their coal-powered engines and ships polluted the air and waterways and their coal-powered factories even more so; while their settlements and cities reshaped and destroyed the existing milieu. The insatiable demand for fossil fuels and other raw materials not only divested the earth of its resources but also fired up manufacturing industries, which contributed to smog, hazardous emissions, irreparable environmental damage and global warning. It is not for nothing that the *Biodiversity Survey of Hong Kong* noted in its 2002 report that 'were it not for human impact Hong Kong's forests might still support elephants, tigers, rhinoceroses, gibbons, pheasants and woodpeckers'.[1]

Humanity has a long history of reshaping the environment and securing dominance in its realm. But industrial globalization added a particularly tragic chapter to the march of what many (but by no means all) nineteenth-century contemporaries considered 'progress' in aid of 'civilization'. And while some of the environmental impacts of the age were obvious to contemporaries, and many scientists certainly became concerned with them through the course of the 1800s, the ecological damage was rarely halted. In most cases, the destruction of the planet's ecology and the decimation or extinction of certain species were unintended but nevertheless fatal. These outcomes of the nineteenth century's industrial revolution were the costs the world endured for industrialization to succeed. Beyond the unintended or unplanned costs, however, were assaults on animals and indigenous food sources that were intended as weapons of imperial warfare. As we shall see, these could prove effective tools of state violence, even genocidal violence, and offered an ideal way for colonizers to exercise sovereignty and control over territory and the natural resources that indigenous communities needed to sustain their way of life.

Although this chapter focuses primarily on the environmental impact of human agency, it is worth pausing at the phenomenal power of nature to dwarf humanity and to do so on a global scale. Consider the eruption in April 1815 of the Tambora volcano, located on the Indonesian island of Sumbawa. Tambora's eruption is the greatest volcanic explosion known to history. It not only caused the death of seventy thousand people in its immediate vicinity, set off earthquakes and tsunamis around the Pacific-rim basin and irreparably altered the landscape of the region, it also had a phenomenal global reach. The massive volumes of sulphur-dioxide aerosols that spewed out of Tambora and into the stratosphere blocked the sun's rays for several years, altering global weather patterns so fundamentally that it snowed at length during the normally hot summer months of June, July and August in Italy in 1816. The snow was tinged with yellow and red dust.

Scientists can now show how Tambora's eruption caused global crop failures, drought and famine; widespread flooding in Europe, China and South East Asia; the spread of cholera and typhus across the planet; and the loss of fish stocks in the waters off the coast of Maine.[2] At the time, this 'year without a summer' (as 1816 was referred to in the United States) was blamed on sun spots and the wrathful gods. The British author Lord Byron penned his poem 'Darkness' in response:

> No love was left;
> All earth was but one thought – and that was death,
> Immediate and inglorious, and the pang
> Of famine fed upon all entrails.[3]

It was only in the aftermath of another major volcanic eruption in the Indonesian archipelago in 1883, this time by Krakatau,[4] that scientists began to make realistic connections between the extreme climate changes of 1815, 1816 and 1817 and Tambora.[5]

Yet even at the time, the weather catastrophes of the 1815–17 period also inspired scientists in Europe and the United States to ask more questions of the interconnections between climate change and human agency. Already in 1805, the Prussian scientist Alexander von Humboldt reflected on the ability of human communities to impact weather patterns. During the 1820s, climatologists began investigating the impact of carbon dioxide emissions on global weather.[6] Geographers, cartographers, botanists, naturalists and a variety of other scientists now paid increasing attention to the correlations between natural phenomena, weather and human activity. With the benefit of hindsight, it is quite clear that their findings offered few effective restraints on industrialization's environmental impact. Nevertheless, such research was as much a product of the first age of industrial globalization as it was a window on the globalized reality of the earth's ecosystems.

Krakatau and Tambora were not the only nineteenth-century weather events to seriously affect communities around the world. One of the tragic intersections between weather patterns and human-made global forces developed in the late 1870s, when a potent El Niño weather system reduced rainfall to critical levels across much of Asia, Africa and South America for three years in succession. The resulting drought cost the lives of between 30 and 50 million people. Though human activity did not create El Niño, the forces of industrial globalization were directly and indirectly responsible for the severity of these famine conditions. It was particularly in the large plantation economies of China, Korea, India, the Dutch East Indies (Indonesia), Africa and Brazil that the impacts of the drought were felt (see Figure 6.1). The lack of rain was decisive. But the fact that many of these regions had shifted to plantation production, growing mainly non-staple crops like cotton, sugar, coffee, oil seeds, rubber trees and tobacco (as opposed to staple foods like rice, wheat and vegetables), contributed to the crisis. Because of the drought, there was not enough produce available to feed the local population. Because of the lack of growth of these other crops, there were also not enough jobs or

FIGURE 6.1 *The Indian famine, 1876–8. The El Niño induced drought of the 1870s resulted in widespread global suffering. Photographs like this one of drought-stricken Madras in the late 1870s highlight the catastrophic impact of three years of reduced rainfall on crops, cattle and communities. Here a farmer, his child and their last remaining cow succumb to the dustbowl conditions of their home. Photographs like this one, of which there were many, not only spoke to the humanitarian disaster that was the 1870s Indian famine but also to their global media reach. They were used in propaganda campaigns around Europe and the United States to invoke charitable responses from their audience, who encountered them in illustrated magazines, lantern-slide shows and newspaper publications. Photography proved to be a powerful medium to communicate suffering and distress and mobilized internationalist activists in a variety of ways through the late nineteenth and early twentieth centuries (for more, see Chapter 8). Source: Tamil Nadu, c.1876, Getty Images, 964859288.*

wages to pay for the meagre food supplies that did exist. Even in places where food crops were grown, the produce was often sold on the global export market or at global export prices, leaving next to none for local consumption or to build up emergency supplies.[7] In combination with the intensification of farming practices on the plantations and the use of foreign seeds and plants, the lack of rainfall only intensified the degradation and erosion of the soil, hampering future growth as well.[8] Industrial globalization inspired the evolution of these industrial plantations, but in so doing eviscerated many ecological safeguards and the food management systems of the pre-existing peasant and indigenous communities. Such developments provided plenty of reason for these communities to resist future change and to blame the mismanagement of imperial and local authorities for their impacts (for more, see Chapter 7).[9]

The expansion of the industrial empires only intensified these ecological evisceration processes. This was particularly true in India, where during the 1870s large volumes of locally grown grain continued to be shipped to high-price markets by their (largely) British owners, maximizing British profits while India's farming communities starved. The Indian famine was so severe that reports of families selling their children into indentured servitude and instances of cannibalism were common.[10] Similar developments also plagued northern China after 1876, where what locals described as the 'incredible famine' killed off anywhere between a third and a half of the Shanxi province's population and more than 10 percent of northern China's total population of 108 million people.[11] The crisis in northern China was deepened by the fact that the Qing dynasty had previously sold its stock of emergency food supplies on the global market to rectify its growing foreign trade deficit. Meanwhile the 'great drought' (grande seca) in Brazil in 1877 and 1878 caused hundreds of thousands of deaths and a vast migration of people out of the northern reaches of the country into the burgeoning rubber plantation economy around the Amazon river. Brazil's rubber barons not only destroyed substantial parts of the Amazon forest but also capitalized on the desperation of the northern climate refugees for jobs.[12]

Though the nature and scale of a tragedy is always clearer in hindsight the fact that similar devastating famines occurred in the same and additional regions in the 1890s and early 1900s demonstrates the failure of governments to take preventative steps to protect agricultural populations against the dual impact of adverse global weather patterns and the appetite of global economic forces.[13] In some instances, they even mobilized famine to their own ends. As an example, consider how during the United States war against Filipino independence fighters (that followed on from the Spanish-American War of 1898), the United States military took advantage of the concurrent famine conditions. By destroying the Philippines' remaining rice stocks, it hoped to suppress local insurgency and enforce its own sovereignty over the islands.[14] Food security was a key weapon of war (for more, see Chapter 7).

These famines did not go unnoticed by the people most advantaged by them in the industrial metropoles of Europe and the United States. Widespread newspaper reporting inspired calls for charitable and humanitarian aid.[15] But pictures of emaciated Indians and Chinese also sensationalized and exoticized these racial 'others' to their mainly white audience. While advocating for aid, these Anglo-Europeans largely failed to recognize their own agency in bringing about the suffering. Furthermore, much of their charity promoted the idea that the white Christian world was taking responsibility for the 'uncivilized' world's inability to support itself. As the editors of the American *Christian Herald* explained in the context of the situation in the Philippines in 1899, the United States was not only tasked with 'redeeming', 'civilizing' and 'Christianizing' Filipinos but also with the 'work of feeding the hungry, clothing the naked and saving the dying from death'.[16] Meanwhile, the English-language *North China Herald* suggested that the 'incredible famine' of 1876 was a product of a 'lack of industry and moral fiber' among the local Shanxi population.[17]

The environmental costs of industrialization were also felt in the heartlands and metropoles of nineteenth-century industry, and particularly in the booming industrial cities. The combination of factory pollution of the air and waterways, densely packed worker quarters and the lack of attention given by officials to sanitation and public health issues made for particularly toxic urban environments. Europe's industrial workers had plenty of reasons to leave the cities and seek 'a better life' in the 'new world'. Its industrial ports were filled with migrants looking to leave (see Chapter 5). Remarkably, and despite sizeable outwards migratory shifts, most of these urban centres were dependent on even larger shifts of people moving in. These 'in-migrants', as the pioneering global historian W. H. McNeill describes them, mostly came from the countryside and sought out city life for jobs.[18] In this context, it is telling that most nineteenth-century cities brooked disproportionately high mortality rates. Deadly outbreaks of cholera, typhus, smallpox and tuberculosis were a constant threat, which spread quickly in unsanitary conditions. In nineteenth-century London, for example, more people died in the city each year than were born, a grim reality in which contagious disease played a major role.

It took a devastating cholera outbreak in 1832 (a global phenomenon which some scholars trace back to the Tambora eruption of 1815)[19] to prompt British authorities to create a Board of Health. Investigations into sanitation systems, water supply and bacteriological contamination followed.[20] In this sense, technological advances, scientific innovations, engineering developments and medical breakthroughs offered solutions for some of industrialization's most deleterious impacts even when the issues seemed too complex to solve. In the densely populated environment of most urban cities, for example, space was at a premium. Even the issue of how to manage an increase in deaths could pose an environmental nightmare as it did in London, where between 1820 and 1850, no less than 1.5 million corpses were buried in a 250-acre area of the metropolis.[21] Major efforts to improve public sanitation with modern sewer systems did not really take off in London until after the 'Great Stink' of 1858, however, when during a particularly hot summer the miasma of the river Thames, which was basically an open sewer, caused a public outcry.[22] Similar concerns emerged in France, where Napoleon III tasked Baron Haussmann to modernize Paris, complete with a new water supply and sanitation system.[23]

In the latter half of the nineteenth century, municipal authorities in many industrial cities looked to improve their sanitation and water-care management systems (see Figure 6.2). Often such reforms were prompted by an outbreak of disease that made the large public investment of funds more politically palatable. This was less true in Asia, Africa, and Latin America, but municipal authorities here did adopt low-cost measures such as boiling drinking water and testing for serious bacteriological contamination, thereby reducing the risk of some contagions. In 1900, and for the first time in history, major urban centres that had undertaken appropriate reforms were able to maintain or grow their population without in-migration from the countryside.[24]

One of the great accelerants of industrial globalization that had severe consequences for the environment was the ongoing search for mineral wealth and resources. Mining is a dirty business. It was by no means a new industry in 1815. The search for gold, silver, diamonds, iron, tin, copper, coal and other elements had long been pursued. Still, the search for fossil fuels to power factories, steam engines and (later) electricity centrals expanded at a

FIGURE 6.2 *The future of pollution, 1895. This powerful illustration published in the Parisian journal* La Vie Electrique *(Electric Life) in 1895 asked serious questions about the future of the world when heavy industries dominated industrial landscapes and caused pollution. The jars contain a specimen of river water (on the left) and air (on the right) replete with dead fish and birds.*
Source: *Albert Robida, illustration in* La Vie Electrique, *1895, Getty Images, 463911569.*

phenomenal rate after 1815, drawing people and machines into 'nature' with devastating results (and not only for global warming). Given its head start in industrialization, Great Britain was the primary source of coal pollution for much of the century. In 1850 it was responsible for no less than 60 percent of global carbon dioxide emissions, and its per capita consumption of coal was ten times higher than that of France and Germany.[25] By 1900, global carbon dioxide emissions had increased tenfold: the United States was responsible for a third of this total, Britain for 21 percent and Germany almost 17 percent.[26]

But nineteenth-century mineral extraction had numerous faces and numerous global consequences. Consider the 1849 California gold rush, for example, which brought three hundred thousand people from across the world to the region looking for quick wealth or to service the newly established mining communities. The gold rush not only expanded the towns of Los Angeles and San Francisco but also turned San Francisco into a major trade port. In the process, it helped to boost trans-Pacific ship movements and extended the reach and importance of all Pacific Ocean ports, including those of Hong Kong, Shanghai and Singapore.[27] The California gold rush turned the Pacific into a major highway of commerce and migration, which was only augmented when gold discoveries in Australia, New Zealand and southern Africa set off new 'rushes' to these regions.

The environmental and ecological costs of the 1849 California ventures were profound.[28] The newly arrived prospectors took almost no account of the rights of the local people, let alone the habitats of flora and fauna. The local Chumash people, certainly, despaired at the costs. From their perspective, the Spanish and Mexicans who had arrived since 1769 were bad enough, introducing cattle herds and foreign grasses and hunting at will, thereby undermining the Chumash relationship to the natural world. According to the testimony of a Chumash elder, Grandfather Semu Huaute,

> Before the Spaniards came to California, the bears and us used to gather berries together. The bears were real friendly. We got along real well. We could talk to each other, and we had a good understanding. When the Spaniards came, they found it pretty easy to shoot the bears. After that the bears wouldn't go berrying with us anymore.[29]

The influx of gold diggers after 1849, however, surpassed even these incursions. The demand for meat from elk, deer, pronghorn, antelope, bighorn sheep and even shore birds killed these animals in the hundreds of thousands and largely eliminated the dominant predators like the grizzly bear and cougar. The draining of marshes, the digging of canals and the growth of domestic livestock herds eroded the natural habitat even further. So too did the insatiable demand for timber to build towns and mining structures. The old-growth redwood, pine and sequoia forests that stretched from modern-day San Francisco to Lake Tahoe were stripped bare of trees. Meanwhile, hydraulic mining techniques not only redirected water supplies and changed the course of rivers but also polluted them so much that they became uninhabitable for fish.[30] Even though some relief was provided when Yosemite Valley became a protected habitat in 1864 and hydraulic mining was outlawed in 1884, it was too late for the Chumash, whose traditional ways of life stood little chance in the face of such wanton destruction.

Of course, humans had long been the architects of doom for other animals. The large flightless ostrich-like moa of Aotearoa-New Zealand (some of which weighed 250 kilograms and stood four metres tall) disappeared by the fifteenth century in large part due to the hunting practices of the local Maori people. The Haast eagle, which preyed on the moa, also died out. Similarly, the flightless Dodo bird disappeared from Mauritius in the seventeenth century as sailors and the various animals they introduced on the island killed them off. The nineteenth century, however, accelerated these human-caused extinction rates. As the historian Franz Broswimmer describes it, 'The Industrial Revolution represents a milestone in the history of ecocide and environmental degradation' as the planet became a 'sacrifice zone' for 'progress'.[31]

As examples, consider how the Great Auk of the north Atlantic region disappeared forever around the middle of the nineteenth century due to European demand for its feathery down, its large eggs and meat. Russian and indigenous Aleut seal hunters reduced the numbers of seals and sea otters in the Russian coastal region and the Aleutian islands to critical levels by the early nineteenth century.[32] Dutch settlers in southern Africa largely wiped out the Quagga zebra by the 1870s as it competed with domestic livestock for forage. The passenger pigeon, that numbered in the hundreds of millions and counted as North America's most numerous bird, was hunted for its meat across the century. The bird was particularly vulnerable as it congregated in great numbers where organized hunters could kill tens of thousands in a day as they did around the Great Lakes until 1880. Often such slaughter of wild animals was undertaken without regard to the management of the hunt or the raising of young. When conservation efforts were introduced, it was too late for many species. The US National Association of Audubon Societies, for example, was founded in 1905. It was unable to save the passenger pigeon, however, whose last-known representative, named Martha, died at the outbreak of the First World War in a Cincinnati zoo.[33]

Other species were not driven completely out of existence but were put under heavy pressure as a result of humanity's greater firepower, increased access to habitat and the greed of global market forces combined. Elephants were among the biggest targets as ivory for carving, combs, piano keys and billiard balls was in heavy demand. In the latter decades of the century, the ivory exchanges in Liverpool and Antwerp relied on the slaughter of tens of thousands of elephants a year.[34] They sourced the ivory from African traders, who also raided villages for slaves while on their elephant hunts. Many of these slaves were sold in the same east African ports that supplied ivory to the world (see also Chapter 5).[35] Increasingly, as the elephant population declined in the central African regions and as demand increased, new hunting areas in the east and south west opened up and trading settlements and caravan routes expanded.[36]

The decline of the elephant population had other ecological effects as well. Elephants are big eaters. When their population declined the plants they ate grew in greater abundance, producing a habitat ideal for the breeding of the disease-carrying tsetse fly. Tsetse fly diseases affected people and cattle in increasing numbers in the late 1880s and early 1890s. As a result, the cattle-herd economy of East Africa suffered a near complete collapse with 95 percent of its animals dying in a great Rinderpest epidemic.[37] Industrial globalization thus linked the fate of African elephants, cattle, insects and people in an inescapable and destructive network of dependence on the global economy and the commodification of ivory to service that economy.[38]

For a similar reason, the many species that lived in or on the edges of the world's oceans came under increasing threat of extinction during the nineteenth century as well. The introduction of steam trawlers in the North Sea in the middle of the 1880s, for example, increased the catch capacity of a single ship exponentially. With heightened competition between rival fishing fleets, the cost to particular fish species was enormous.[39] Advances in cartography, communication networks, harpoons, lances and bombs also made humans more lethal than ever as hunters of the largest of all creatures, the whale. While whales were hunted well before 1815, sometimes near to extinction,[40] the nineteenth century's steam-powered whaling vessels and explosive hunting equipment turned whale hunting into an industrial enterprise. As early as 1840, such ships launched from the whaling capital of New Bedford, Massachusetts, embarked on three-year-long voyages that might kill as many as three thousand sperm whales per vessel.[41]

Whales had exceptional value in the nineteenth-century's commodities market. Whale oil served as a fuel for lamps and as a key ingredient in margarine, candles and cooking oil as well as a lubricant for factory machinery. Whale bones made corsets, umbrellas, buggy whips, collar stays, toys and ground up into fertilizers. Sperm whale teeth made piano keys, chess pieces and the handles of walking sticks. Whaling was big business. The products whales yielded were invaluable to the growth of the industrial economy. In the end, only two things saved the whales from extinction, namely the replacement of lamp oil with alternate fossil fuels (including electricity) and the fact that the drastic reduction of whale numbers made whale hunting less predictable and hence manufacturers looked for alternate materials. Petroleum increasingly replaced whale oil lubricants, for example.[42] Still, the damage done to whale pods and the oceanic environment was severe: grey, arctic bowhead and southern right whales were particularly affected.[43]

Another surprisingly important animal commodity that fed the growth of nineteenth-century industrialization was bison (buffalo). The destruction of north America's bison herds through the course of the century went hand-in-hand with the expansion of the American frontier, the expulsion and eradication of indigenous communities and the growth of factories globally. For thousands of years, indigenous Americans hunted and killed bison, sometimes in great numbers and concentrated form. For example, at the annual buffalo jump at Heads Smashed In (now a World Heritage site in southern Alberta, Canada), the Blackfoot people stampeded bison herds off a cliff and then butchered and processed the entire animal into food, clothing, tools and construction materials.[44] Bison sustained the way of life of the many indigenous communities of the Great Plains' region.

The economic, political and military forces of the nineteenth century changed all of this both for the bison, which was driven close to extinction,[45] and for the local people. The pressures on many indigenous peoples were steadily increasing and the movement of settlers and the miners of 1849 across the region brought deadly disease that killed as many as three-quarters of the dominant Comanche people of the southern plains by 1840.[46] Still, before 1860, indigenous communities were able to supply the global demand for bison robes and leather by trading these with European and American merchants, a trade that yielded about one hundred thousand bison hides a year.

When tanners in Germany and the United States developed a process to turn bison leather into long-drive belts for industrial machinery, however, the demand for bison hides boomed.[47] The arrival of railways into the Great Plains area at around the same time made extracting the animal hides easier and faster as well. After the American Civil War (1861–5), then, the United States government supported a massive hunting campaign to kill the bison, take their valuable hides for production and undermine the way of life of the Great Plains' tribes who resisted the United States' policies. As a result, by the 1870s the peoples in the southern plains were reduced to poverty, while the wolf population soared as they feasted on the massive piles of bison carcasses left behind by the white hunters and skinners. Millions of buffalo died in these slaughters. Between 1872 and 1874 alone, nearly 10 million buffalo hides were shipped by rail from the southern plain's region.[48] Rather macabrely, some of the hunters even became celebrities, including 'Buffalo' Bill Cody, who killed thousands of buffalo himself and sold the meat to the Pacific Railroad Company construction crews as the railway and the slaughter advanced. The rich and famous joined him for the hunt from time to time and eventually he transformed his profession into that of an entertainer in his 'Wild West' shows.[49]

As with many of these other environmental developments, there was some resistance to the bison slaughter, and not only from within indigenous communities. During the Red River War (1874) that was launched by the United States Army to remove the Comanche, Kiowa, southern Cheyenne and Arapaho tribes from the southern plains into designated 'reservations', General Philip Sheridan explained the stakes,

> We took away their country and their means of support [the bison], broke up their mode of living, their habits of life, introduced disease and decay among them, and it was for this and against this they made war ... Could anyone expect less?[50]

Nevertheless, over the next two decades the destruction of the bison and the people of the Great Plains became the focal point of the United States military and the Northern Pacific railway, which carved a path through even the 'protected' Indian reservations. 'Manifest destiny' (as described in Chapter 4) came with a huge amount of bloodshed and the ultimate defeat of the Great Plains' peoples.[51] The Sioux people's struggles against the United States, for example, came to a tragic end at Wounded Knee in 1890 when about 450 followers of Sitting Bull (who had been killed two weeks earlier) were shot by the US Seventh Cavalry, as one rare survivor described, 'like we were buffalo'.[52]

While industrial globalization caused the destruction of many peoples and species, it also occasioned the spread of biodiversity across oceans and continents. Some of this migration was intentional, but like many human activities the introduction of new species had both positive and negative impacts. The massive settler migrations of the nineteenth century (as described in Chapter 5) were decisive. By bringing familiar animals and plants with them, these settlers reshaped the 'new world' to look and feel more like 'home'. But in so doing, many indigenous environments were irretrievably altered. Consider the impact of European plants and animals in New Zealand's unique ecosystem, for example, which before Maori arrived in the thirteenth century sustained no indigenous terrestrial mammals other than bats.[53] During the nineteenth century, the introduction of more mice and rats, then stouts, ferrets and weasels (to control the mice and rats), Australian possum and deer (for hunting) and ever-increasing numbers of grazing mammals like sheep, cows and pigs (including the Asian kunekune variety) alongside domestic cats and dogs decimated the country's flightless bird population, as well as many of its frog, lizard and invertebrate species.[54] The introduction of trout, whitefish and salmon to New Zealand rivers and lakes may have improved fishing conditions for settlers and tourists alike but did so at the cost of the indigenous upokororo (grayling) and the ecological balance of New Zealand's waterways.

Meanwhile, the introduction of some new plants and crops also had unexpectedly devastating impacts. Many of these came with the country's new settlers. The yellow-flowered gorse bush (or broom), introduced in the middle of the century to provide hedging for farms, swept across New Zealand's islands with impunity and remains a noxious weed today.[55] The expansion of Chinese market gardens and the spread of gardening culture among the country's cosmopolitan communities resulted in numerous other exotic species being planted as well. As the historian James Beatty shows, the abundance of these plants in New Zealand registers how globally connected the nineteenth-century plant trade was and how central a role the Chinese played in it. Rhododendrons, azaleas, chrysanthemums, camellias, peonies, narcissi, gingko trees and many maples originated in Asia, after all.[56] Intoxicating as the sweet smell of jasmine might be, when such foreign exotics (and others like ginger and agapanthus) escaped the controlled space of settlers' gardens and naturalized in New Zealand's environment, the new invasive species strangled native plants, poisoned root systems and smothered the soil.

The expansion of settler communities across New Zealand during the nineteenth century as well as the growing demands for timber on the global market also expanded the country's logging industry causing serious deforestation. So much of New Zealand's native forest was lost that by the 1890s, new fast-growing species of exotic pine trees were planted to feed the ongoing demand for wood locally and globally. In this, New Zealand mimicked global forces. Industrial capacity and demand had fundamentally altered (and in some cases completely removed) old-growth forest landscapes in the Americas, Africa, Australasia, India, South East Asia and across the Pacific. Steam-powered sawmills, railway networks and growing market demand transformed the clearing of land into a major export business. The impacts were devastating. To take but one example, by the 1850s in the Midwestern Great Lakes' region of the United States, 153 million acres (an area that is roughly the size of France) had been cleared for farming. Another area twelve times greater in size was cleared of trees for their industrial use. By 1900, only 13 percent of the original forest remained (see Figure 6.3).[57]

Equally devastating was the nineteenth-century decimation of the sapodilla forests of South East Asia. The indigenous peoples in Malaysia, Borneo and Vietnam had long used sapodilla's sap (gutta-percha) to make tools, knife handles and walking sticks but its many properties and potential uses were dramatically expanded in the 1840s when German and British researchers discovered the thermoplastic insulation value of gutta-percha. Over a million

FIGURE 6.3 *Sequoia logging in the United States. The massive forests of old-growth sequoia trees in the United States were liberally felled across the nineteenth century as sources of fuel, lumber and wood fibre. In this photograph, forestry workers take a moment's rest on top of a giant sequoia tree trunk before it is loaded onto a waiting railway car heading for a lumber mill.*
Source: Getty Images, 615229236.

kilos of sap were imported to Britain in the decade that followed and gutta-percha covering for telegraph wires and submarine communication cables was soon the industry standard. As gutta-percha sap had substantial properties of bio-inertness, it was also used to make surgical and dental items. Furniture and toy manufacturers as well as golf enthusiasts embraced gutta-percha's properties as well. The 'gut' core of a new generation of golf balls invented in 1848 by Robert Adams Paterson changed that game until rubber cores replaced them in the 1890s.[58] Furthermore, the wood from gutta-percha trees proved an excellent ship-building material. In combination, industrial demand for gutta-percha propelled the harvesting of tens of millions of sapodilla trees and devastated most of its forests within a few decades.[59]

Industrial capitalism thus ensured that the old-growth forests of much of the world, like so much else, were transformed into commodities up for trade, sale and exchange. Not only did the loss of so many trees globally impact climate change (as trees absorb carbon dioxide and release oxygen), where-ever trees were removed so too did local ecosystems disappear, threatening animals and plants alike. The lives and cultures of many indigenous peoples who depended on these forest-ecosystems were threatened too. And since the Anglo-European world had already cleared most of their own forests before 1800, their industrialization depended on these foreign sources, offering a particularly poignant environmental consequence of their version of industrial imperialism.

Though the overall impact of the destructive changes that the industrial world brought to the environment and its various forms of life was sizable throughout the first age of industrial globalization, it was not the case that nothing was done to try to slow its damaging course or limit its reach. Certainly, a rising understanding of the environment costs grew as forests disappeared and once prevalent communities of animal species declined. By the early 1800s, Europeans were already aware that the loss of their own old-growth forests resulted in soil erosion, increased flooding and reduced rainfall.[60] They were also aware that the unrestrained killing or harvesting of animals could result in their extinction. For the most part, however, the cultural reflex of these Anglo-Europeans was to imagine a future when more scientific development and the extension of their 'civilization' was the key to 'solving' such problems. As such, their understanding of conservation depended on the precept of the human mastery of nature (humans shaping the environment). Many indigenous communities, in contrast, advocated for a symbiotic model of conservation that placed humanity as being 'at one' with nature.

Concepts of symbiosis, however, rarely sat well with the greed of global capitalism. Still by the 1890s, the study of ecology in the Western world had evolved substantially, including pioneering work by the English-born New Zealand resident Leonard Cockayne, who in 1911 noted that 'introduced plants' may

> at first appear better suited to the soil and climate than indigenous species ... but this is only the case where draining, cultivation, constant burning of forest, scrub, and tussock, and the grazing of domestic animals have made absolutely new edaphic conditions which approximate those of Europe, and where it is no wonder that the European invader can replace the aboriginal.[61]

Increasing numbers of people globally (and, thus, not only the indigenous communities who had resisted and protested many of these industrial and imperial developments from the outset) started asking serious questions about the loss of natural habitats. This popular conservation movement inspired governments in many regions to establish national parks, conservation reserves and to pass laws protecting natural heritage sites. Yellowstone park in the United States was the world's first national park (although other natural reserves already existed, including Yosemite noted above). Established by federal law in 1872, Yellowstone stretched across two million acres of northwest Wyoming. Its purpose was to preserve the area's pristine natural beauty and guarantee access to its waterfalls and geysers for the enjoyment of the American people.[62]

Even here, however, the main idea was that the 'wilderness' could be improved upon by humans.[63] As the historians Bernhard Gissibl, Sabine Höhler and Patrick Kupper explain, national parks enabled industrializing states to 'civilize, territorialize and categorize' nature and in so doing place clear boundaries on what might be exploited and what could be protected and studied. In so doing, these governments managed to confine and localize conservation efforts (thereby enabling the ongoing exploitation of other natural resources) as much as they could trumpet them as symbols of 'civilization'.[64] In many ways, these parks and reservations also aimed at controlling and excluding indigenous communities from utilizing the parks' resources or exercising their own traditions in managing them. Conservation for many industrial states was about controlling the earth and its people according to prescribed Western ways.[65]

Yet when indigenous communities mobilized in support of the creation of national parks, as some Maori tribes did in New Zealand for example, they also managed to keep their own taonga (treasures) from being exploited by investors, settlers, tourists and the state. In 1887, Ngati Tuwharetoa's chief Te Heuheu Tukino III gifted his iwi's sacred lands around the Tongariro volcano to the New Zealand government for safekeeping. The country's first national park was established from this gift in 1894.[66] It would be followed by many others. Such parks offered some kind of reprieve for local Maori from the expansion of colonial settlements, railway lines and other foreign incursions. Still, it was not a complete reprieve, as these parks also became popular tourist and recreational destinations. Artist communities, health spas and hiking trails all developed in and near such areas and many of these celebrated the benefits of nature and its wonders in Western ways. The creation of national parks was not enough to stop industrial globalization or the spread of colonies and 'blue-water' empires, but it did shelter some areas from its most invasive ecological impact.

By 1914, it was clear that the globally connected world had sustained significant ecological damage from the previous hundred years of industrial development. The First World War, which erupted in July–August that year, would alter the geopolitical foundations of these global connections. The years of total industrial warfare had their own damaging impact on these ecosystems. The war may have interrupted and ended the 'first age of industrial globalization' but it did not end the planet's ecological or pathogenical interconnectedness. In fact, the unprecedented numbers of troop movements across the globe in aid of the war effort contained within them the seeds of the war's most destructive impact, namely that of the 'Spanish flu' pandemic. This version of influenza, which scholars now show began in China,[67] struck in 1917 and raged across the planet in three deadly waves over the following two years, killing between 50 and 100 million people. No continent (bar Antarctica) and almost no community was left unaffected. Only the communities that imposed strict quarantines escape the flu's ravages.[68] From the highly placed to the humble, the 'Spanish flu' virus waged its own global campaign. Its global impact speaks to the environmental powers of the first age of industrial globalization. Rather ironically, it was this flu that further destabilized the already tendentious human endeavours to construct a global peace after this long and terrible war had undermined much of the political and economic order of the nineteenth-century world.

Study questions

1. How did industrial globalization impact the earth's ecosystems between 1815 and 1914? In what ways were these impacts the product of human intent?

2. How did imperial endeavours contribute to the erosion of natural habitats and the destruction of species around the world in the long nineteenth century?

3. What types of measures were taken to inhibit or prevent the destruction of the environment and its species after 1815?

4. How did scientists engage with these global ecological changes?

5. What role did environmental damage play in eroding indigenous communities and ways of living?

Recommended readings

David S. Barnes, *The Great Stink of Paris and the Nineteenth-Century Struggle against Filth and Germs*. Johns Hopkins Press, 2006: 'Introduction', pp. 1–11.
James Beattie, 'Eco-cultural networks in southern China and colonial New Zealand: Cantonese market gardening and environmental exchange, 1860s-1910s' in James Beattie, Edward Mellilo, Emily O'Gorman, eds, *Eco-Cultural Networks and the British Empire: New Views on Environmental History*. Bloomsbury, 2015, pp. 151–79.
Karen Brown, 'Conservation and utilisation of the natural world: Silviculture in the Cape Colony, c. 1902–1910', *Environment and History* 7, 2001, pp. 427–47.

Mike Davis, *Late Victorian Holocausts: El Niño Famines and the Making of the Third World.* Verso, 2001: Chapter 1 'Victoria's Ghosts', pp. 29–65.

Jelle Zielinga de Boer, Donald T. Sanders, *Volcanoes in Human History: The Far-Reading Effects of Major Eruptions.* Princeton UP, 2002: Chapter 6 'The eruption of Tambora in 1815 and the "Year without a summer"', pp. 138–56.

Kathryn Edgerton-Tarpley, 'Tough choices: Grappling with famine in Qing China, the British empire and beyond', *Journal of World History* 24, 1, 2013, pp. 135–76.

Georgina Endfield, Samuel Randalls, 'Climate and empire' in James Beattie, Edward Mellilo, Emily O'Gorman, eds, *Eco-Cultural Networks and the British Empire: New Views on Environmental History.* Bloomsbury, 2015, pp. 21–43.

Dan Flores, 'Bison ecology and bison diplomacy: The southern plains from 1800 to 1850', *Journal of American History* 78, 2, 1991, pp. 465–85.

Benjamin Lieberman, Elizabeth Gordon, *Climate Change in Human History: Prehistory to the Present.* Bloomsbury, 2018: Chapter 6 'Humans take over', pp. 133–55.

W. H. McNeill, *Plagues and Peoples.* Anchor Books Doubleday, 1998: Chapter 5 'The ecological impact of medical science and organisation after 1700', pp. 242–95.

Anne Rasmussen, 'The Spanish flu' in Jay Winter, ed., *The Cambridge History of the First World War.* Volume Three, Cambridge UP, 2014, pp. 233–357.

John Shultis, 'Improving the wilderness: Common factors in creating national parks and equivalent reserves during the nineteenth century', *Forest and Conservation History* 39, 3, 1995, pp. 121–9.

John Tully, 'A Victorian ecological disaster: Imperialism, the telegraph, and gutta-percha', *Journal of World History* 20, 4, 2009, pp. 559–79.

7

A world of war after 1850

From 'satanic mills' to colonial outposts, the growth of nineteenth-century industrialization involved significant amounts of human suffering as well as enduring environmental damage. Globalization's primary impact, namely the 'threading together of human communities' in a complex web of interconnections,[1] was seldom achieved by peaceful means, nor was it left uncontested. The expansion and building of the century's industrial empires, be they formal or informal, also came with considerable and ongoing degrees of discord, protest and resistance 'from below', including by colonial subjects. Governments were rarely restrained in using military power to suppress such resistance, whether it occurred at home or abroad. Warfare and *state violence* (as conducted by soldiers, the police or by other agents of the state) were a marked feature of the nineteenth-century world and a clear characteristic of this 'age of empire'.

This chapter focuses on the period of 'industrial and imperial consolidation' that came in the second half of the nineteenth century. It makes a case for the global interdependence of wars and military actions in the period and argues that in consolidating their imperial and economic dominion over others, the industrializing governments relied both on strategies of *war avoidance* and *war mongering*. Above all, it acknowledges Antoinette Burton's powerful conceptualization of armed revolt as 'endemic' to nineteenth-century imperialism. The foundations of nineteenth-century imperialism were built not only on the technological, economic and systemic advantages offered to the industrializing powers but also relied heavily on the repression of resistance. Dissidence and disruption pervaded all nineteenth-century empires.[2] In many respects, then, the 'age of revolution' did not end in 1848, as resistance 'from below' to power wielded 'from above' remained a dominant feature of the late nineteenth-century world as well.

There were a lot of wars conducted in the nineteenth century and they had some telling characteristics.[3] First and foremost, it was generally understood that the use of violence by a government (be it to conduct a formal war against another state or to police a population) was both legitimate and expected. In the 1830s, the influential Prussian military strategist Carl von Clausewitz described the right of governments to go to war as follows: warfare is a 'continuation of politics by other means'.[4] The choice for war, be it against enemies within the state or as a campaign waged against another state, was made by a government based on a range of considerations and interests. The choice for war was almost always constrained in some way by the international environment (a government's relationship with other governments and the range of imperial, diplomatic, economic and political interests at play), although these limitations rarely meant that a particular instance of warfare was in any way restrained in terms of its violent impact. The technological advances made in the weaponry of war – be it the quick-loading rifle, iron- or steel-clad warship or the invention of dynamite and the aeroplane – also had the potential to make warfare more destructive and, thus, to provide particular advantages to the wielders of these industrial weapons.

As we saw in Chapter 2, the use of military force to suppress revolutions and enforce the power of the state was a common feature of the 'age of revolution/restoration' (1815–48). But even after 1848, in the expansion and consolidation of their formal and informal empires, few industrializing governments or their representatives hesitated in using such force. They certainly felt compelled to keep armed troops on hand to respond to the wide range of resistance activities at play across their country and empire. The historian Charlotte MacDonald's project *Soldiers of Empire*, for example, highlights just how essential Britain's colonial armed forces were to imposing and maintaining their version of 'law and order' around the globe.[5] Antoinette Burton, furthermore, highlights how commonplace everyday acts of resistance against these foreign rulers and rules also were. That was as true in the age-old empires ruled by the Qings, Romanovs, Habsburgs and Ottomans as it was in the newer 'blue-water' realms of the British, French, Dutch, Belgians, Germans, Americans and Japanese. Layers of state violence, ranging from police actions to 'burn-village'[6] and 'scorched earth'[7] tactics, underwrote the building and sustenance of the nineteenth-century global imperial order.

Yet from the perspective of interstate relations, the nineteenth century was a relatively peaceful century, one in which 'formal' wars between recognized states occurred, but when they did, they were carefully managed and constrained. Diplomatic historians of Europe often reflect on the relatively limited number of 'formal' wars conducted between 1815 and 1914.[8] These historians take the principles of the 'concert system' and of 'limited war' (as described in Chapter 2) as foundational to explaining the existence of a 'long'

European peace. Geopolitically speaking, of course, they are not wrong. By restricting the geopolitical impact of an interstate conflict, these governments shielded their collective security against internal revolutions and external threats. In so doing, they protected the stability of the international system and consolidated their international positions of power which many of them utilized to project their 'formal' and 'informal' empires outwards into the rest of the world. The European concert system and the American Monroe doctrine enabled these industrializing states to draw the whole world into their webs of economic, political and cultural control while avoiding a great war erupting between the industrial powers.

Of course, from the perspective of the people who were ruled by these industrializing states, the nineteenth century was far from peaceful. The juxtaposition between a 'world of Anglo-European peace', as diplomatic historians might describe it, and a 'world of imperial violence' offers a powerful explanation for why social-cultural historians are often dismissive of traditional diplomatic history.[9] Yet the wars of the nineteenth century, where-ever they occurred, were closely interrelated events: peace and security in one region enabled war in another. Furthermore, the widening web of information exchange through the course of the century also made the sharing of news and ideas about warfare more commonplace. Globalization made all wars, however localized, potential subjects for global media attention and thus for global responses at a state and popular level.

How important the changes in the global media environment was to comprehending the role played by warfare in contemporary understanding is well illustrated by the Crimean War (1853–6).[10] In this war, war correspondents followed the armies in the field, reporting directly back to their newspapers at home by means of the postal system (by ship) or via telegraph transmission.[11] The war also saw the adoption and use of military photographers (see Figure 7.1). Recent inventions (including telegraphy, the steamship and the daguerreotype camera) ensured that news about the war fronts could reach a newspaper reader within a day or two. In the past, such news might take many weeks and sometimes even months to publish. The relative immediacy of war news had decisive political consequences, particularly when the portrayal was far from glorious. In Britain, for example, military bungling convinced many Britons that the war was a wasteful and needless endeavour. This, despite the popularity of Alfred Lord Tennyson's poem 'Charge of the Light Brigade' (which depicted the bravery of the cavalrymen who were slaughtered in a frontal assault on the Russian position at Balaclava in 1854) and the romanticization of nurse Florence Nightingale's activities treating the wounded. Reports of thousands of casualties – 22.7 percent of the British forces succumbed in the conflict due to lack of proper medical facilities, disease and the cold – inspired widespread critique of the war.[12] Such perceptions helped to promote

FIGURE 7.1 *Crimean War photography. This daguerreotype photograph from the inside of the destroyed Russian fort at Sevastopol during the Crimean War (in 1855) was published in the French magazine L'Illustration in 1905. Daguerreotype was the first commercially available form of photography, invented by Louis Jacques Mandé Daguerre in the 1830s. It was an extremely expensive form of photography as each individual image was projected on a silvered copper plate. Still by 1900, photographs frequently featured in newspapers alongside the more traditional black-and-white woodcut. Illustrated magazines had also become increasingly popular. The imagery of war in these periodicals showed up the destructive power of war and helped contemporaries to question the role warfare played in their lives and in international relations generally. Photographic methods would improve so much during the course of the nineteenth century that by 1888, handheld cameras loaded with flexible plastic roll-film were invented (first introduced by the Kodak company), enabling anyone who could afford to buy a camera to take snapshots of their daily lives. In conjunction with the invention of the phonograph (capturing sound on a replayable disc) in 1877 and moving pictures in the 1890s, the photograph had a revolutionary impact on the ways in which contemporaries saw, heard and considered the world around them.*

Source: *Photograph of Russian fort, Sevastopol' L'Illustration 3267, 7 October 1905, Getty Images, 931986378.*

a post-war British foreign policy of neutrality, at least when it came to the wars of Europe: why go to war when there were so few advantages to be had in doing so?[13]

This is not to say that mid-century Britons were not militaristically minded nor that they were not proud of their military and naval achievements and history. On the contrary, their belief in the superiority of the British empire and the Royal Navy, in their 'right to rule' other people and in the necessity of enforcing British power globally dominated British political culture after the Crimean War. So too did the idea that military service defined masculinity.[14] Similar concepts of imperial duty and the value of soldiering flourished in the other industrializing metropoles during the 1800s and early 1900s as well. They thrived in part because contemporaries framed their understandings of the value of imperialism and warfare within their perceptions of how the international system functioned and what their place as 'civilized people' was within it. Warfare, then, was a normalized and celebrated part of late nineteenth-century Anglo-European, Japanese and American life. But this did not mean that these contemporaries considered all wars or even all soldiers as equal.

Within the Anglo-European framing of the nineteenth-century international system, three types of warfare existed: *interstate wars, civil wars* and *imperial wars.* Interstate or 'formal' wars were easily identifiable, namely as military conflicts undertaken by a recognized state against other recognized states. An interstate war had distinct characteristics: it usually involved a formal declaration of war by a government as well as many neutrality declarations by the non-belligerent powers. It also usually involved the mobilization of a country's armed forces. Only recognized sovereign states, members of the 'family of civilized nations', conducted such wars. As a result, an interstate war was subject to a variety of diplomatic protocols, such as the expulsion of enemy diplomats and envoys. It also tended to progress according to the precepts of the international law of war, even if the terms of that law remained contested (and could be reinterpreted). Interstate wars, then, were defined as much by the diplomatic relationship of the warring governments and their neutral neighbours as they were by the economic and military damage inflicted during the conflict. Rather paradoxically, contemporaries often described such wars as 'civilized wars', for they were supposedly restrained conflicts, proscribed by the principles of 'civilization' as determined by the international law of war.

Beginning with the Declaration of Paris of 1856, such legal principles were increasingly written into multilateral treaties. In settling on a universal 'law of war' that bound them all, these governments believed that they could stabilize the principles of diplomatic restraint, neutrality and war avoidance that were embedded in the congress system that had defined the international environment since 1815. As a result, they could more easily protect their own right to neutrality when others were at war, safeguarding the economic security of global commerce from unwarranted naval attack and protecting access to their 'blue-water' empires at the same time. While the law of war during the nineteenth century certainly allowed for enemies to attack each other's commerce, the primary ambition was to prevent belligerents from unduly interfering in the commercial affairs of non-belligerents. After all, they also hoped to profit from their own non-belligerency when others were at war.[15]

Another major reason to proscribe interstate warfare after 1856, as many of the industrializing governments saw it, was to offset the impact of the rapid development of industrial military technology. The nineteenth century was an age of invention and innovation, including in new weaponry. Enterprising entrepreneurs and inventors made their fortunes on investing in industrialized armaments production. Alfred Nobel, whose fortune and will would establish the Nobel Peace Prize, invented dynamite in 1866, which revolutionized both the mining industry and expanded the reach and explosive capacity of artillery fire.[16] Hiram Stevens Maxim designed the first rapid-firing machine-gun (the Maxim gun) in 1884, which had a devastating impact on land warfare.[17] While these technological breakthroughs made the acquisition and policing of empires easier, the fear of not keeping up with the armaments' advantages of a rival state (or with the organizational changes made by forward-thinking armed forces) had the potential to upset the balance of power within Europe as well. Wealthy states – like the industrializing powerhouses of Great Britain, Prussia/Germany, France, the United States and, by the 1890s, Japan – could afford to invest in the new technologies. Privately owned armaments firms happily supplied them with their wares. By 1900, armaments investment had become one of the ways in which these industrial powers registered their global power. They did so by comparing the relative strength of their armies and navies. Great power rivalry over armaments' acquisition would be a major contributing factor to a changing international landscape in the early years of the twentieth century and leading to the First World War (for more, see Chapter 9).

But even the European wars of the 1860s brought out the interplay between local politics, congress system principles, new military technology and global economics. Between 1859 and 1871 a number of short but decisive conflicts were fought in Europe that reshaped the geographic boundaries of key states and created two new nation-states: Germany and Italy. Contemporaries considered the wars of Italian and German unification as interstate conflicts, pitting existing governments and their armed forces against neighbouring states. In both cases, and much like the Greek Wars of Independence fought in the 1820s (see Chapter 2), the European great powers helped to micromanage the course and impact of these wars so that they did not threaten general European war nor interfere too greatly in the global economy.

The 1859 second war of Italian unification,[18] for example, saw 240,000 French and Sardinian troops clash against 220,000 Austrian soldiers in an attempt to determine who would rule the northern Italian states. The conflict quickly drew in the other Italian states and forces, including those led by the Italian nationalist Giuseppe Garibaldi (who, as an anti-imperialist, had learned the art of guerrilla warfare in Brazil and Uruguay in the 1830s and 1840s). The first wave of warfare lasted only a few months. It was brought to a quick conclusion when the French Emperor Napoleon III personally negotiated peace terms with the Austrian Emperor Franz Joseph I. Shocked by the forty thousand casualties sustained in the space of nine hours during the Battle of Solferino, both monarchs also feared the uncertainty of what might happen if the war expanded into central Europe. The Prussian government had mobilized its armed forces and announced it would remain neutral only as long as no major changes were wrought in the balance of power in the Italian region. The Peace of Villafranca, hurriedly signed in June 1859, ended Austrian and French military involvement in the war and kept Prussia neutral. It also left the Sardinians alone to face the wrath of the other Italian states. The changes wrought in Italy by the 1859 conflict inspired Garibaldi's guerrilla forces to launch a populist war in southern Italy that would combine with the Sardinian campaign to bring the remaining Italian kingdoms into a singular nation-state under the rule of the King of Piedmont and Sardinia.

The wars for Italian unification were products both of local agency (the actions of the various Italians involved) and great power diplomacy. It was in large part because the great powers restricted their involvement in the wars that Italy could unify in the manner that it did. These wars barely impacted the global economy (although it offered a boon for arms sales). It also confirmed the general commitment to neutrality of most of the other European states, which, in turn, ensured that a unified Italy did not upset the general principles of the existing concert system. After its creation, the newly formed Italian state only gained from avoiding war with its great power rivals. It also profited from the wars of others, acquiring Venice from Austria in 1866 (as the Austrians faced defeat in the Austro-Prussian War) and Rome in 1870 (as the French removed their garrisons from the city during the Franco-Prussian War).

The concurrent wars for German unification, fought by Prussia in Denmark in 1864, against Austria in 1866 and against France in 1870–1, were more of a challenge to the European congress system, in large part because they collapsed the German Confederation, ended the sovereign independence of 37 German states and reshaped the Habsburg empire.[19] In the aftermath of the 1859 Italian war, the Prussian army had professionalized. Making the most of these improvements, the Prussian chancellor Otto von Bismarck used judicious diplomacy and successful battle plans to expand the Prussian kingdom's regional influence and economic reach. The war fought with Denmark over who controlled the provinces of Schleswig and Holstein offered Prussia easier access to the North Sea (and thus to the global economy). The war against its primary Confederation rival, Austria, presented Prussia with a decisive victory at the Battle of Königgrätz. Prussia's success in both wars depended in part on the neutrality of the other great powers, particularly Britain, Russia and France. These conflicts also highlighted how technological and industrial advances could have a decisive impact on the waging of war. By 1867, Prussia was considered a great military power, while the Austrian empire was considered to be in danger of internal collapse. Its removal from the German Confederation also occasioned a domestic political crisis that resulted in its restructuring as the Dual Monarchy of Austria-Hungary.

The final war of German unification was largely accidental. The Franco-Prussian War of 1870–1 began as a dispute over a dynastic succession, namely about who would take over the Spanish crown after the 1868 Spanish revolution. Napoleon III took offense when Prussia proposed a Catholic Hohenzollern prince for the role. Refusing to accept Prussia's interference in the succession crisis, Napoleon III declared war on Prussia, a move that quickly backfired when Prussia's superior military forces invaded France, besieged Strasbourg and Paris and captured the French emperor at Sedan. France capitulated, the Parisians revolted and Napoleon III, though released by the Prussians, fled the country to live in exile in Britain. The war inspired the other German states (but not Austria) to join with Prussia and form a new nation-state, Germany, ruled by the erstwhile Prussian king now known as Germany's Kaiser Wilhelm I. Germany's creation signaled the rise of a potentially powerful industrial rival to the other European empires, one that frightened the French, concerned the British and Russians and destabilized the Austrians.

Traditionally, diplomatic historians describe the Franco-Prussian War as the 'beginning of the end' of the concert of Europe system. They argue that with the creation of Germany, the diplomatic equilibrium in Europe was shot, presenting it as a key reason why the First World War erupted in 1914. But while many contemporaries feared what a powerful German nation might do to the European equilibrium, the war of 1870–1 seemed to actually uphold many of the key principles of the concert system.[20] For one, the permanent neutrality of Belgium was left unaffected. Both the Germans and French agreed to respect Belgian neutrality, despite the geostrategic advantages the use of Belgian territory might have provided. The key reason for not breaching Belgian neutrality was the fear that the war would then draw in the British, the Austrians and the Russians (and with them all of Europe). At any rate, all three of these powers as well as the smaller non-German European states were determined to remain neutral.[21] They also campaigned hard for diplomatic recognition of their neutral rights as defined by international law.[22] Furthermore, on the conclusion of the war in 1871, the new German government looked to its own long-term security by finding new ways to avoid war in Europe. It repeatedly declared its own neutrality when others went to war and orchestrated collective responses to a number of international crises, including the Congresses of Berlin in 1878 and 1885. General peace, not war, reigned supreme on the European continent for more than forty years after 1871.[23]

The European wars of the 1860s also highlight how vitally important the rule of international law was considered to be by contemporaries. These laws defined the accepted limits of belligerent and neutral agency. Significantly, the legal framework that governed the conduct of interstate warfare in Europe extended to all recognized states that were members of the 'family of civilized nations'. The Asian and Latin American governments certainly underscored the legitimacy of their existence and voice in the international system on this basis by pointing to their own observance of these laws. During the Sino-Japanese (1894) and Russo-Japanese (1904–5) wars, for example, the Japanese even appointed international lawyers to trek with their armies to make sure they did not breach any of the rules.[24] In so doing, the Japanese government claimed full status as a 'civilized' state and confirmed its right to participate fully in international governance alongside the other industrializing powers. Adherence to international law further legitimated its ambition to acquire its own industrial empire, which it did by taking over Taiwan from China (1894–5), conquering Korea (1907) and infiltrating Manchuria.

The involvement of forty-four governments, at least half of which were non-European, in the 1907 Hague conventions further legitimated the importance of international law as a regulatory principle that governed how states across the globe behaved towards each other.[25] The Latin American states even developed their own arbitration mechanisms, aimed at avoiding war between them, particularly war over contract debt. In so doing, they hoped to be able to compete more effectively as economic and diplomatic agents on the international stage and, in the process, assert their own sovereignty against the growing power of the United States and the informal imperialism of several European states.[26] As Chapter 9 shows, the expansion of the number of states taking part in formal diplomacy had a significant impact on the international environment, but also recognized how dominant the Anglo-European system of international law and diplomatic agreement had become by the early twentieth century.

The turn to neutrality by many governments was also internalized into the national identities of many states, including the United States and many in

Latin America. Such identities focused both on the self-serving interests of the country (along the lines of 'we can prosper as neutrals supplying the world with our goods') and also on the potential for the neutral to do good in the world, including as humanitarian actors ('as neutrals, we are essential to global peace and prosperity').[27] As a result, the prevalence of neutral states helped to promote the value of international laws that aimed at war avoidance, war limitation and humanitarianism. When their neighbours were at war, neutral communities were known to send ambulance units to the frontlines; they took in refugees and sent provisions to refugee camps. During the Franco-Prussian War, for example, British charities sent money, medical provisions and food to the besieged citizens of Paris. During the second Anglo-Boer War (1899–1902), the Dutch sent warships to southern Africa to rescue Afrikaner women and children, while Red Cross societies from a number of neutral European countries sent ambulances and medical aid.[28]

The turn to neutrality for so many nation-states in the second half of the nineteenth century also inspired the growth in humanitarian activism and internationalist endeavours. The International Committee of the Red Cross (ICRC) and the Geneva Conventions, for example, were established in the permanently neutral state of Switzerland in 1863 and 1864. They aimed at offering medical care to the victims of (interstate) warfare. The conventions (initially signed by 12 governments) aimed at enabling Red Cross medical units to travel to a warfront as 'neutrals' and then provide care to all who needed it, regardless of the side they fought on. The Geneva conventions signaled how essential the framing of universally applicable rules was to the shaping of the international environment. Such rules could help to stabilize expectations about what could and could not happen when war threatened. Like the Hague Conventions of 1899 and 1907, the Geneva Conventions were reworked in 1906, when they were renegotiated by thirty-five governments. They also speak to the power of neutrality as a force to define the international environment, not least because without neutral Switzerland the ICRC could not continue to exist. Neutrality protected the humanitarian purpose of the ICRC.[29] Neutrality even helped to promote a rhetoric among some late nineteenth-century idealists who considered the possibility of a world in which war would not exist. Other more pragmatic internationalists imagined an international order in which war was the last option for states that had exhausted all other diplomatic and legal alternatives to settle their disputes. In other words, by the turn of the twentieth century, the idea that neutral states could aid the international system and protect it from warfare only grew.

Of course, in all almost all these imaginings, the professed 'good' of neutrality was embedded within an international system that enabled and allowed for a range of other kinds of warfare and state violence to exist, including by neutral governments in the expansion of their own industrial empires. Neutrality, then, was only ever a reference point in time of interstate warfare. The Geneva Conventions did not apply to imperial or civil warfare even if, in practice, Red Cross medical staff often worked on the frontiers of state violence, imperial and civil wars.[30] Neutrality, then, did not keep governments from violence, but it did help many of them from going to war with other states.

Though limiting war and avoiding war were key aspects of neutrality, industrialized neutrals were often also the nineteenth century's greatest armaments suppliers (see Figure 7.2). The permanently neutral state of Belgium, for example, had one of the most advanced metallurgy and armaments industries in the world, which it happily sold on to foreign buyers. Britain excelled as a supplier of naval ships to the world, while the United States was renowned for the high quality of its small arms industries.[31] The German Krupps manufacturers, for their part, supplied top-of-the-range artillery cannons. In 1914, Krupps counted fifty-two countries among its customers and 51 percent of its artillery manufactures left Germany.[32] Keeping the world's seas and oceans open to neutral trade thus also meant keeping the world open to the growth in armaments sales.[33]

And here we reach another one of those distinct nineteenth-century paradoxes. For on the one hand, neutrality helped to spur nineteenth-century discourses on humanitarianism, the care for the 'other' and the utility of war avoidance. Because there were so many neutral countries, neutral media reporting helped to advance the notion that 'civilized' states should behave according to a set of internationally defined norms and avoid war if possible.[34] Certainly, neutral populations raised awareness of the human suffering endured during warfare. These discourses also helped to define the acceptable 'limits' of warfare in the global media. They set in motion a normative language that sustained the idea that a world run by international law would improve all humanity. Such ideas helped to promote the principle that governments could not just do whatever they liked when they were at war.

On the other hand, however, and this is a very big however, the sustenance of neutrality and of the international system ruled by the Western powers enabled these same powers to generally avoid war with powerful states and instead use violence to acquire, control and suppress subjects in their own empires. The international laws that applied to 'civilized' states in time of 'formal' warfare did not extend to any of their actions against 'non-civilized' communities on the frontiers of their empires or to their policing actions within their own country or empire. International law, after all, only applied to the relationship *between* formally recognized states, members of the 'family of civilized nations', and not to the behaviour of a government and its agents *within* the state or in relationship to what they considered 'uncivilized' communities.

FIGURE 7.2 *Neutrality and armaments. This German cartoon from the First World War, brought out the connection between neutrality and armaments supply. It shows the United States as the 'angel of peace', serene in her peaceful demeanour, yet supplying the belligerents with a cornucopia of weapons, artillery, shells and munitions to sustain the war. United States arms suppliers (and the United States economy more generally) grew very wealthy during the First World War.*
Source: Carl O. Peterson, 'Der Amerikanische Friedensengel' Kriegszeit Künstlerflugblätter. 52, 31 August 1915, Library of Congress, LC-USZ62-31829.

FIGURE 7.3 *'Civilized' Europeans at war. This colour lithograph, designed by A. H. Zaki in 1908, depicts a French and British soldier celebrating their imperial successes in ruling the north African countries of Morocco and Egypt. Both soldiers stand on the skulls and bones of the dead their imperial wars have caused, while Casa Blanca blazes in the background and a man is hanged in Egypt.*
Source: A. H. Zaki, Cairo Punch, c.1908, Getty Images, 640474833.

As a result, as the historian Joanna Bourke so powerfully reminds us, across the nineteenth century the concept of barbarism increasingly took up 'residence in the house of the civilized'.[35] This is not to say that citizens in these empires did not consider their imperial warfare as violence (see Figure 7.3). They certainly did. Some of them were also highly critical of the violence and debated its rightful limits.[36] But, by and large, these contemporaries differentiated such conflicts from interstate ones, namely as 'wars of the people'. They tended to distinguish two kinds of 'people's warfare': *civil or revolutionary wars* (wars conducted by a group or community against each other or within a recognized state to overthrow its leaders and achieve control over that state), and *imperial warfare* (wars or police actions that aimed at acquiring or consolidating a state's control over a region or community).

Be it an imperial or revolutionary war, people's wars were generally considered less controllable because the stakes for all involved were so high. The very existence of who ruled and who defined what could and could not happen in a community, region or country was at stake. People's wars were often but not always framed by 'do or die' ideologies ('if we do not succeed in our goal then the enemy will force their way of being onto us'). In people's wars, violence often ruled supreme. Because of the stakes involved, few expected that participants would limit their violence, whether they be citizens of a 'civilized empire' or not. Rather conveniently from the perspective of the imperial authorities, the rule of international law seemed less applicable in people's wars because at least one set of the participants was not a formally recognized state in control of a formally recognized armed force.[37]

Of course, it is one thing to say that 'formal' and 'informal' wars and state violence were distinct. In reality and in large part because all warfare (regardless of how it began) was unpredictable and disruptive, the nineteenth-century's 'formal' and 'informal' wars often bled into each other. Because they involved the state, all wars had the potential to impact (and be impacted by) the workings of the international diplomatic and economic system. Furthermore, state violence in whatever shape it occurred also impacted how people perceived of the various agents and causes at play. Those perceptions influenced their own actions in response and sometimes had surprising short- and long-term results. The global media then could, and often did, play a decisive role in how wars evolved.

As examples of the fluidity of warfare, consider these two nineteenth-century civil wars: the Taiping Rebellion (1851–64) and American Civil War (1861–5). The Taiping Rebellion was the deadliest of the nineteenth-century's many wars. It evolved in response to the declaration of a Protestant-style heavenly kingdom by the Chinese leader Hong Xiuquan and led to the attempted overthrow of the Qing dynasty. The civil war cost more than 20 million people their lives and affected all regions of the Chinese empire. It was a Chinese war influenced by global ideas (not least the appeal of millenarian Christianity) and, in the end, was won by the Qing dynasty after it appealed for military and technological aid from the Western powers.[38] The civil war signaled to the world that the Chinese empire was not as cohesive as it ought to be and offered encouragement for the other empires to seek economic concessions from the Qings (see Chapter 3).

The American Civil War evolved out of the inability of the government of the United States to enforce federal law, in this case on the seven southern states, whose constituents looked to expand slavery. After declaring their secession from the Union, 'the South' declared war on 'the North'. The conflict was brutal, costing more than 1 million people their lives (about 3 percent of the United States' population).[39] Yet while it met all the conditions of a 'civil war', this American conflict also quickly grew into an internationally significant interstate event. Because the United States was a key player in the global economy and because both sets of belligerents sought weapons, naval ships and other supplies from neutral sources, the laws of war and neutrality applied. Not only did this bring both American belligerents into protracted (and sometimes heated) negotiations with the various neutral governments, but it also had a decisive impact on the global economy. For one, the inability to access the cotton supplies of the southern states, resulted in new plantations being established in India, Egypt, China and across the Pacific. They thrived while the war ran its course. With the resumption of American cotton supplies at war's end however, some of these new plantations faced severe economic hardship, resulting in heightened workers' agitation and resistance.[40]

Even the Franco-Prussian (1870–1), Spanish-American (1898) and Russo-Japanese (1904–5) wars, which were clearly defined as interstate wars at the time, morphed into 'people's wars' of a sort. The Franco-Prussian conflict, for example, shocked many observers for its military violence, not least by the use of *franc-tireurs* (civilian guerrilla fighters) by the French against the invading German armies. The German armies were relatively unrestrained in their treatment of these civilian-soldiers, who did not meet the definition of 'formal' soldiers. Furthermore, when the German siege of Paris turned Parisians against their own government, another revolution rocked France. Napoleon III was forced to abdicate and a new French Republic was established. In this war, then, two new nation-states were created: Germany and France. The ongoing instability of the new French republic was a major reason why France looked to avoid involvement in any further European wars after 1871.

For their part, the Spanish-American and Russo-Japanese Wars pitted two powers against each other to determine who would control a key imperial outpost. The Spanish-American War was quickly lost by Spain. The American forces in the Philippines, Puerto Rico and Cuba, however, then faced a concerted effort to suppress the militant resistance of local peoples against the imposition of a new imperial ruler. In Korea, Manchuria and parts of China, the imposition of a Japanese empire also brought with it considerable and ongoing resistance from the local populations, who were unwilling to accept Japanese authority. Meanwhile, the Russian war effort in East Asia in 1904–5 inspired what would become known as the first Russian revolution (the second and third Russian revolutions would occur in 1917). The Tsar survived this first revolution in part because he agreed to adopt political reforms, in part because he ended the war with Japan and in part because he used his armed forces to suppress his subjects.

The most common forms of state violence throughout the 'long' nineteenth century, then, were not 'formal' interstate wars or even civil wars but *imperial wars* conducted by the agents of an empire to acquire territory and resources or to suppress unrest and resistance by a 'subject' people. There were certainly no formal rules that determined what a government could do to enforce 'law and order' or to police its sovereign territory. The agents of this kind of warfare employed the rhetoric of opportunism, racial prejudice and the 'right to rule' to justify their use of violence, including genocidal activities.[41]

To describe imperial warfare in the nineteenth century is to acknowledge humanity's propensity for extreme violence. Furthermore, since no empire was immune from anti-imperial resistance, few imperial governments exercised restraint in curbing that resistance. They were all agents of this form of violence. Consider, for example, how the British empire clamped down on incidents of major rebellion. The resistance of a number of North Island hapu (Maori tribes) to the seizure of their land by government authorities saw eighteen thousand British troops travel to New Zealand in the 1860s to quell the uprisings. The New Zealand Wars lasted several years and involved numerous bloody battles (many of which were won by the hapu). They were not fully suppressed until 1872, and even then, resistance against the imposition of British rule continued.[42] Similarly, what came to be known in Britain as the great Indian Mutiny of 1857 and in India as the 'First War of Indian Independence' was not fully suppressed by the British colonial authorities until 1859. The uprising, which began in the Dum-Dum arsenal on the outskirts of Calcutta (Kolkata), ultimately involved military actions and repressions across the sub-continent and the death and torture of hundreds of thousands of local Indians at the hands of the British imperial forces.[43] Even though the mutiny heralded the effective end of the Mughal empire, popular resistance against the British Raj never let up.

The daily management of empire also involved a slew of other forms of state violence. The expansion of British control over Australia from 1788 on, for example, witnessed innumerable incidences of orchestrated murder and massacre by white settlers against the continent's aboriginal peoples.[44] Such activities continued well into the twentieth century and helps to explain the decline of Australia's indigenous population of about 750,000 in 1788 to 31,000 by 1911.[45] In Africa, agents of the British state repeatedly exercised 'scorched earth' tactics to keep resistance from the various African communities in check. They also mobilized pre-existing animosities between the various communities and chieftains to advance their own imperial ends. When orchestrated well, divide and conquer policies could work. To this end, it is important to recognize that empires were built by more than violence. Local agency worked in a surprising number of ways to accommodate and reject imperial power and culture, global infrastructure and global capitalism.[46]

In all these activities, 'subject' peoples understood very well what they were resisting and what was at stake: autonomy and control over their own future, their culture and for many, their very existence. As the Xhosa Chief Sandili explained at the outbreak of a rebellion against settlers in the Cape Colony in 1851, 'God made a boundary by the sea, and you White Men cross it to rob us of our country. … if you kill me my bones will fight, and my bones' bones will fight. I will rise up and fight against the White Man for ever.' In response, the *Port Elizabeth Telegraph* newspaper noted that 'A war to Life or Death has commenced' on the Cape. Few restraints were exercised in bringing the Xhosa rebellion to an end.[47]

There was also nothing extraordinary about Britons' use of violence against their 'subject' peoples: the British empire was as violent as any other industrial empire of the time, including those maintained by the Dutch, Belgians, French, Germans, Americans, Russians and Japanese. The United States expanded its formal control across the north American continent during the nineteenth century often by means of warfare as well as unequal treaty agreements with indigenous First Nations' communities. The French empire held little back in quelling resistance in Algeria, Tahiti, Melanesia, Madagascar, Morocco, Mauritania, Niger and Indo-China. As Robert Aldrich explains, the French nineteenth-century empire was acquired at great human cost and never fully successfully. The anti-imperial military campaigns waged against the French by local communities were 'cohesive, well-organised and articulate efforts' that underwrote an ongoing anti-colonial political movement long after France repressed the initial resistance.[48] Meanwhile, the Russians were responsible for several waves of pogroms and ethnic cleansing in the empire's contested border regions, including the 'pacification' of anywhere between 450,000 and 1 million Muslims out of the Caucasus between 1859 and 1864, 40,000 Chechens in 1860 and more than 200 attacks on Jewish communities in the empire's eastern European holdings during the 1880s.[49]

The Dutch also expanded their influence and control over the Indonesian archipelago during the 1800s by violent means. Its war in Aceh, which waged on and off for decades after 1870, cost 7,700 Dutch soldiers and anywhere between 30,000 and 100,000 Acehnese their lives.[50] In the Congo meanwhile, the personal rule of the Belgian king Leopold II enabled an increasingly violent environment where locals were forced to work in abysmal conditions in chain gangs on plantations, in mines and factories. Any resistance was quelled by the most terrible means. German colonial authorities in south west Africa, too, held little back when the local Herero and Nama people took up arms in 1904 to rebel against incursions of the Damarraland Treaty of 1885 (which guaranteed them key rights). The ensuing genocide, saw up to 80 percent of the Herero and 50 percent of the Nama population murdered.[51]

Few of these events went unnoticed by the rest of the world. They were reported on and sensationalized in many newspapers. As a result of the newspaper revolution of the 1890s, condemnation and criticism of such violence were also increasingly reported in the media on a global scale. In other words, while industrial imperialism allowed and enabled a vast amount of state violence, not everyone in those empires agreed or supported such activities. The exponential growth in printing techniques, photography and film (moving pictures) also made the visual evidence of atrocity more compelling.[52] The popular voice raised against the use of extreme violence from within the industrial metropoles, even when it was conducted outside the terms of interstate warfare or the parameters of international law, only grew in the early years of the twentieth century.[53] Still, while the popular critique had an occasional success (rulership over the Congo was taken away from Leopold II in 1908, for example), in general the violence did not let up. The reason was clear: the governing elite in most empires considered that any resistance had to be suppressed as hard and fast as possible for fear it might spread. For if conversion and persuasion could not sway the people to accept your rule, then needs must.

Of course, suppressing political resistance was a marked feature of all nineteenth-century states. The multi-ethnic land-based Russian, Austrian, Chinese and Ottoman empires had certainly practiced such methods for centuries. As the historian Dominic Lieven reminds us, there was also little difference between the challenges to imperial power presented in Austria-Hungary or the Ottoman empire in the nineteenth century and those facing the British, Germans or French.[54] They all had subject communities to deal with. Where there was a difference between the landed and 'blue-water' empires, was that in the former, the anti-imperial resistance was undertaken sometimes within the heart of the metropole. When the Balkan peoples challenged the authority of the Ottoman or Habsburg empire, for example, they did so in a way that could serious undermine the ability of the ruling elite to rule.

Yet the ongoing and endemic violence prevalent within the 'blue-water' empires of the nineteenth century also spoke to the inherent weaknesses of these empires. It certainly reminded the imperial governments that they could not take their power or 'right to rule' for granted. The strength of any empire was in constant flux: a product of local, imperial and global forces, negotiations and actions. Furthermore, where globalization aided many industrial imperial endeavours, it also enabled individuals and communities with a common enemy (be it a specific empire or the 'white world' in general) to communicate and coordinate their resistance efforts. The renowned Indian nationalist and anti-imperialist, Mahatma Gandhi, spent much of his pre-1914 years travelling across the Indian Ocean region advocating for greater rights to be given to subject peoples. He edited a journal, the *Indian Opinion*, which was published in four languages and reached readers in southern Africa, India and the Middle East. It aimed at promoting Indian rights within empire.[55] The African-American leader W. E. B. DuBois also travelled the world preaching African unity, membership of the Pan-African Congress and anti-imperial resistance.

Such activities and many others meant that globalization not only served the powerful.[56] Its networks and structures also gave those who would resist the means to challenge and ultimately bring an end to the overseas empires of the Anglo-European world in the twentieth century.

Study questions

1. Traditionally, how do diplomatic and social historians differ in their approach to writing the history of warfare and state violence in the nineteenth century?

2. Do you agree that the whole nineteenth century (1815–1914) could be described as an 'age of revolution'? Justify your answer.

3. In what ways did neutrality impact the course and conduct of 'formal' (interstate) and 'informal' (people's) warfare in the nineteenth century?

4. In what ways did 'formal' and 'informal' wars bleed into each other?

5. How can we account for the extreme violence of nineteenth-century imperial warfare?

Recommended readings

Maartje Abbenhuis, *An Age of Neutrals: Great Power Politics 1815–1914.* Cambridge UP, 2014: Chapter 5 'Neutrality as an international and patriotic ideal', pp. 144–77.

Robert Aldrich, *Greater France: A History of French Overseas Expansion.* St Martin's Press, 1996: Chapter 6 'The French and the "Natives" ', pp. 199–233.

Christon I. Archer, John R. Ferris, Holger H. Herwig, Timothy H. E. Travers, *World History of Warfare.* University of Nebraska Press, 2002: Chapter 11 'The west conquers the world: War and society in the age of European imperialism 1757–1914', pp. 440–82.

Joanna Bourke, 'Barbarisation v. civilisation in time of war' in George Kassimeris, ed., *The Barbarization of Warfare.* New York UP, 2006, pp. 19–38.

Antoinette Burton, *The Trouble with Empire: Challenges to Modern British Imperialism.* Oxford UP, 2015: 'Introduction', pp. 1–23.

E. Thomas Ewing, 'A most powerful instrument for a despot: The telegraph as a trans-national instrument of imperial control and political mobilization in the Middle East' in I. Löhr, R. Wenzlheumer, eds, *Governing Globalization Processes in the Nineteenth and Early Twentieth Centuries.* Springer, 2013, esp. pp. 83–100.

Jeffrey Grey, *A Military History of Australia.* Third edition, Cambridge UP, 2008: Chapter 2 'The military and the frontier, 1788–1901', pp. 28–40.

Douglas Howland, 'Sovereignty and the laws of war: International consequences of Japan's 1905 victory over Russia', *Law and History Review* 29, 1, 2011, pp. 53–97.

Benjamin Madley, 'Tactics of nineteenth-century colonial massacre: Tasmania, California and beyond' in Philip G. Dwyer, Lyndall Ryan, eds, *Theatres of Violence: Massacre, Mass Killing and Atrocity throughout History*. Berghahn, 2012, pp. 110–25.

Charles S. Maier, 'Leviathan 2.0' in Emily Rosenberg, ed., *A World Connecting, 1870–1945*. Harvard UP, 2012: 'Introduction', pp. 29–39.

John Newsinger, *The Blood Never Dried: A People's History of the British Empire*. Second edition, Bookmarks, 2013: Chapter 'The great Indian rebellion, 1857–1858', pp. 73–91.

Tom Pessah, 'Violent representations: Hostile Indians and civilized wars in nineteenth-century USA', *Ethnic and Race Studies* 37, 9, 2014, pp. 1628–45.

Jean H. Quataert, 'A new look at international law: Gendering the practices of humanitarian medicine in Europe's "small wars" 1879–1907', *Human Rights Quarterly* 40, 3, 2018, pp. 547–69.

Stefan Rinke, 'No alternative to extermination: Germans and their "savages" in southern Brazil at the turn of the nineteenth century' in Matthew P. Fitzpatrick, Peter Monteath, eds, *Savage Worlds: German Encounters Abroad, 1798–1914*. Manchester UP, 2018, pp. 21–41.

Peter N. Stearns, *Peace in World History*. Routledge, 2014: Chapter 6 'Peace in an industrial age', pp. 91–114.

Christina Twomey, 'Framing atrocity: Photography and humanitarianism' in Heide Fehrenbach, Davide Rodogno, eds, *Humanitarian Photography*. Cambridge UP, 2015, pp. 47–63.

Theodore H. von Laue, *The World Revolution of Westernization: The Twentieth Century in Global Perspective*. Oxford UP, 1987: Chapter 1 'How the concept originated', pp. 13–17.

Peter H. Wilson, 'European warfare 1815–2000' in Jeremy Black, ed., *War in the Modern World since 1815*. Routledge, 2003, pp. 192–216.

8

Where local meets global: Ideas and politics on a global scale

According to the idiom: all politics are local. Throughout the course of the nineteenth century, however, the local was increasingly influenced and affected by global developments, events and ideas. Given the enormous changes wrought by the nineteenth-century age of industrial globalization on communities around the world, it is really no surprise that this century also witnessed the expansion and global application of a wide range of political concepts. These ideas covered a spectrum of claimed rights, privileges, identifiers and statuses. Some helped to situate individuals within a community (or on the 'outside' of a community) and looked either to protect or alter existing circumstances to improve or defend that community's situation. Others focused on the international environment itself and advocated for improvements to benefit all, be it in the name of humanitarianism, 'civilization' or 'progress'. The global also offered motivation, inspiration and context to underwrite political activity at every level of application.

As Christopher Bayly's book *The Birth of the Modern World* explains it, nineteenth-century globalization both inspired a massive shift to greater *uniformity* in social life and a concomitant shift to a heightened sense of *difference.*[1] Where people came to organize their social existence according to more uniform practices (be it in the way their state was run or how laws were created or applied or to how they themselves dressed or spoke), they also became more aware of how they differed from 'others' and came to consider those differences as fundamental. Globalization both offered opportunities to consider the 'human condition' as a universally shared experience and to compartmentalize communities according to the perceived differences between them, including how well or how much they had modernized. It bears worth saying that it was almost never possible to remain faithful to the ideals offered to humanity in this era (or any other) when they were actually put into practice. Nonetheless, the nineteenth century was a great age of competing visions, ideals and movements that were shaped by globalization and in turn contributed to its development.

It is, as the historian Jürgen Osterhammel explains, extremely difficult to generalize about social and political ideas as they applied to individuals and communities in any one moment.[2] Still, many nineteenth-century intellectuals tried and it is chiefly from the documentary record of this strata that the history of ideas is written. All the forces that we have discussed in earlier chapters – including industrialization, capitalism, globalization, warfare, revolution, the lived realities of daily life and environmental damage – shaped the context of the intellectuals and politically active peoples of the era. Many of them considered the international environment as a key influence on local, communal and individual identity and political agency. Certainly, many individuals and communities in the nineteenth century mobilized behind particular sets of ideas to affect change. The growth in global communications and the rise of a global media environment helped these ideas to go global as well.

The concept of *nationalism*, for example, thrived in the nineteenth century in large part as a response to the modernization of societies, the creation of new states and the increasing interconnectedness of these states and societies. At its heart, nationalism offered a frame of reference to link strangers from a common cultural or ethnic background to a common cause ('the nation') and to differentiate those strangers from other 'others' who belonged to a different cultural or ethnic community or nation. Nationalism could be a powerful force for change (e.g. when coupled to claims of self-determination from within an empire) as well as a powerful force for defending established practices (e.g. when mobilized in time of war to defend a nation or empire).[3] In the nineteenth century, nationalism both helped to create new states out of a number of pre-existing communities (as occurred in the unification of Italy and Germany for instance) and undermined the legitimacy of other pre-existing states (like the multi-ethnic Ottoman and Austrian empires). Nationalism could inspire local action and identity and help to define the international environment. Nationalism, then, could serve many ends. For some it was a political idea that could be used as a weapon to galvanize the anti-imperial ambitions of a particular ethnic community seeking independence from an empire. For others it was the language of the people as 'citizens' mobilizing against traditional aristocratic and monarchical rule. In contrast, conservative monarchies such as the Prussian Hohenzollerns, used German nationalism in the aftermath of the 1848 revolutions as a unifying ideology to mitigate class struggle and regionalism and strengthen social-political cohesion. Nationalism was also a highly personal concept, which could be interpreted differently depending on the individual or community involved. Local and global contexts influenced the reception, adoption and adaptation of most political ideas.[4]

Another powerful nineteenth-century concept was that of 'civilization'. Depending on who you asked at the time, to be considered 'civilized' in the nineteenth-century age of industrialization largely depended on a society's ability to modernize: to accept and adopt change and innovation as a 'good', to find ways to rationalize the organization of states and societies according to uniform rules and to participate fully in the international arena as economic agents. Intellectuals around the world considered 'civilization' and 'enlightenment' largely in terms of modernization. What their discourses had in common was the notion of looking forward to a future where change, progress and adaptation to industrialization and capitalism were necessary. Where they differed was in how their ideas were mobilized to advance the power and politics of different groups, states and communities at a local and global level. Despite what many traditional histories of 'the rise of the West' argue, Anglo-Europeans did not have a monopoly on enlightenment theory or its multiple applications.[5] But, as this book shows, as Anglo-Europeans advanced their industrial empires and increasingly dominated the international system through the course of the nineteenth century, their versions of 'enlightenment' and 'civilization' also came to dominate the norms of global interaction at a diplomatic, economic and legal level.

The most important political concept to come out of the multiple global discourses around 'civilization' and 'enlightenment' was the notion of an individual having 'political rights', or rather having a right to have a voice in how their life was governed. Such claims to rights originated in the pre-1815 early modern period. The American War of Independence, for example, began in 1775 with the declaration that the British crown had no right to make laws and impose taxes on the thirteen American colonies when its colonial subjects had no formal representation in the British parliamentary system. The phrase 'no taxation without representation' echoed around the globe through the ensuing revolutionary period, as did the catchphrase of the 1789 French revolution, 'liberty, equality, fraternity'. The freedom of movement, the freedom of speech, freedom of religion, legal equality and the communal interests served by protecting these claimed political rights underwrote many anti-monarchical and anti-imperial revolutions over the ensuing decades. They were also vociferously resisted by traditional elites and many religious authorities, who feared what granting such rights might do to their own power and influence.

In the clash between differing interpretations of 'rights' and 'privileges' lay many of the conflicts of the nineteenth century at a local, national, imperial and international level. For where there were many powerful ideas that aimed at defending established ways (be it by the ruling elite in Europe or in the traditions of 'subject peoples' facing incorporation within an industrial empire), there were also many that aimed at destabilizing, resisting and reconfiguring that established power. Claims to political rights came in a number of forms: be it to count as citizens, be it to gain a right to vote or to establish a tradition of parliamentary politics, be it to acquire greater self-determination or independence from an empire, be it to gain equal rights in law, be it to alter existing laws, develop social welfare policies or create a new constitution or be it to overthrow the existing political system entirely. Some of them reflected on the nature and promise of globalization and the universality of humanity; others focused fearfully on the changes that might be wrought by industrialization.

Consider, for example, the basic principles that lay at the heart of the 'concert of Europe' system established at the Congress of Vienna in 1815 by Europe's landed aristocracy. The Vienna agreements looked to protect the rights and privileges of monarchs and rejected many of the claims to citizenship, representative politics and legal equality asserted by the proponents of the French revolution. Across the ensuing century, the promotion of the rights of Europe's traditional elite – the aristocracy – came to be embedded in the political principles of *conservatism* and *protectionism* (as in, protecting the 'old' ways). Political conservatives of the nineteenth century tended to look for ways to defend aristocratic privilege, including their right to rule, to own land, to create laws and to determine the foreign, economic and military policies of the state.

Through the course of the century, these conservatives faced many challenges not least as their economic power had to adapt to the rise of industrial capitalism (which enabled those with money to reap great profit) and to the claims of middle-class industrialists (the *bourgeoisie*) to share in political power. Many conservatives were reactionary: repressing political opposition as and when necessary. Where these conservatives were adaptable, however, as some had to be in the wake of the 1848 revolutions, they came to present their conservative principles as useful pillars of stability that could serve the wider needs of the general populace. As a result, many monarchies looked to promote themselves as essential symbols of the nation (or empire) and its people. Conservatism thus survived the industrial revolution, even if autocratic aristocratic rule rarely did.

Nobles across the world encountered fundamental challenges to their 'right to rule' during the age of industrial globalization, which was particularly but not only true in the many communities that were forced to adapt to the imposition of foreign imperial rule, laws and cultures. After the Meiji restoration in Japan, for example, the samurai class of nobles faced dissolution in the face of significant societal change brought about by industrialization, urbanization, the bureaucratization of the Meiji government and the creation of a nationalized military force. The samurai leader, Saigo Takamori, inspired a major rebellion against these changes in 1877 hoping to restore traditional rights and privileges to the samurai class and avert economic disaster for samurai families. After months of war, the Japanese army (consisting of conscripted Japanese men trained, organized and equipped to replicate the German army) thwarted the last of the samurai resistance. After 1877, the samurai disappeared as a recognized social stratum in Japanese society. In its place, the Meiji leadership established a new conservative elite to govern Japan, modelled on Britain's peerage system.[6]

Where nineteenth-century conservatives aimed at protecting the established order, *liberals* aimed at affecting changes in that order. *Liberalism* was the ideology that sat at the heart of industrialization and of political revolution in most industrializing metropoles until 1848. Liberals were essentially anti-monarchical and anti-aristocratic in their outlook. They aimed to overthrow the political and economic structures of the landed aristocracy and replace them with the basic principles of capitalism: free trade, market economies, private enterprise and the protection of individual rights.[7]

For liberals, the purpose of the state was to protect the individual and their pursuits from undue interference. From a liberal perspective, a nation should exist for all citizens as equals and should enshrine their individual rights in its laws. Liberals demanded the opening up of the political arena to a greater number of political actors and particularly to those who had economic power (mainly middle-class men, who owned enough capital). To protect the principle of the equality of all citizens (but not necessarily all subjects), liberals looked to the creation of constitutions and to the establishment of parliaments, consisting of enough free and equal men, who could defend the constitution. Liberalism was an incredibly powerful nineteenth-century political concept. It inspired numerous anti-imperial rebellions, revolutions and changes to the political landscapes of the industrializing empires.

The principles of free-trade liberalism also propelled industrial capitalism on a global scale. Free traders argued against restrictive economic policies and looked to open up the world to the free movement of goods and money (if not necessarily for all people nor of all ideas). While many early nineteenth-century liberals claimed that they were anti-imperial (i.e. they disapproved of the aristocratic old-world empires of the Romanovs, Qings, Habsburgs and Ottomans), they nevertheless enabled 'blue-water' and economic (informal) imperialism to thrive.[8] Liberals were also foremost promoters of international law and treaties aimed at stabilizing economic and political relationships at a local and global level. The liberal international order that evolved in the nineteenth century privileged the growth in power and wealth of the industrializers and the industrializing empires.

Unsurprisingly, as liberalism came to dominate the political landscape of many industrializing empires, it also came to be perceived as rather conservative in its ambitions and applications. These new winners now had much to defend against the claims of others. Most liberals were not true democrats. Even when they considered that their principles aided all people, they purposely excluded those without economic assets from sharing political power. When liberals established new constitutions and formed parliamentary systems (as happened in many countries), the right to vote was almost always limited to men with money, disqualifying the majority of lower middle-class men, all working-class men, all women and all subjects (as opposed to citizens) of an empire or nation. The exclusion of the majority of a country's (or empire's) adult population from the franchise in itself led to political dissatisfaction. Why, so the disenfranchised asked, should they also not be represented in the halls of power? Why should the right to vote be restricted to those with wealth or only to men or only to the white citizens of empire? The ideal of *democracy* (political representation for all) inspired a range of political activities and resistance movements in the nineteenth century, both within metropoles, across empires and globally.

In combination, the idealism of liberal thought and the appeal of democracy sat at the heart of many nineteenth-century political movements, including a number that challenged the legitimacy of the industrial capitalist international system. As noted in Chapter 2, for example, the claims of indigenous peoples to political rights and independence in the early nineteenth century were embedded in the revolutionary claims of 'liberty, equality and fraternity' as much as they were in indigenous identities and traditions.[9] As their empires expanded, imperial elites had to contend not only with active resistance to their rule but also with the growth of claimed political rights from subject groups and communities. Identity politics framed the ideals of many of these groups, who organized themselves at a local, parliamentary, national, imperial and transnational level and spread their ideas far and wide utilizing the international communications networks that were available to them. By the latter decades of the century, political parties with set policy platforms also vied for voters in most countries with parliamentary systems. The origins of the twentieth-century age of mass party politics can be found in these developments.

Nineteenth-century identity politics operated at many levels of abstraction. One of the most important was determined by socio-economic status. Karl Marx and Friedrich Engels's *Communist Manifesto*, for example, argued that the history of all previous societies was driven by class struggle. They saw the impact of industrial capitalism as decisive. They divided humanity into three strata of classes, each with its own function and collective identity in the industrial capitalist world: the upper-class elite (landed aristocracy) whose day had passed as its wealth and power was being steadily overthrown by the middle-class *bourgeoisie* (those with the new form of economic power, who owned the capital or industrial 'means of production') and the lower-class workers (who were divided between agricultural and industrial workers). The relationship between the classes and within the structure of global industrial capitalism made it inevitable, so Marx and Engels thought, that the industrial workers or *proletariat* (who did all the work and were in the majority in the most advanced industrial economies) would stage a revolution against the *bourgeoisie* (who made all the profit) just as the *bourgeoisie* was staging its own revolution against the landed aristocracy. A post-capitalist world, as imagined by the followers of Marx and Engels, would see a different economic structure replace capitalism, where the means and products of industrialization would be collectively owned and equitably shared. Nineteenth-century Marxists (some of whom were known as *communists*) effectively argued for the rights of workers and against the principles sustaining liberalism, capitalism and 'blue-water' imperialism. They were internationalists and argued that it was only when the 'workers of the world unite' would global capitalism be overthrown.

Like other forms of *socialism* (the principle that a government should provide for the basic needs of its subjects), Marxism thrived as a political ideology in the aftermath of the 1848 revolutions. But there were many types of socialists in the nineteenth century. What they had in common was the belief that governments should offset the social costs of industrialization and create a more equitable society. Unsurprisingly, the principles of socialism attracted industrial workers, particularly those in large urban settings, who encountered the abject conditions of industrial life first-hand. Many formed their own political organizations, including trade unions and political parties, to promote their ideas, advocate for change and proffer communal support in time of economic or political hardship.[10] Some of the most effective political movements of the time were founded on the principles of social democracy.[11] They aimed broadly at improving the lives of workers and the poor. They also aimed at promoting the establishment of social welfare systems, the end to child labour and slavery, the provision of universal access to reliable healthcare and a secular education for all.

Nineteenth-century socialists were often democrats, who looked to expand the franchise to include all men. Others were more radical and aimed to include all women as well; yet others, all of humanity, contesting the artificial differentiations many governing elites made between 'citizens' (those who rule) and 'subjects' (those who are ruled). The more extreme socialists, like the Marxists, ultimately looked to a revolutionary future, where the entire industrial–imperial–capitalist international system would be overthrown and replaced with a global working-class utopia. *Anarchists* were even more radical, aiming for the overthrow of established political authority according to the principle that, as K. Steven Vincent describes it, 'human beings possessed sufficient rational capacities or powerful enough moral sentiments to hold society together' without 'institutions like the state', which they considered 'artificial, unnatural and oppressive'.[12] Anarchists aimed for organic human social organization, based on local solidarities and community building impulses rather than power structures wielded coercively 'from above' by elites who aimed at the exploitation of the masses. The most extreme of these believed that the effective decapitation of the power structure was necessary to free humanity. They engaged in assassination campaigns that killed hundreds of aristocrats, leading government officials and even the Tsar of Russia, Alexander II, in 1881.

What conservatives, liberals and socialists all had in common was their desire to impact the political landscape in such a way as to influence how their society was run and what values were prioritized. Given the numerous shifts to greater bureaucratization and the growing influence of the state and its rules in the everyday lives of citizens and subjects (as discussed in Chapter 4), the latter decades of the nineteenth century also witnessed a shift to the professionalization of politics. In countries with parliamentary systems, the expansion of the franchise made the mobilization of political parties with distinct policy platforms that aimed to attract a wide public audience essential. Conservatives, for example, mobilized themselves into political groups that aimed at promoting religious traditions, traditional social structures or traditional economic practices (such as those of farming communities). Liberals grouped themselves into parties that supported liberal policies like free trade or the power of international law to promote global prosperity and peace. Liberals and conservatives alike tended to fear the politics of the working classes, the power of trade unions and strike action. They dreaded the revolutionary activities of the more radical socialists. As a result, oppositional politics came to influence the political landscape of most countries and certainly all empires.

The professionalization of political organizations was a marked feature of the latter decades of the nineteenth century as well. The range of such organizations also grew to cover all manner of identity platforms and political ideas. In the industrializing empires, for example, many women's organizations formed seeking to mobilize women of varying socio-economic backgrounds behind key ideas. Some of these groups began as single-issue organizations, like the Women's Christian Temperance Union (WCTU), an organization of aristocratic and middle-class women set up first in Ohio, which aimed to eradicate alcoholism and other temporal 'sins'. WCTU branches spread around the world and soon expanded their political platforms to include a number of other pressing issues affecting women globally, including: their lack of political rights, the introduction of effective social welfare policies, religious education for children and support for key international developments like the prevention of warfare and the advance of international arbitration.[13] Dedicated women's suffrage groups equally vociferously advocated for granting women the vote (see Figure 8.1). Many of them connected up with like-minded women's organizations in other countries to advance this collective goal. Yet others, like the International Council of Women (ICW) and its many national and imperial branches aimed more generally to create a transnational forum for women to

FIGURE 8.1 *Women's suffrage in the United States. This 1920s photograph of members of the United States National Woman's Party celebrate Susan B. Anthony's attempt to cast a vote for the presidential elections of 1872. Anthony was arrested for breaking electoral laws, as women were not legally entitled to vote in the United States. They would not be granted that right until the passing of the 19th Amendment to the American constitution in 1920. The banner states 'no self-respecting woman should wish to work for the success of a party that ignores her self'. Voting rights for African American men were enshrined in the 15th Amendment to the Constitution of 1870. However, voter registration impediments, including poll taxes and literacy tests, kept many African Americans in the southern states from fulfilling this right of citizenship. Source: Universal Images Group, 1920, Getty Images, 9002560.*

discuss common concerns and issues. By 1900, the ICW included member organizations from across the world including in India, Japan, the Middle East and Latin America.[14]

In similar ways, indigenous and colonized communities also mobilized into politicized organizations aimed at acquiring political rights and celebrating identity. W. E. B. DuBois's Pan-African Congress, for example, sought to unite African peoples on a global scale from its base in the United States to the African continent itself.[15] The Aborigines' Rights Protection Society, which was established in Ghana in 1897, mobilized globally to end the misappropriation of African lands by European colonizers and entrepreneurs.[16] The Pan-Slavic movements of central and eastern Europe looked to unite and promote Slavic cultural identity and political representation within empires and as a nation-building enterprise.[17] In 1897, Theodor Hertzl developed the principle of Zionism to establish a permanent nation-state for Jews in Palestine. Zionists too were globally connected and, like these other organizations, aimed at influencing the global public sphere through effective circulation of information and propaganda events.[18]

In almost all cases, the above political organizations were influenced in some way by another key identifier of the time, namely *nationalism*. The concept of 'the nation' as a collective of people from an identifiable racial or cultural background was a powerful mobilizer of political consciousness then (as now). Nationalism was also a multidimensional idea that could underpin and augment a range of political and religious concepts. By 1900, the conservative elite in most empires endowed their empires with national virtues: their citizens existed to defend the empire in the name of 'God, king and country'. For their part, liberals were no less patriotic but tended to promote a more secular and legal definition of nationhood, citizenship and civic duty (even if, in practice, they excluded many 'others' from enjoying the full benefits of citizenship on racial, religious, gender or economic grounds). Ethnic nationalists, in turn, focused on the racial, linguistic and religious differences that existed between communities and claimed that every distinct ethnic community should have the right to self-governance on their own terms.

Nationalism was a useful concept to link individuals to the state as citizens. If the state existed for its citizens (as opposed to its subjects), then citizenship of a nation implied rights and duties. The right to vote, to have a say, to determine the focus of the state were increasingly embedded in the claimed political rights of citizens. Nationalism helped to make those rights part of the identity of the individual. Nationalism thus also helped to advance the concept that citizens had duties: to defend the country, to serve in its military forces and to pay taxes. To that end, citizenship helped to draw people from different socio-economic backgrounds into a shared sense of an 'imagined community': the nation.[19] Nationalism helped to offset some of the detrimental social impacts of industrialization, like urbanization and the destruction of traditional communal loyalties and offered a powerful ideology for elites to mobilize the general populace behind the state.

But nationalism also offered an effective ideology to isolate and 'other' and to protect the power and privilege of certain citizens as against those of non-citizens or subjects. 'Othering' was a powerful way to deny political rights to certain groups within a state or empire. Many governments justified the expansion of their industrial empires by claiming the right to rule 'subject' peoples on the grounds that they were not 'civilized' enough to rule themselves or because they did not meet the requisite competencies of full citizens. Using similar rationales, women were often excluded from the franchise and from exercising full political and economic rights as citizens on the basis that they were not considered biologically able to fulfil the duties of military service or, for that matter, to fully function in public and economic life (as opposed to men who could). The key point to make here is that while these patriarchal and racist concepts dominated the nineteenth-century world and shaped many of its contours, the century also witnessed a bourgeoning set of counter-narratives. Oppositional politics thus existed on many levels: be it the claim to 'self-rule' or gain suffrage for the disenfranchised, be it to protect a traditional heritage or culture or be it the ambition to revolutionize a nation, empire or even the international system itself.

The growth in political activism on a range of identity issues was made possible by the expansion of communications networks across the planet (enabling like-minded people to find and communicate with each other), the growth in literacy and the expansion of global publishing. The nineteenth-century age of globalization also made awareness of the 'international' as a space where people, ideas, money and identities interacted more prevalent. It is really not surprising to find that the international environment itself was also opened up to reimagining during this century. Not only did many groups mobilize their identity politics across borders, they also organized international congresses, engaged the international media and brought a range of new ideas into being that focused on improving 'the international' for the betterment of people like themselves and sometimes for the betterment of all.

Internationalism was a peculiarly nineteenth-century term that described a range of political developments aimed at reshaping or influencing the international environment. Like nationalism, internationalism was a broad catch-all concept with numerous applications. Internationalists by definition crossed borders, but they often connected their own local interests (be it to claim or protect rights and identities or to protest against persecution) to a wider international ambition. Shared identities, shared opportunities or a shared sense of suffering helped to advance a range of internationalist endeavours. Given their global interconnectedness, most internationalists also understood the importance of influencing the global public sphere to promote their ideas and affect meaningful change. They utilized available media channels and other international forums aiming both to influence the corridors of power and spread the acceptance of their ideas among a wide audience.[20]

Some of the most successful global movements of ideas and identity in the nineteenth century were mobilized by the major religions. Of course, Islam, Judaism, Christianity, Hinduism and Buddhism were already global religions in 1815. The nineteenth-century age of industrial globalization, however, reinvigorated many of them. Christian missionaries, for example, were particularly influential in infiltrating many Pacific Island communities but also expanded their reach throughout China and Africa. More than one hundred thousand European Christian missionaries operated in Africa by 1900.[21] In that sense, Christianity was an imperial ideology that helped the agents of the Western industrial empires justify their 'civilizing' mission. But religious idealism also sat at the heart of many anti-European responses to industrial imperialism. For example, the international appeal of Islam grew in the nineteenth century in part because it offered a powerful counter to the 'civilizing' dogma of the Christian empires. This was particularly true in Africa, India and South and South East Asia where numerous communities consolidated their commitment to Islam in opposition to the claimed sovereign rights of the local (largely Christian) colonial rulers.[22] For its part, the promotion of Confucianism in China as a national religion (as opposed to a set of classical texts on ethics and duty) helped to sustain the idea that China was a uniform nation able to sustain its own version of modernization, as opposed to a backward-looking multi-ethnic empire.[23]

At another level, the protection of local and familial religious and cultural practices also helped colonized peoples to defend and promote their own identities, in the process ensuring that many colonial spaces remained multidimensional in their cultural diversity. These religious practises also globalized as their adherents migrated. Where-ever people moved, they built mosques, churches, temples and synagogues. These religious buildings came to dominate many nineteenth-century urban landscapes and lent identity, community and character to an area. The most cosmopolitan cities situated on the world's oceanic highways embraced them all and became important sites for the publication and exchange of religious texts and ideas. By 1900, for example, Singapore boasted several Christian churches (including St Andrews Anglican Cathedral, opened in 1861, and the Armenian Church, built in 1835), Taoist temples like the Thian Hock Keng (built in 1842), Confucian temples (including Yueh Hai Ching, which was built in 1826), Hindu temples (including the Sri Mariamman, constructed in 1827), Jewish synagogues (like the Maghain Aboth founded in 1878) and Islamic mosques (including the Masjid Sultan built

FIGURE 8.2 *Singapore South Bridge Road, c.1900. This photograph, taken around 1900 of Singapore's South Bridge Road, shows both the Hindu temple of Sri Mariamman (built in 1827) and the Islamic Masjid Jamae mosque (built in 1826). Like many cosmopolitan port cities in the nineteenth century, Singapore was home to numerous religious communities and houses of worship, whose physical presence lent a cosmopolitan character and identity to the city's landscape.*
Source: Photographic Views of Singapore, G. R. Lambert, 1900, np.

in 1826 and the Masjid Hajjah Fatimah erected in 1846) alongside a wide array of other religious spaces and joss houses (see Figure 8.2). The communications revolution of the nineteenth-century age of industrial globalization enabled both the spread of traditional ideas and cultures and discourses on how to adapt to modernization, imperialism and industrial capitalism.

That there were numerous cities where global religions, global politics and global communities encountered each other on a regular basis also helped to spur the growth in the concept of universal *human rights*: that all human beings are equal and deserve to be treated equally and, thus, that they have the same rights to citizenship and political agency.[24] *Universalism* (the concept that at heart all human beings should be treated the same) influenced numerous nineteenth-century international political developments as well. Universalism covered the gamut of nineteenth-century idealism that ranged from the basic premise of most global religions ('all humans are equal in the eyes of our god(s)') to the claims of many secular liberals that 'all individuals are equal in law' to Marx and Engels's conceptualization of humanity to collectively share the world's human and material resources.

Universalism in its multiple forms also helped to advance the concept of *humanitarianism*: the concept that vulnerable 'others' deserved protection from violence and exploitation. By the early twentieth century, charitable aid networks stretched across empires and transnationally often in response to newspaper reports and pictorial representations of warfare, famine and violence in some other part of the world. The International Red Cross movement, for example, established in the context of the Geneva Conventions of 1864 became a popular public movement for providing humanitarian aid across borders.[25] The International Red Cross Society of Shanghai, for example, formed in the context of the Russo-Japanese War (1904–5) as an indigenous Chinese initiative within a wider world environment where neutrals increasing provided aid in time of war. To that end, the Shanghai Red Cross coordinated the evacuation of 130,000 refugees from Manchuria, supervised relief centres and hospitals near the war fronts and raised more than 120,000 taels of silver by public subscription. The organization's relief efforts were so effective that it transformed into the Red Cross Society of China after the conflict as an empire-wide endeavour, offering aid regionally and globally, including to the victims of the 1906 San Francisco earthquake.[26] The Japanese Red Cross Society, for its part, was the largest national Red Cross organization in the world by 1903, with a phenomenal membership of nine hundred thousand individuals. By 1918, it would count 1.8 million members (the American Red Cross only had thirty-one thousand members at the time). As the historian Sho Konishi argues, in Japan and China, universalist humanitarianism was already well established before the onset of the industrial age, but in the context of the 'first age of industrial globalization' its reach extended well beyond the local.[27]

By the latter stages of the nineteenth century, acting globally to affect political change was also becoming more commonplace. Globalization, in effect, aided the growth in resistance to industrial imperialism as it could bring people and their ideas together faster and more easily. As an example, consider how globally interactive three prominent groups of Indian revolutionaries were. According to the historian Kris Manjapra, the Khilafat, Swadeshi and Ghadar movements had different foundations yet worked in tandem and with other global anti-imperial groups to achieve a common goal, namely the end of the British Raj.[28] The Khilafat movement was principally an Islamic organization that maintained strong links with other Islamic communities fighting their own anti-imperial crusades across the globe, including in Africa. The Swadeshi movement's principle objective was to overturn the British decision to partition Bengal in 1905. Its activists mobilized public support for their cause in the global press and established support groups across India and in London, Paris, New York, San Francisco and Tokyo. Swadeshi revolutionaries aimed at military intervention and connected with anti-imperial, anarchist and socialist revolutionaries in Ireland, Russia, Japan, China and the United States. For its part, the Ghadar movement began among Punjabi migrants living in California who looked to establish an independent Punjabi state in India and were willing to take up arms to achieve this end. They also mobilized support across South Asia and globally through the dissemination of pamphlets, holding political meetings and influencing newspaper reporting. Significantly, all three movements received monetary and infrastructure support from Britain's imperial rivals, including the Japanese, Ottoman and German governments, who saw only opportunity in destabilizing the British empire from below.

These Indian revolutionaries were by no means original in mobilizing the international environment to aid what might be perceived as a local or nationalist cause. After all, they rightly recognized that to successfully defeat the British empire would require a global effort. The historian Benedict Anderson shows similar international connections in describing the contours of Filipino independence fighters' anti-American activities in the early twentieth century in his magisterial *Under Three Flags: Anarchism and the Anti-Colonial Imagination*.[29] As Anderson describes them, these revolutionaries aimed to free the Philippines from American imperial rule after the Spanish-American War of 1898. They connected with socialist and anarchist revolutionaries across the United States imperial sphere (including in Puerto Rico, Cuba and the Dominican Republic) as well as in Europe. They placed representatives who could agitate for their cause in every major international city, including in Paris, Hong Kong, London and New York. They influenced and to some extent coordinated their activities, uprisings and political techniques with ethnic nationalists everywhere, including in China and southern Africa. As Anderson explains, the late nineteenth century's globalized world ensured that for 'the first time in world history ... such trans-global coordination became possible'.[30]

Socialist internationalists were equally globally mobilized. They aimed at organizing the plethora of socialist, communist and anarchist groups that existed and affect effective change locally and globally. The First International, as it was called, formed in London in 1864. When its leadership failed to agree on effective priorities – Marx and the anarchist Mikhail Bakunin, did not get along – it dissipated. In 1889, however, the Second International was set up at a meeting of socialists and trade union activists during the Paris World Fair held that year. The Second International's purpose was to coordinate the numerous nationally focused socialist political parties (like the German SPD, which by the 1890s received close to 25 percent of the vote and by 1912 helped to form the government coalition) as well to coordinate effective action on key issues affecting working-class communities. From this point on, the Second International met regularly.[31]

As noted earlier, women's groups were also highly adept at mobilizing themselves in the international sphere. In large part because political agency was denied to many of them within the nation-state or empire, the transnational environment proved a useful medium for advancing women's identity and activism.[32] After women gained the vote in New Zealand in 1893, for example, the female representatives of the New Zealand suffrage movement became heroic figureheads for suffrage campaigns globally.[33] They travelled far and wide to help advance the cause.[34]

Many of these women were also members of other liberal international organizations that aimed at improving international relations and affairs. The Inter-Parliamentary Union (IPU), for example, set up in 1889 as a transnational lobby group for parliamentarians. Their aim was to influence the domestic political landscape of each of their countries by advancing a shared vision of international cooperation. The IPU's vision revolved around introducing key improvements at an international level to advance conflict resolution mechanisms between governments and heighten the power of international law to prevent and alleviate the impact of war.[35] With a similar aim in mind, twelve lawyers from around the European continent met in the Belgian town of Ghent in 1873 and set up the *Institut de droit international* (Institute of International Law). By 1914, the Institute had expanded its membership to include legal representatives of every sovereign state in existence. Its annual reports and recommendations were a powerful influence on diplomacy and multilateral treaty-making practices. On an equally serious note, Ludwik Zamenhof invented the language of Esperanto in 1887, hoping to inspire its universal adoption so that people from different linguistic backgrounds could communicate with each other on equal terms and so that no one nation or culture would have a distinct advantage in global communication.[36]

In their activism, many liberal internationalists took their lead from the various Quaker and other religious charitable movements that advocated for global peace, the abolition of slavery and, increasingly, for the promotion of international law as a medium to prevent war, promote conflict resolution mechanisms and, in some cases, advance universal human rights.[37] The notion that international politics and international diplomacy could be improved to limit the spread of war and, even more radically, to decrease human suffering became more common through the course of the nineteenth century. As we will see in the next chapter, by the time of the first Hague peace conference, held in 1899, the idea that ordinary people could affect the diplomatic priorities of their governments was also becoming more prevalent. Certainly, the global media enabled greater engagement with the world as an interconnected space.

The second half of the nineteenth century also witnessed numerous occasions where globality was celebrated by the world's elite in ostentatious ways.[38] London's Great Exhibition of 1851 was one of the most magnificent of these events. Set in the resplendent surroundings of Hyde Park, the event offered the industrial empires a chance to display their imperial glory. More than 6 million visitors from around the world came to London in 1851 to partake of the fair's many attractions, including a massive glasshouse named the Crystal Palace. The exhibition displayed the paradoxes of mid-nineteenth-century industrial globalization in marvellous array. Where on the one hand it celebrated trade as the world's great 'peacemaker', as Queen Victoria described, on the other it also heightened a sense of imperial competition and national prowess.[39] It drew stark attention to the racial differences within the world's population. Still, the event also brought the world's political thinkers and activists to London, aiming to find ways of utilizing it as a way to improve the global environment.

The Great Exhibition inspired numerous repeat events. The Universal Exposition of 1889 held in Paris, for example, celebrated the centennial of the French revolution and foregrounded global relations. The iconic Eiffel Tower was built for the event, a symbol of the technological advance of French engineering and the latest developments in iron work (see Figure 8.3). It towered over the city and the other countries' pavilions, including a number from Latin America. Like the 1851 Exhibition, the 1889 event presented the accomplishments of the white industrializers bringing 'civilization' to the world, including in displays of new machinery, weaponry, electricity and trade commodities. Displays of colonial subjects placed in make-shift 'indigenous' environments, veritable human zoos, were a highlight for many of the 32 million visitors to the event, signaling yet again how racialized everyday conceptions of humanity were in the heartlands of industrial imperialism.[40] Yet this event too brought the world's global thinkers and activists together aiming to improve the world. No less than sixty-nine international congresses were held in the course of the fair. The Second International inaugurated at the event as did the IPU. The ICW held its first major congress at the fair.[41]

The subsequent 1893 Columbian Exposition held in the middle of the American continent in the great railway hub of St Louis had 27 million visitors and included a World Congress Auxiliary and a World Parliament of Religion.[42] The 1900 world fair in Paris outdid this event again, with no less than 50 million visitors. The International Olympic Committee (set up in 1894 to organize a world sporting event, itself a major internationalist endeavour) agreed to hold the second modern Olympic Games to coincide with the 1900 Paris fair. When St Louis held a repeat Columbian Exposition in 1904, it also hosted the third Olympic games.

Altogether then, through the course of the nineteenth century, thinking globally became a normalized part of political action and personal identity

FIGURE 8.3 *The Paris Expo, 1889. The world fair of 1889 was held in the French capital of Paris. It coincided with the centennial celebrations of the French revolution and brought the world's visitors and media attention to Paris. Baron Gustave Eiffel's impressive wrought-iron tower, constructed for the event, aimed at showcasing the industrial and engineering mastery of the French. It towered over a colourful array of exhibition halls from thirty-five different countries. Intended as a temporary structure, the Eiffel Tower became an iconic symbol of the nineteenth-century era of industrial globalization.*

Source: Roger Viollet, photograph, 1889, Getty Images, 56225544.

for many people (although certainly not all people). The global environment could both inform and challenge local priorities and activism. The familial, communal, national, imperial and international often coexisted in a complex and messy relationship (what some historians call 'entanglement' and others describe as a 'social world of colliding forces').[43] Such ideas both informed those with power and enabled the promotion of their power and privilege and underwrote alternate identities, some of which shaped in resistance to those with power, others evolved to meet the intrinsic needs of the person or community. The sense of the world connecting and, in connecting, opening up a space for international engagement presents a key change and development of the nineteenth-century age of industrial globalization. This global arena would become increasingly important for defining the shape of local, national, imperial and global politics in the twentieth century as well.

Study questions

1. Explain how the forces of industrial globalization both inspired greater uniformity in social life during the nineteenth century and heightened contemporaries' sense of difference. Why does it matter?

2. Define the basic tenets of the following nineteenth-century political ideas:

   a. conservatism
   b. free trade liberalism
   c. socialism
   d. ethnic nationalism
   e. anarchism
   f. liberal internationalism

3. In what ways did individuals and communities around the world claim political rights in the nineteenth century?

4. How did events like the world fairs or Olympic games movement impact on nineteenth-century thinking about international interconnectedness?

Recommended readings

Maartje Abbenhuis, *The Hague Conferences in International Politics 1898–1915.* Bloomsbury, 2018: Chapter 1 'How the nineteenth century shaped the Hague conferences', pp. 9–20.

Michael Adas, *Machines as the Measure of Men: Science, Technology and the Ideologies of Western Dominance*. Cornell UP, 1989: Chapter 5 'The limits of diffusion: Science and technology in the debate over the African and Asian capacity for acculturation', pp. 271–342.

Constance Bantman, 'Introduction: The foreign political press in nineteenth-century London: Local and transnational contexts' in Constance Bantman, Ana Cláudia Suriani da Silva, eds, *The Foreign Political Press in Nineteenth-Century London: Politics from a Distance*. Bloomsbury, 2018, pp. 1–14.

Christopher Bayly, *The Birth of the Modern World 1780–1914*. Blackwell, 2004: Chapter 9 'Empires of religion', pp. 325–65.

Christopher Bayly, 'European political thought and the wider world during the nineteenth century' in G. S. Jones, G. Claeys, eds, *Nineteenth-Century Political Thought*. Cambridge UP, 2011, pp. 835–63.

Duncan Bell, 'Empire and imperialism' in G. S. Jones, G. Claeys, eds, *Nineteenth-Century Political Thought*. Cambridge UP, 2011, pp. 865–92.

Sebastian Conrad, 'Enlightenment in global history: A historiographical critique', *American History Review* 117, 4, October 2012, pp. 999–1027.

Daniel Gorman, *International Cooperation in the Early Twentieth Century*. Bloomsbury, 2017: Chapter 1 'Ideas of international order, empire and anticolonialism', pp. 15–37.

Richard Bach Jensen, 'Daggers, rifles and dynamite: Anarchist terrorism in nineteenth-century Europe', *Terrorism and Political Violence* 16, 1, 2004, pp. 116–53.

Marilyn Lake, Henry Reynolds, *Drawing the Global Colour Line: White Man's Countries and the International Challenge of Racial Equality*. Cambridge UP, 2008: Chapter 10 'International conferences: cosmopolitan amity or racial enmity?', pp. 241–62.

Daniel Laqua, *The Age of Internationalism and Belgium 1880–1930: Peace, Progress and Prestige*. Manchester UP, 2013: Chapter 2 'Empire', pp. 45–79.

Mark Mazower, *Governing the World: The History of an Idea 1815 to the Present*. Penguin, 2013: Chapter 3 'Brotherhood', pp. 31–64.

Clare Midgley, 'Bringing the empire home: Women activists in imperial Britain 1790s-1930s' in Catherine Hall, Sonya O. Rose, eds, *At Home with the Empire: Metropolitan Culture and the Imperial World*. Cambridge UP, 2006, pp. 230–50.

Frank Ninkovich, *Global Dawn: The Cultural Foundations of American Internationalism 1865–1890*. Harvard UP, 2009: Chapter 1 'Global civilization', pp. 15–46.

Jürgen Osterhammel, *The Transformation of the World: A Global History of the Nineteenth Century*. Princeton UP, 2014: Chapter 15 'Hierarchies: The vertical dimension of social space', pp. 744–78.

Fiona Paisley, 'Resistance in exile: Anthony Martin Fernando, Australian aboriginal activist, internationalist and traveller in Europe' in Desley Deacon, Penny Russell, Angela Woollacott, eds, *Transnational Lives: Biographies of Global Modernity, 1700-Present*. Palgrave MacMillan, 2010, pp. 183–94.

Caroline Reeves, 'Developing the humanitarian image in late nineteenth- and early twentieth-century China' in Heide Fehrenbach, Davide Rodogno, eds, *Humanitarian Photography: A History*. Cambridge UP, 2015, pp. 115–39.

Emily Rosenberg, 'Exhibitionary nodes' in Emily Rosenberg, ed., *A World Connecting, 1870–1945*. Belknap Press, 2012, pp. 886–918.

Sarah Steinbock-Pratt, 'It gave us our nationality: US education, the politics of dress and transnational Filipino student networks, 1901–45' in Stephan F. Miescher, Michelle Mitchell, Naoko Shibusawa, eds, *Gender, Imperialism and Global Exchanges*. Wiley Blackwell, 2015, pp. 181–204.

Theodore H. von Laue, *The World Revolution of Westernization: The Twentieth Century in Global Perspective*. Oxford UP, 1987: Chapter 3 'The cultural revolution', pp. 27–34.

9

Industrial globalization and the origins of the First World War

In 1886 the Scottish-Canadian inventor, surveyor and engineer Sir Sanford Fleming reflected on the impact of globalization on how people experienced the simultaneity of everyday life. Since the onset of the telegraph, Fleming recognized how the growing interconnectedness of communities opened the world 'to the observation of civilized communities and leave[s] no interval of time between widely separated places proportionate to their distances apart'.[1] Fleming was particularly knowledgeable on the subject. He helped to develop the principles behind global timekeeping, was responsible for planning Canada's cross-continental railways and designed Canada's first postage stamp. For Fleming, the fact that news travelled globally and that information could circulate relatively easily and faster than ever before ensured that increasingly more people were aware of the globality and interdependence of their existence. Fleming's reflections are an example of what the historian Glenda Sluga describes as the 'new self-consciousness of the internationality of everyday life', which blossomed across the planet by the turn of the century.[2] That global awareness is a key marker of how much had changed across the world since 1815.

The world of 1900 was evolving at a rapid rate. The impact of industrialization and modernization processes in most states, the growth of an interconnected global capitalist economy and the spread of industrial empires ensured that the world of 1900 looked quite different from that of 1815. Yet, importantly, the international power dynamics at play in this interdependent world were in many respects the products of the great power decisions made in 1815. The foundations of the 'concert of Europe' system – particularly the aim of avoiding war between the great power empires – had enabled these same powers to reap great benefits. They were the first to be able to take full advantage of the industrial revolution and as a result they were able to shape and dominate the economic, diplomatic and even cultural precepts that dominated the nineteenth-century international system. In 1900, the winners in the international environment were the states that had industrialized relatively easily and relatively fast, which included many European countries, the United States and Japan.

These industrial powerhouses thrived in the global economy because their citizens maximized their access to global markets and global trade routes as well as dominating the building of (and profiteering from) global infrastructure projects. They also thrived because they managed to expand their formal and informal empires (frequently by violent means) and stretched their economic and imperial power across much of the world. The world of 1900 was dominated by the power and values of the industrializing empires. While their collective power depended in no small part on the willingness of their governments to avoid war with each other, this world order was also built on the intense economic and imperial rivalry between them. Capitalism flourishes on the back of competition, after all. The rush to acquire territorial and legal sovereignty over land, people and resources in the latter decades of the 1800s aimed first and foremost at beating out competitors. That competition made the sustenance of the diplomatic principles of the 'concert system' increasingly difficult.

Furthermore, the global impact of the first age of industrial globalization ensured that by 1900 the notion that the five European great powers (Britain, France, Russia, Germany and Austria-Hungary) could micromanage all international crises between them became increasingly untenable. Not only were their rivalries globalized in response to the globalization of their empires and economic interests, but there were now many more global players operating in the international arena. For one, Japan and the United States had become key partners in many multilateral arrangements. For all seven industrial powers, the waning stability and strength of the Chinese and Ottoman empires warranted careful attention and increased the potential for a major international crisis to evolve. The rise in economic power and political influence of a growing number of smaller states in Europe, Asia and Latin America (some of which had their own formal 'blue-water' empires, most of which were intricately involved in the intricate web of informal 'empires of business' that stretched across the planet) also complicated the maintenance of the diplomatic equilibrium between the major powers.[3] Significantly, the governing elite of all these states were highly alert to the possibility of a future war, at least to a future war involving one or more of their imperial rivals. In preparation for that eventuality in the period 1890 to 1914, they substantially increased the size of their armies, invested in new military and naval technology and initiated a number of alliances and 'friendly' treaties with potential future allies. The potential of a great power war – although not necessarily the prospect of a global war – infused the international politics of the time.

The other major shift in the global diplomatic order that marked 1900 so clearly apart from 1815 was the growth of public awareness of the international diplomatic order and of diplomatic crises more generally. Fleming's notion of simultaneity and Sluga's concept of the 'internationality of everyday life' remind us that engaged individuals around the world learned about major events almost as they happened and assessed the political impact of those developments on their own lives and priorities. As the previous chapters show, by 1900, large numbers of them used that awareness to promote change both at a local and global level. The interdependence of the global economy, the interconnectedness of the global media environment and the growth in political activism of ordinary people marked the world of 1900 off from that of 1815. This is not to say that there was no global interconnectedness in 1815 – the numerous revolutions and wars of independence fought across the Atlantic world at the time speak to those connections – but it is to say that by 1900, many more people than ever before thought about who they were within a local and global context and conducted their lives within that context as well.

As a result, not only did the great powers operate in a more globally dynamic international environment in 1900, but their governments regularly faced what they considered dangerous threats to their political authority and security, both from within their empires and from without. Dealing with these challenges as a collective multilateral enterprise became increasingly difficult. After all, the disadvantages facing one industrial empire surely presented an advantage or opportunity for another when they competed for the same share of the international pie?

The history of the origins of the First World War is often written as a 'path to war' story in which the growing competition and rivalry between the European great powers in the decades leading up to 1914 offer a convincing explanation for the outbreak of the war.[4] At times, such histories even become teleological and describe the war as an inevitable outcome of imperial competition. This was, for example, Vladimir Lenin's thesis in his 1917 treatise *Imperialism: The Highest Form of Capitalism*, in which he argued that since there was nothing left for the industrial great powers to conquer by 1900, their economic competition increasingly became acrimonious resulting in inevitable warfare between them.[5]

Later historians have posited alternate versions of the 'inevitable war' thesis, many of which present a case for any one of the five European great powers' willingness to provoke a system-breaking conflict. According to these accounts: Austria-Hungary felt increasingly isolated in a world of great power competitors and willingly risked war with its rival Russia in order to protect the integrity of its empire in the Balkans; Germany willed war in support of Austria-Hungary for it feared the future resurgence of a militarily strong Russia; Russia sought to protect its power in the Balkan region and willed a war against the unwarranted interference of Austria-Hungary; France supported a Russia-led war against Germany so it could exact revenge for the Franco-Prussian War; and Great Britain considered a war in Europe as a useful distraction from domestic challenges including the Irish Home Rule question and the suffragette movement.

There is much to be said about highlighting the growing challenges facing the European great powers in sustaining the principles of restraint and war avoidance (this chapter will highlight several more). But to characterize the inevitability of a European great power war as an endemic feature of the period fails to recognize that many contemporaries did not imagine such a war as inevitable. Some did not even consider its possibility at all. Many 'path to war' arguments fail to recognize not only the developments that seemed to sustain the diplomatic principles of the concert system but also those that advanced and heightened them. Asking the question 'why was Europe at peace for most of the period 1871–1914?', as the historian William Mulligan so persuasively does, rejigs our alertness to the paradoxes of the time.[6] For while there were many pressures that amplified global rivalry, competition and a 'will to war' among the great industrial empires of the age, there were also many that seemed to mitigate and alleviate such pressures.

As with the entire history of the first age of industrial globalization, this chapter highlights some of these paradoxes and brings out a range of global implications. For while in July 1914, Europe did go to war, dragging the rest of the world with it, before 1914 no one considered the prospect of global industrial warfare as inevitable. Most assumed that the principles that had kept the great powers from going to war with each other since 1815 would continue to operate. That they did not in July 1914 is, thus, highly significant, but it takes nothing away from the fact that the First World War came as surprise to most contemporaries: a disastrous surprise.[7]

The origins of the First World War lie unequivocally in Europe. Stronger still, they lie in the decisions made by the governing elite of the same five great European powers that had orchestrated the Congress of Vienna a century earlier, namely: Great Britain, Germany (then Prussia), Austria-Hungary (then Austria), France and Russia.[8] Historians have unpicked the minutiae of the timetable to war – the so-called 'July crisis of 1914' – in tens of dozens of books and journal articles. The outbreak of the First World War remains one of the most debated and controversial topics in international history. It is possible, for example, to find reputable explanations for why any one of the five European great powers could (and some of them argue should) be held accountable for the war. These arguments all show that, at a certain level, all five governments were either preparing for or willing to risk some kind of military conflict breaking out between at least some of them. If we can say anything conclusively about the cascade of war declarations that followed Austria-Hungary's ultimatum to Serbia on 23 July 1914, then, it is that the 'will to risk some kind of great power war' was greater than the 'will to prevent all war'. In every moment of international crisis before this point of time, that same willingness to risk 'some kind of great power war' did not exist in quite the same way.

In a thoughtful and powerful essay about the dynamics of the nineteenth-century international system, the historian Paul Schroeder posits that 'peace is always caused', 'wars sometimes just happen'.[9] Schroeder's focus on peace as a manufactured reality is essential to explaining many of the arguments presented in this book. After all, the concert of Europe system could only be maintained as long as all the great power governments were wedded to its basic principles. That those principles helped to keep Europe (and with Europe, the rest of the world) from general war between 1815 and 1914 is highly significant. That they failed to do so in July 1914 is most important, but that does not necessarily mean that they collapsed because there was a general will to ignore them. It seems more likely that war came in 1914 despite the established practices of the concert system. This chapter explores some of the reasons for the outbreak of war in July–August 1914 and situates those reasons within the context of a globally connected and industrializing world.

On 28 June 1914, the heir to the Austrian Habsburg throne Archduke Franz Ferdinand and his wife Sophie toured the city of Sarajevo in an open-topped car. Their tour was ill-judged.[10] Sarajevo was the capital city of the Balkan territory of Bosnia-Herzegovina, a region annexed by the Austro-Hungarian empire in 1908 amidst much international controversy (Russia was particularly incensed) and the source of considerable local resistance (some Bosnians looked for an independent state, others for incorporation into the neighbouring Slavic state of Serbia). As representatives of an unpopular imperial authority, Franz Ferdinand and Sofie were potential targets for political action. The secretive and clandestine Serbian-Slavic Black Hand organization certainly saw only opportunity in the royal couple's visit, stationing six of their members as assassins on the advertised tour route. After the first five members failed in their missions, it was only by luck that the sixth, Gavrilo Princip, was in a position to shoot and kill.

Although it made for impressive newspaper headlines and triggered some anti-Serb riots across the Austro-Hungarian empire, the assassination of Franz Ferdinand and Sophie was otherwise unremarkable. Political assassinations were a common feature of the era. Numerous political leaders, monarchs, politicians and diplomats had succumbed to deadly acts by terrorists, anarchists, revolutionaries and the like in the decades leading up to 1914.[11] In this age of the assassin, every year brought new media sensations including the deaths of: Empress Elisabeth of Austria in 1898, the president of the Dominican Republic General Heureaux in 1899, the Italian king Umberto I in 1900, American president William McKinley in 1901, the Russian minister for the Interior Dmitry Sipyagin in 1902, the Serbian king Alexander Obrenovic and queen Draga in 1903, the Russian governor general of Finland Nikolay Bobrikov in 1904, Grand Duke Sergei Alexandrovich of Russia in 1905, thirty bystanders of the Spanish king Alfonso XIII's cortege in 1906 (the monarch escaped injury), the Bulgarian prime minister Dimitar Petkov in 1907, King Carlos I of Portugal in 1908, the Japanese resident-general in Korea Ito Hirobumi in 1909, the Egyptian prime minister Boutros Ghali in 1910, the president of Mexico, Francisco I in 1911, the Russian prime minister Pyotr Stolypin in 1911, and the Greek king George I in 1913. Each of these events, alongside a much larger number of attempted assassinations, occasioned some form of political upheaval and considerable media attention. None of them resulted in a major international crisis or war. There was nothing about the attack on Franz Ferdinand and Sophie that suggested that their deaths would result in a global calamity. In fact, since it occurred at the outbreak of the European summer, most of Europe's governing elite went on holiday. The German Kaiser Wilhelm II, for one, left for his summer vacation in the Norwegian fjords.

The origins of the First World War lie not in Franz Ferdinand's death but in the political opportunism it occasioned in Austria-Hungary.[12] Two leading figures in the Austro-Hungarian government, namely Foreign Minister Count Leopold Berchtold and Chief of General Staff Conrad von Hötzendorf, saw in the assassination an opening to solve what they considered the ever-growing problem of Serbia. In the context of the recent Balkan Wars (1911–13), which had removed the Ottoman empire as a formal authority in the Balkan Peninsula and had established a number of independent nation-states, the Austrian authorities were all too aware of the dangers presented by the growing number of anti-imperial political movements within their own empire. The rise of Serbia during these wars as a virulent and powerful Slavic state on the border of the Austro-Hungarian empire served as a beacon of hope for a range of ethnic nationalists, including Pan-Slavic irredentists. That Austria-Hungary was considered a weaker industrial power only spurred the ambitions of these independence seekers. That the Young Turks' revolution had succeeded in overthrowing the government of the Ottoman empire in 1908 and that the Xinhai revolution ended the Qing dynasty in 1911 signalled all too clearly to Austria-Hungary's ruling elite that its own age-old dynasty might be in danger too. Keeping its dynastic integrity intact against rebellion 'from below' remained a key priority.[13]

From the perspective of Berchtold and von Hötzendorf, Franz Ferdinand's assassination presented an opportunity to do something about Serbia. Exactly what that 'something' might be however was more difficult to decipher. For the two Austrians, the best outcome would be a small war leading to a military victory over Serbia, which would put the Pan-Slavic movement firmly in its place and repress the nationalist ambitions of other ethnic groups in the empire alongside. In many respects, then, the Austrian government's will to go to war with Serbia was in keeping with the traditions of the concert system. The suppression of rebellion was a primary reason for why the congress system was established in 1815 after all and, from the perspective of the empire's elite at least, Serbia clearly posed a threat to the internal security of Austria-Hungary. Furthermore, the Austro-Hungarian government had good reason to believe that the Serb government had sponsored the Black Hand organization. A reasonable *casus belli* thus existed. Surely, no other power would reject these grounds for a small-scale conflict against a dangerous and militant small nation-state?

But the Austro-Hungarian government was not confident enough that its anti-imperial rationale for going to war with Serbia would satisfy the other great powers.[14] The greatest danger came from Russia. The Russian government had long abandoned the principle of supporting their neighbours' anti-imperial activities in aid of stabilizing the concert system. It had not, however, abandoned the concert principle of finding multilateral diplomatic solutions in time of crisis. With the collapse of Ottoman power in the Balkans over the previous years, however, the Romanov government had become more alert to any unilateral actions taken by any of the other great powers in the region. It saw Austria-Hungary as its main competitor and saw its annexation of Bosnia-Hercegovina in 1908 as a unilateral act.[15] Given the volatility of the peninsula in the wake of the Balkan Wars, Austria-Hungary also could not risk alienating any of the great powers either, but neither was it willing to give up on its own imperial security and Balkan interests. Above all, it could not afford a war with Russia, whose government had its own geostrategic and political interests in the Balkan region to protect. In an attempt to keep Russia from interfering in its proposed war with Serbia, the Austro-Hungarian government thus approached its German ally for support: Russia would surely not escalate a diplomatic crisis involving both Germany and Austria-Hungary?

The German government's reply to the Austro-Hungarian request came swiftly: of course, the Serbs need to be dealt with; of course, we support any course of action you see fit; of course, Russia needs to be deterred from interfering. This response, which historians often describe as a 'blank cheque' (giving Austria-Hungary any and all resources to aid their cause), has received a considerable amount of historical attention.[16] Did the Germans seek a war with Russia at this point of time? Possibly. Certainly, a number of high-ranking military personnel in the German High Command (much like their Austrian counterparts) considered that a war with Russia was inevitable at some point in the intermediate future.[17] Given that Russia was modernizing its armed forces, the opportunity for a war now, as opposed to one fought later when Russia was stronger, made sense strategically speaking. However, it is far more likely that the German message sent to Austria-Hungary on 6 July 1914 aimed at signalling that the German government supported a small-scale war with Serbia and that it was willing to lend its diplomatic weight behind any action that would keep Russia from getting involved.

From the Russian perspective, Serbia was all important. Not only did the Serbs help to protect Russian interests on the Balkan Peninsula, but as a Slavic state and declared ally of the Serbs, the Russian government could not afford to 'lose face' as they had done in 1908, when Austria-Hungary annexed Bosnia-Herzegovina unopposed. Russia's determination to protect Serbia was complicated by an ultimatum sent by the Austro-Hungarian empire to the Serbian government on 23 July, which demanded (among other things) that the Serbs hand sovereign authority over their judicial system to the Habsburgs or face war. The Austro-Hungarians did not want or expect that the Serbian government would accept the conditions of the ultimatum.[18] On the advice of the Russian government, however, Serbia nevertheless accepted all but the judicial demand on 25 July. But by this stage, Austria-Hungary was fixated on a short war and invaded Serbia on 28 July. Whether the war would remain localized in the Balkans, however, was not determined by the Austro-Hungarians. That fate depended on the decisions of the Russians and Germans. In the aftermath of the ultimatum, the Russian leadership estimated that only a show of military strength would inspire Austria-Hungary and Germany to keep from going through with the Serbian conflict. It issued its first pre-mobilization orders on 26 July (and mobilized its armies fully on 30 July). The Russian government had not behaved this aggressively towards another European great power since the conclusion of the Crimean War in 1856.

Significantly, neither of Russia's closest friends, France and Britain, made any serious moves to keep the Russians from taking these actions.[19] There is some evidence to suggest that the French even encouraged the Russians in taking a strong stance against the Austrians. After all, a Russian-German war would decrease the burden on the French to defeat a militarily stronger Germany in the future. Meanwhile, the British government did suggest a conference-style diplomatic solution to the Serbian crisis in keeping with the diplomatic practices of the past, but the suggestion was as good as ignored by the other powers. Instead, what began as an opportunity to advance the security needs of a weakened multi-ethnic empire (Austria-Hungary) quickly snowballed into a dangerous diplomatic crisis involving all the European great powers.

The speed of diplomatic communications only intensified the urgency of the crisis. Urgency rarely inspires wisdom. Given the fact that all the great powers also had detailed military plans in place that prioritized early mobilization to maximize the use of railways and seize a military advantage, the speed at which the July crisis deepened presented a recipe for disaster.[20] Given the size and scale of the military forces involved (Russia commanded a conscript army of nearly 6 million, Austria-Hungary 3 million, Germany 4.5 million and France 4 million), everyone recognized that a war between these powers was potentially calamitous. But if one side was to come out victorious, they also believed that it had to be the first to fully mobilize. As a result, any mobilization declaration by one power panicked the military commanders of the others. No matter how defensively minded, the mobilization of one resulted in the mobilization of all. Russia's mobilization decrees of 26 and 30 July thus risked the expansion of a Balkan war in unprecedented ways.

The military context was particularly hazardous for Germany, whose military blueprint for defeating Russia also involved going to war with France. In the context of the July crisis, the inflexibility of Germany's Schlieffen Plan accelerated the likelihood of a Europe-wide war.[21] Since the Germans did not have any alternate plans available that enabled a defensive mobilization aimed only at Russia, any German mobilization against Russia necessitated aggression against France. Furthermore, the Schlieffen Plan relied on a slow Russian mobilization and a speedy German mobilization so that France might be attacked and defeated in western Europe before Russia posed a threat to Germany's eastern borders.

Thus, when Russia began mobilizing its armed forces on 30 July in support of the Serbs, the German High Command was placed in an extremely difficult situation. It decided to put extra pressure on the German government to mobilize and prepare for war with France. Once it declared war on Russia on 1 August, Germany had to go to war with France, which it duly did on the night of 3 August. But not only did it go to war with France, it also invaded neutral Belgium and Luxembourg. The Schlieffen Plan imposed this course of action so that the French armies might be more easily defeated (as the Belgian-French border had fewer fortifications). Germany's declaration of war on two permanently neutral countries was highly significant. It was a blatant act of unprovoked aggression that undermined the basic principles on which the nineteenth-century international system were built. It enabled Germany's enemies to present the Central Powers (as the coalition between Germany, Austria-Hungary and, later, the Ottoman empire, was known) as the 'wrongdoers'. While Germany did not cause the crisis that brought about the First World War, its government's actions certainly aggravated the Serbian crisis and expanded what might have remained an east European war, localized in the Balkans, to the rest of Europe.

While Germany willingly breached Belgium's and Luxembourg's neutrality, it nevertheless predicated much of its pre-war planning on the expectation that Great Britain would remain neutral. Britain had, after all, declared its neutrality in all of Europe's wars since 1856. Much like the Austro-Hungarian government assumed that Russia would not dare risk general war over Serbia if the Germans were involved, the German government miscalculated what the British government would do when war came to western Europe. Decades of British commitment to neutrality and the protection of the freedom of the seas suggested a long-term British commitment to war avoidance. The success of the concert system since 1815 also depended, at least in part, on the willingness of great power states to avoid military involvement in the wars of their neighbours. And throughout the July crisis, it remained a close call. Right up until the German invasion of Belgium on the night of 3 August, the British cabinet prevaricated about its duties to France, to Russia and to Belgium (should Germany invade).[22] In the end, the possibility of a German hegemon appearing in Europe loomed as a frightful prospect: if Germany was victorious against France and Russia, it would become an unbeatable industrial and imperial competitor to the British empire. Britain's cabinet thus declared war on Germany late on 4 August 1914 in defence of its own global economic and imperial interests. In public, it presented its cause as one of justice and 'civilization', in defence of treaty law (by invading Belgium and Luxembourg, Germany had breached the 1839 Treaty of London), the protection of the sovereignty of small states and the principles of international law and neutrality that underwrote the international system. Almost as an afterthought, Britain and France declared war on Austria-Hungary on 12 August.

The momentum for a small localized war was lost somewhere between 23 July (when Austria-Hungary issued its ultimatum) and 28 July when its armies invaded Serbia and shelled its capital, Belgrade. In the space of four more days, the European great powers shifted the focus of their war planning from the Balkans to their shared borderlands in Galicia, Poland, Belgium and Alsace-Lorraine. A Balkan War had become a European war. But it was Britain's war declaration on 4 August that globalized the war in one foul swoop. That act made belligerents of the British empire's 446 million global subjects, turned every outpost of the European belligerent powers' empires into potential warzones and rendered the global economy a powerful tool of industrial warfare (see Figure 9.1).[23] No community situated anywhere on the complex web of interconnected networks of trade and communications that crisscrossed the globe was left untouched by these developments. Given its central importance to the machinations of the global web that was the international system in 1914, a neutral Britain might have kept the world from war, a belligerent Britain could not. The consequences of this development are explored in the next chapter.

Where then should we assign responsibility for the outbreak of the First World War? The governments of Austria-Hungary, Russia and Germany bear a lion's share of the blame for accentuating an avoidable crisis in a tense region. France and Britain might be blamed for not doing more to arbitrate or mediate those tensions. They certainly helped to globalize the consequences of the choices that were made by Europe's governing bodies. What we can say about the outbreak of war in July and early August 1914 is that a handful of aging European statesmen dragged the world into the maelstrom of calamitous conflict that would quickly become the First World War. If we read their actions kindly, we might argue that they did so 'by accident', that by aiming to avoid general war they actually (and accidentally) provoked it. Or as the British prime minister David Lloyd George at the time suggested, in July 1914 Europe 'slithered over the brink into the boiling cauldron of war'.[24]

But to call the outbreak of the First World War an 'accidental war' is to miss the obvious point that at no point between 1815 and July 1914 did these same great powers situate themselves in a similar predicament.[25] At all times in the hundred or so years before July 1914, the risk of a general war was deemed too great. Even the course and conduct of the Crimean War (which involved three European great powers and the Ottoman empire) was pockmarked with diplomatic restraint, great power neutrality and ambitions to limit and localize the spread and economic impact of the war. The contours of the two other major great power wars fought since 1856, namely the Franco-Prussian War of 1870–1 and the Russo-Japanese War of 1904–5, were determined in large part by the neutrality of the non-belligerent great powers. Slithering blindly into war was not something diplomats in the early twentieth century did easily or well.[26]

At any rate, the exercise of restraint and diplomatic cooperation had served the great powers well right up until July 1914. The Treaty of London signed at the conclusion of the first Balkan War in 1913, for example, involved all the European great powers even though none of them had fought in the war. That agreement aimed at mitigating the impact of the declining power of the Ottoman empire on the volatile Balkan region and on establishing a renewed equilibrium between a compliment of smaller ethnically cohesive states, including Serbia. In so doing, the great powers were continuing a long tradition of micromanaging and localizing international wars and crises in an attempt to keep themselves out of a disadvantageous conflict. It was not a case of avoiding all warfare but rather of minimizing the negative impact of becoming involved in a general war.[27] During the Boxer Rebellion crisis of 1899–1900, for example, the seven great powers (including Japan and the

United States) and several smaller imperial powers (like the Netherlands) even combined their efforts to suppress the Yihequan rebellion in China by sending troops and naval ships to the region. Their collective aim was to protect the Qing dynasty from collapse and thereby also protect their collective imperial interests in upholding the rights to their own treaty ports and trading rights in China.[28]

Likewise, during the Russo-Japanese War (1904–5), all the great powers aside from Russia and Japan remained determinedly neutral. They even collectively mobilized their diplomatic efforts to ensure that the two belligerents upheld the collective neutral rights of the other powers.[29] When these rights were breached – as Russia was particularly adept at doing – the neutrals governments did everything in their power short of going to war to force Russia and Japan's hands. In so doing, they aimed at localizing and minimizing the impact of the war on the international system as well as sustaining the general balance of power in Asia and China. Both Japan and Russia adapted their wartime practices to accommodate many (although not all) of these neutral governments' expectations. Furthermore, once it had obtained a military advantage over Russia, the Japanese government invited the president of the neutral United States, Theodore Roosevelt, to mediate the conflict. An early conclusion would be preferable to a drawn-out and expensive continuation of the war. The Russo-Japanese War signalled that for all the great powers, interstate warfare offered an effective tool of diplomacy but one to be used sparingly.

Thus, what was clearly different in July 1914 was the willingness of at least three great power governments (Austria-Hungary, Russia and Germany) to use a show of military force to effect diplomatic change. Some historians explain this willingness to utilize military power to enact foreign policy as an outcome of the growing imperial competitiveness between these states. Others attribute it to the failure of the concert system to protect the internal cohesion of the landed multi-ethnic empires. In both cases, they contextualize this imperial competition by focusing on the prevalence of militarism, arms races and a general tone of military one-upmanship in the public diplomacy exercised by these imperial rivals in the decades leading up to 1914.

Here again, the paradoxes of the time come to the fore. There is no doubt that the period 1890–1914 witnessed numerous arms and naval races between the industrial great powers, who expanded their conscript armies and invested in a range of new and powerful military equipment.[30] All the major powers, Japan and the United States included, invested vast sums of their wealth in expanding their military might. They also initiated a number of alliances so that the collective power of the Russians, British, French and Japanese could off-set that of the Germans, Austrians and Italians. In combination these alliances and military expansions helped to advance the oft-quoted maxim from the time, *si vi pacem para bellum* (if you want peace, prepare for war). Such acts were interpreted in part as a means of protecting the balance of power. Military deterrence aimed at avoiding war after all. Still most contemporaries also understood that military expansionism heightened the expectation of using that military power, which boosted popular perceptions of imperial rivalry, xenophobia and nationalism. Popular conceptions of war heightened in all these industrial empires in the years leading up to 1914.

In part, the growth in the militarization of the industrial empires was also a result of the exponential growth of the global armaments industry.[31] Like many successful nineteenth-century industries, most armaments firms were privately owned. They sold their wares on the global market to the highest bidder whenever possible. They made the most profit in time of war. A neutral state could (and often did) grow substantially wealthy from allowing its private citizens and firms to supply the wartime needs of the belligerents. The Balkan Wars (1911–13), for example, were supplied by the armaments firms of the world's neutral industrial states.[32] The profits neutrals could make from war highlight that neutrality, like much foreign policy, was rarely a benign enterprise. Wealthy governments, in turn, used their wealth to invest in armaments to bolster the security of their states and empires. As a result, the arms and naval races that evolved from the 1890s on were both a product of imperial rivalries and an ongoing agent of those rivalries. But they were also a product of the age of limited warfare and neutrality. For it behoved the economic and power interests of many states to remain neutral and supply the war needs of others rather than actually to go to war themselves.

As a result, we should not look for the origins of the First World War in the dynamics of the late-nineteenth-century industrial-military complex alone. As the historian David Stevenson argues, armaments may have been the 'wheels and pistons of the locomotive of history' but they were 'not the steam'.[33] Having said this, however, it is important to acknowledge that the global industrial armaments industry helped to determine the nature and impact of the global industrial war that evolved after July 1914 (for which see the next chapter). Similarly, while the existence of popular nationalism, militarism and imperial rivalry in the years leading up to 1914 are an important context for understanding the decisions made by the European governments to go to war in July 1914, they were not the driving reason for these governments' decisions either. Still, all these ideas were mobilized by the belligerent states once war broke out to mobilize support from their citizens and subjects for the conflict. They are then essential to understanding the nature of the war that evolved after July 1914.

It is also important to note that before 1914, many contemporaries were duly concerned about the potential impact of industrial warfare, arms races, conscription quotas and popular militarism. Popular nationalism, imperialism and militarism were not universally valued.[34] Citizens and subjects in all the world's industrial empires also questioned and protested their governments' political and material investments in warfare. Most socialists in the Second International, for example, were strident anti-militarists, advocating against conscription and warfare (even if some of them acknowledged the right and necessity of communities to defend themselves against attack and others expected a revolution 'from below' to be exacted by violent means). For their part, many liberal internationalists (most of whom were strident opponents of socialism) were advocates of international arbitration and aimed at improving the international laws of war to keep governments from going to war with each other. If these liberal internationalists had their way, interstate wars were to become less prevalent. Furthermore, they aimed at improving the laws of war to protect the rights of non-belligerents and thus sustain the global balance of interstate peace.

Like many of their contemporaries, both socialists and liberals frequently invoked the concept of 'civilization' to make a case for altering or improving (as they saw it) the international environment. As we have seen, by the early twentieth century, the concept of 'civilization' implied many things. Civilizational ideas sustained a deeply unequal, racially defined and divided international environment. But even when they were aware of these inequities, many contemporaries did not necessarily approach the concept of 'civilization' cynically. They endowed it with hope and ambition. Increasingly, the norms of 'civilized' behaviour, including the prescription that 'civilized' nation states should behave in 'civilized' ways towards each other and towards all communities, permeated the global media environment. Whether their representatives actually behaved in a 'civilized' manner or not, the notion that a 'civilized' state, its soldiers and agents should uphold the precepts of international law and act in a 'civil' manner was normalized. So much so, in fact, that media reports of warfare and state violence in the early 1900s frequently analysed whether these acts conformed to the laws of war or upheld the terms of any treaties signed by the parties involved in the violence.[35]

That all the great powers were actively involved in legislating the laws of international arbitration, war and neutrality at the two Hague conferences of 1899 and 1907 then was significant. They registered a willingness by the great power governments to expand the principles of diplomatic cooperation and war avoidance beyond Europe. Significant too was the fact that the first Hague conference evolved out of a request made by the Russian tsar Nicholas II in 1898 to reduce the collective burden of the existing arms races. No doubt, Nicholas II's rescript (as his announcement was called at the time) aimed to win time and give Russia a chance to catch up to the levels of armaments investment and production as their imperial rivals.[36] Certainly, none of the other great power governments wished to actually disarm. Yet the popular appeal of the rescript among the global newspaper-reading public forced these governments to discuss the issue alongside a range of other popular internationalist concepts, like international arbitration and the regulation of the laws of war.[37] The prospect of industrial warfare worried many.

Representatives of twenty-six countries, including the seven great powers, China, the Ottoman empire and a number of smaller states in Europe and Asia, attended the first Hague conference in 1899. In 1907, forty-four governments attended, including most of the Latin American countries. The second Hague conference represented the first genuinely global diplomatic forum in which almost all sovereign states in existence took part. Aside from making extraordinary strides in establishing universally applicable laws of war and neutrality, the Hague Conventions of 1899 and 1907 also established an international judicial forum, the Permanent Court of Arbitration, offering governments an accessible and universally recognized mechanism to solve interstate disputes. In all these ways, the Hague conferences signal how globally connected the diplomatic environment had become. They also heralded the power of international legal agreements and multilateral treaties to impose norms onto the international environment. The expansion of the Geneva Conventions, which were originally introduced in 1864 with twelve governments signing on, in 1906 expanded to include thirty-five signatory states. In combination, The Hague and Geneva conferences highlighted the power of internationalism and humanitarian idealism as alternative visions for guiding global interaction.[38]

Of course, the great powers dominated the negotiations at The Hague in 1899 and 1907 and Geneva in 1906. The agreed upon Hague and Geneva Conventions also spoke volumes about the power of these same industrial empires to dictate terms to the rest of the world. At one level, then, these multilateral forums highlight the power of the industrial empires to continue to micromanage the international environment in 'concert of Europe' style, extending their 'custodial duty' to international balance (as the political scientist Hedley Bull described the purpose of the Congress of Vienna) outwards over the whole world. At another level, they also reflect how the issues facing the major powers were no longer contained regionally within Europe but stretched globally and involved a greater number of states, peoples and international ambitions. At the very least, the Hague and Geneva negotiations highlight that concepts of international governance and multilateral negotiation were normalized and expected means of dealing with international concerns. Furthermore, these international conferences reinforced the notion that global interconnectedness made all political crises, wars and instances of state violence globally relevant events.[39]

The July crisis of 1914 was orchestrated by a small number of European elites. But the world watched the crisis unfold in their newspapers. From reading these reports, it is quite clear that they did not expect a European war to develop after the death of the Archduke Franz Ferdinand and Duchess Sophie. Even after Austria-Hungary's ultimatum to Serbia, many newspapers decried the possibility. The idea that a Balkan War would lead to global war was also considered unlikely. As the historian Michael Neiberg shows, most people at the time expected that the European governments would keep from going to war with each other as they had time and time again in the past.[40] When war did come, it was met by shock, confusion, fear and uncertainty.[41] It took the reality of war to harden attitudes on all sides, belligerent and neutral alike, as to why it was occurring and who was to blame. Regardless of their perspective, this war was unlike any seen before. The great powers who had preserved the peace of the seas for nigh on a century and had used that peace to advance their own power, wealth and glory and did so at the expense of millions of other people, now dragged themselves into a global industrial war that would prove calamitous.

Study questions

1. To what extent was the outbreak of the First World War an outcome of the collapse of the 'concert of Europe' system?

2. Do you agree with David Lloyd George that in 1914, the European great powers 'slithered over the brink into the boiling cauldron of war'? Was the war an 'accidental event'? Explain your reasoning.

3. Situate the British government's declaration of war on Germany on 4 August 1914 within a global context? What impact did this decision have globally?

4. What role do you think we should attribute to the following developments in explaining the outbreak of the First World War?

    a. ethnic nationalism
    b. imperial governance
    c. great power diplomacy
    d. popular militarism
    e. arms races
    f. internationalism

Recommended readings

Maartje Abbenhuis, *The Hague Conferences and International Politics 1898–1915*. Bloomsbury, 2018: Chapter 7 'When the world showed up: The second Hague conference, 1907' pp. 145–68 or Chapter 8 'City of peace: The Hague 1907–1915' pp. 169–84.

Hogler Afflerbach, 'The topos of improbable war in Europe before 1914' in Holger Afflerbach, David Stevenson, eds, *An Improbable War? The Outbreak of World War I in European Political Culture before 1914*. Berghahn, 2012, pp. 161–82.

C. A. Bayly, *The Birth of the Modern World 1780–1914*. Blackwell, 2004: Chapter 13 'Conclusion: The great acceleration c.1890–1914' pp. 451–67.

Eric Dorn Brose, *A History of the Great War: World War One and the International Crisis of the Early Twentieth Century*. Oxford UP, 2010: Chapter 1 'The long descent' pp. 3–20 and Chapter 2 'From peace to war' pp. 21–44.

Andrew Scott Keefer, 'An obstacle, though not a barrier: The role of international law in security planning during the *Pax Britannica*', *International History Review* 35, 5, 2013, pp. 1031–51.

Dominic Lieven, *Empire: The Russian Empire and its Rivals* Yale UP, 2001: 'Dilemmas of empire 1850–1917' pp. 274–87.

Gordon Martel, *The Month that Changed the World: July 1914*. Oxford UP, 2014: 'Prologue: The long European peace' pp. 22–55.

William Mulligan, *The Origins of the First World War*. Second edition, Cambridge UP, 2018: especially Chapter 2 'Security and expansion: The great powers and geopolitics, 1871–1914' pp. 25–94 and Chapter 6 'The July Crisis' pp. 210–29.

Eugene Rogan, *The Fall of the Ottomans: The Great War in the Middle East 1914–1920*. Penguin, 2015: Chapter 1 'A revolution and three wars 1908–1913' pp. 1–28.

Paul W. Schroeder, 'International politics, peace, and war, 1815–1914' in T. C. W. Blanning, ed., *Nineteenth Century: Europe 1789–1914*. Oxford UP, 2000, pp. 115–49.

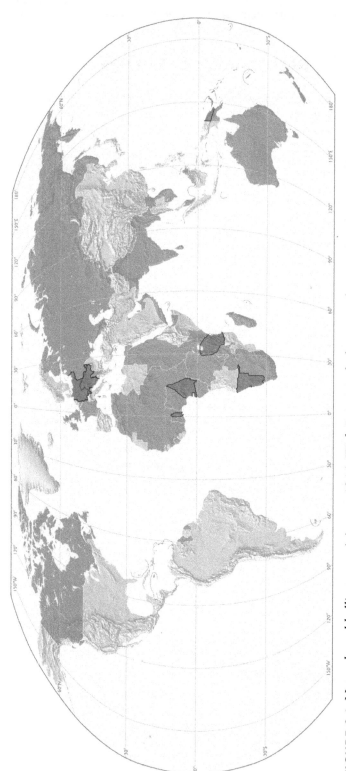

FIGURE 9.1 *Neutrals and belligerents, 4 August 1914. With Britain's declaration of war on Germany in the evening of 4 August 1914, the war globalized to the outposts of the British, German and French empires. This map highlights the various belligerents in dark grey (the British, German and French empires. This map highlights the various belligerents in dark grey (the Central Powers marked in extra dark grey) and the rest of the neutral world in very light grey.*
Source: Igor Drecki (designer), 2018.

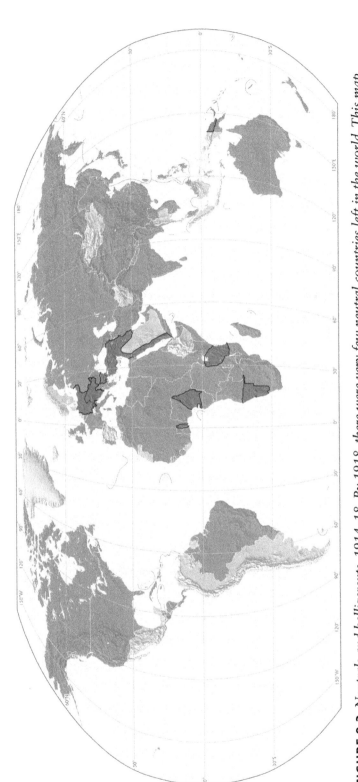

FIGURE 9.2 *Neutrals and belligerents, 1914–18. By 1918, there were very few neutral countries left in the world. This map shows all the belligerents (in dark grey, with the Central Powers marked in darkest grey) who fought in the war, leaving only a few neutrals.*

Source: Igor Drecki (designer), 2018.

10

Industrial globalization at total war, 1914–18

In his book *South America and the First World War*, the historian Bill Albert explains how decisive the impact of the war was on the South American continent, this despite the fact that for much of the 1914–18 period the Latin American states were neutral and geographically removed from any military theatre by an entire ocean.[1] Albert opens his volume by describing how the remote Canete valley in Peru, a region situated 150 kilometres south of the city of Lima and reachable only by coastal steamer or horseback ride, was affected by the outbreak of war. Much of the Canete valley was planted in cotton and sugar crops aimed for the export market. The region employed about three thousand workers. On 10 August 1914, Canete's sub-prefect called a meeting of local merchants and estate owners to discuss the burgeoning crisis. They well understood that with Britain's declaration of war on Germany on 4 August, the global economy ground to a halt: uncertainty about the reliability of the seas (might a ship be attacked by a warship, sunk by a mine or captured as a prize?), the availability of shipping insurance (if any of the above happened), the accessibility of belligerent ports and even the value of money itself only heightened the anxiety. Around the world, merchant and passenger ships lay idle in ports, crops rotted on docks, shops emptied of goods, banks closed their doors and stock markets stopped trading. As the historian Richard Roberts explains, within the space of a few days, the 'whole elaborate mechanism' that was the nineteenth-century age of international finance 'broke down'.[2]

As Albert describes it, as of 4 August 1914, Canete's 'life support system had been disconnected'.[3] The same was true for much of the rest of the world.[4] The impact was immediate. Fearing the worst, the Peruvians at the

10 August Canete meeting discussed how best to alleviate pending food shortages, rising unemployment and social unrest. The sub-prefect sought support from his colleagues to request relief from the Peruvian government, hoping it would send cash to the region so that workers could be paid in the short-term. Given that many of the sugar plantations in Canete were funded by British bank loans or owned by British investors, they considered not only the immediate emergency but also the potential long-term impact of a global war involving a belligerent Britain.[5] Their concerns were well-founded. Peru's larger cities were also experiencing intense disruptions, including the closure of banks, factories and workshops. In the end, many of Canete's plantations shut down or cut production with drastic consequences for the well-being of the local population.[6]

Similar stories of crisis and anxiety can be found across the neutral world.[7] In the neutral Netherlands, for example, the government took strenuous steps to vouchsafe the economic stability of the nation. The Amsterdam and Rotterdam stock exchanges had already closed on 29 July. By 3 August, shops ran out of essential goods, people emptied their bank accounts and sought payment in silver and gold (as opposed to paper money). Government and municipal authorities responded by issuing a series of emergency decrees: they allowed banks to shut their doors (to keep them from bankruptcy); they distributed emergency paper currency to replace silver coinage (so that workers could be paid and everyday purchases be made); they issued price guarantees and requisitioned essential goods (so that farmers and merchants would not profiteer too greatly from the public's panic-buying instinct); and they discussed how to protect the longer-term social and economic stability of the country and its empire when their immediate neighbours (Belgium, Germany and Great Britain) were at war.[8] On the other side of the globe, the residents in the cosmopolitan and neutral port city of Shanghai were just as worried. Unemployment skyrocketed as ships lay idle and no new orders for silk (a luxury at the best of times) came in for the local silk industry to supply. Money became scarce as banks and gold shops shut down and Shanghai's stock market closed.[9] For all these neutral communities, fears about the impact of a longer-term economic crisis occasioned by the war were all too pressing. They shared these anxieties with almost every community connected to the global economy, be it belligerent or neutral. Even in the industrial powerhouse economy of the United States and in Japan, the weeks immediately following the outbreak of war were crisis-torn.

With good reason, much of the history written about the First World War focusses on the European continent. After all, the war began in Europe and was orchestrated by the European great powers. Within days, it pitted 18 million soldiers against each other along massive battlefronts in Poland, Galicia, Belgium, northern France and Serbia. By December 1914, many millions of these troops counted among the war's ever-growing list of casualties, either killed, captured or seriously wounded, including a third of the Russian army (a staggering 1.4 million men).[10] Millions of civilians in these same regions also fell victim to the waves of war which destroyed their homes, farms, villages, towns and cities, leaving them either displaced as refugees or ravaged by the personal violence that so often accompanies the advance of armies in the field. Invasion, occupation and the destruction of land, property and lives became an increasingly common experience across Europe from August 1914 on. This violence did not let up over the ensuing years. There is no question that the First World War was the most deleterious conflict to have impacted Europe up to this point of time.

But to concentrate on the importance of the war for Europe and Europeans alone fails to acknowledge the global contours of the conflict. For as of 4 August 1914 and thanks to the globally connected industrial economy and the fact that many of the European belligerents ruled over a 'blue-water' empire, the war in Europe dragged the rest of the world into its maelstrom. By analysing the contours of the world of war between 1914 and 1918, the full extent of the interconnected reality of the 'first age of industrial globalization' comes to the fore and does so in the starkest and most profound of forms. For the war of 1914–18 not only altered the future of Europe, it also altered the future of the world.

That the stakes in the war were global were recognized by the great power belligerents from the outset. On the night of 4 August, the British Royal Navy cut Germany's all important trans-Atlantic telegraph cable.[11] On 6 August, a joint British-French military expedition invaded German-controlled Togo, destroying Germany's key telegraph station in Africa.[12] Alongside the blockade of Germany's North Sea and Baltic ports, the ability of the Central Powers to continue their international business and trade arrangements, let alone their global communications or overseas travels were seriously hampered. After 4 August 1914, they either had to use neutral communication channels or enemy ones, which posed the risk of surveillance and attack. Either way, the Central Powers' ability to sustain their global interactions were seriously compromised.

The invasion of Togo set of a series of further attacks by the Allies on German colonies globally. By late August, New Zealand soldiers invaded the islands of German Samoa while Australians captured German-held Papua New Guinea within the following fortnight.[13] Both actions aimed at removing Germany's ability to use these colonies as coaling stations and as telegraph hubs. For their part, a German naval squadron patrolled the vast Pacific Ocean looking to hamper Allied shipping and sink Allied warships. On 22 August, the SMS *Scharnhorst* and *Gneisenau* bombarded the French Tahitian port town of Pape'ete causing substantial damage to the town and killing two civilians. The war's violence did not stay contained in Europe.[14]

In Africa, the military campaigns initiated on 6 August only expanded. By February 1915, South African troops had invaded German South-West Africa (present-day Namibia). In central Africa, German-friendly Tutsi tribes attacked rival Hutu communities in Belgian-controlled Congo. Eventually, the Belgian government would lead an expeditionary force made up of mostly local African soldiers and thousands of conscripted labourers and porters against neighbouring German territories in Burundi and Rwanda. The war fought in East Africa (in and around present-day Tanzania) was even more devastating. The German commander Paul von Lettow-Vorbeck amassed a sizeable army, which fought British- and (later) Portuguese-led troops in a lengthy guerrilla campaign that lasted for the entirety of the war. Both sides requisitioned food, cattle and labourers from locals without consideration of their impact, which was nothing short of calamitous. More than a million East Africans died in direct service of these military campaigns.[15] Many more suffered from the short- and long-term consequences of the war situation. The Wagogo people of Tanzania, for example, ascribe the word 'Mtunya' (the scramble) to the drought that followed the military requisitioning of their cattle, produce and people. Mtunya evoked the worst possible of consequences: abandoned villages, empty fields, starvation, death, even cannibalism and the sale of children into enslavement.[16] The social cohesion of the Ugogo communities failed to recover from Mtunya. Only the Wagogo elite managed to hold on to their cattle and manoeuvred their positions of wealth to extend power and control over the rest. The First World War was as destructive in this part of the world as anywhere else.

If in August 1914, the great power belligerents harboured hopes that the war might be short-lived and conducted according to the 'limited war' principles of the past, by December 1914 it was clear that any 'business as usual' model of warfare was doomed. A 'short war' proved unwinnable. The western front in Europe had stalemated across a 400-kilometre line of entrenched defences that would over the coming years draw in millions more soldiers and support staff, including hundreds of thousands of non-European troops and labourers. In eastern Europe the picture was no less dire. Meanwhile, the Austro-Hungarian invasion of Serbia resulted in a wave of more than three hundred thousand refugees (a third of Serbia's population) attempting to flee Austrian occupation across the country's mountainous border regions. Tens of thousands died along the way. By war's end, 150,000 Serbs would die of typhus.[17]

The shift to a long-war strategy that occurred in all belligerent societies in December 1914 was fundamental. It entailed recognition by both sets of belligerents that victory now depended on the effectiveness of the resourcing of their war effort. The side that could out outproduce its enemies in terms of weaponry, military equipment, food and fuel supplies and in terms of human labour (be it as soldiers or industrial and agricultural workers) had a decisive advantage on the battlefield. The prospect of victory was tied to a state's ability to mobilize all available resources and, thus, also to target and destroy the human and material resources of its enemies. No one, be they soldier or civilian, neutral or belligerent was left unaffected by this shift to global economic warfare. In this 'total war' (*guerre totale*), as the French journalist Léon Daudet described the conflict in 1916, everything and everyone was under siege, including all 'political, economic, commercial, industrial, intellectual, legal and financial domains'.[18]

In this industrial war, the odds favoured the Allies, who could mobilize more wealth, global resources and, ultimately, industrial capacity than their enemies.[19] This was especially true after the United States joined the British, French and Russian side in April 1917. But no European state came out of this war enriched. All the European belligerents were bankrupted by the phenomenal costs of sustaining millions of soldiers in the field with the latest industrial weaponry and ammunition. By 1918, the French government had borrowed 175.5 billion francs, which accounted for 83.4 percent of its total budget that year.[20] The German government owed more than 101 billion Reichsmarks,[21] while Britain's national debt had grown to 5.9 billion pounds while it also underwrote the bank loans of its French and Russian allies in the United States.[22] The Ottoman and Austro-Hungarian empires, for their part, were respectively spending 360 and 528 percent more than their revenue income that year.[23] These financial costs had an inevitable impact on the domestic economies and social and political cohesion of all the affected states and played a key hand in determining the contours of the post-war economic and diplomatic order.

From early 1915 on, the waging of the First World War expanded in unprecedented ways and did so as a global phenomenon. The principle of victory at (almost) any cost rapidly magnified the war's violence. The conflict drew in increasing numbers of belligerents, a development that made upholding neutrality and the principles of diplomatic restraint that had defined the 'concert system' during the nineteenth century increasingly difficult. In this respect, the First World War was a system-breaking conflict. By 1918, only a very few states managed to remain neutral (see Figure 9.2) and even these suffered from the socio-economic impact of the global war. By 1918, out of a total global population of 1.8 billion people, more than 1.4 billion were officially at war (see Table 10.1). The 1914–18 conflict brought the 'first age of industrial globalization' to an end and brought a highly volatile 'second age of industrial globalization' into being, an era which the historian Eric Hobsbawm so poignantly describes as the 'age of extremes'.[24]

There are many ways to chart the fundamental impact of the First World War on the systemic principles of the 'first age of industrial globalization'. An ideal

TABLE 10.1 Belligerent populations, 1914–18

In millions of people

Country	End 1914	End 1916	End 1918
Allies			
Russia empire	176.4		
French empire	87.8		
British empire	446.1		
Serbia (and region)	7		
Liberia	1.5		
Japanese empire	74.2		
Italian empire		37.6	
Portuguese empire		14.7	
Romania		7.7	
United States empire			106.3
Latin America			34
Greece			4.8
Siam (Thailand)			8.4
China			441.5
Total	**793.3**	**853.3**	**1,271.7**
Central Powers			
German empire	61.3		
Austria-Hungary	67		
Ottoman empire	23		
Bulgaria		4.8	
Total	**151.3**	**156.1**	**156.1**

Source: Stephen Broadberry, Mark Harrison, 'The economics of World War One: An overview' in Stephen Broadberry, Mark Harrison, eds, *The Economics of World War One*. Cambridge UP, 2005.

one is presented by the war's impact on neutral states and on the international economy. In late July and early August 1914, many governments declared their country's neutrality according to the requirements of international law. They expected that the belligerent powers would respect these rules, not least because they had only recently been ratified at the Hague conferences of 1899 and 1907 and in the Declaration of London of 1909. As noted at the outset of this chapter, however, as soon as Britain went to war, it was all too obvious that the conflict would in no way resemble 'business as usual'. As the historian Mark Bailey shows, new financial, insurance and trade systems had to be created to accommodate the change to total economic warfare.[25]

The shift to total war was fundamental to neutrals and belligerents alike.[26] From early 1915 on, neutral governments, neutral merchants and neutral banks had to balance their interests with those of the competing belligerents for war supplies, war loans and preferential economic treatment.[27] Sustaining a country's neutrality was no longer an automatic right nor only an exercise of upholding the international laws that dictated the rights and duties of neutral states and protecting territorial neutrality (although those requirements were trying enough). Increasingly, neutral governments conducted lengthy and complex diplomatic negotiations to sustain their own rights to economic security, international trade and supplies. Their populations projected their own moralized representations of neutrality and its humanitarian value outwards into the world of war.[28] Still, the idea that neutrals were little more than war profiteers also proliferated. Certainly, many neutrals grew wealthy by supplying the belligerents with all their wartime needs. This was especially true in 1915 and 1916 and remained true for the United States throughout the war. But by 1917, as the war at sea in the Atlantic and Mediterranean heightened, and increasing numbers of neutral ships were sunk or intercepted by the belligerent navies, most neutral economies and societies also faltered under the strain of rising inflation and widespread shortages.

The choice to join the war was not always left to the neutral either. Much like Belgium and Luxembourg were invaded, neutral Persia (Iran) and Greece succumbed to the will of the major belligerents.[29] Other neutral governments chose for belligerency seeking to maximize the potential advantages of doing so. Japan, for example, declared war on Germany on 23 August 1914. The outbreak of war in Europe left a decisive power-vacuum in the Asia-Pacific region, which Japan all too readily looked to fill. It invaded the German–Chinese concession port of Qingdao late in August. It also captured the German-controlled Marshall, Caroline and Mariana Islands and Jaluit Atoll.[30] As European merchants disappeared from the region, Japanese merchants replaced them. Across the war years, the value of the Japanese export market tripled, its shipping tonnage doubled and its investment in the plantation economies in the region grew alongside.[31] By 1917, Japan controlled

55 percent of the Pacific mercantile trade market, which in 1914 had been dominated by British merchants.[32] These developments had a decisive impact on Japan's post-war status as a key power in the region. It also guaranteed ongoing rivalry with the United States.[33]

The Ottoman empire chose for war on the side of the Central Powers as quickly as the Japanese chose to support the Allies. Its government recognized that any war involving the European great powers and Russia would leave it vulnerable to attack and to the whims of the victors. Better to be on the side of victory. On 31 October 1914, the Ottoman empire formally went to war, opening up major military fronts against the Russians in the Caucasus and Persia and against the British and French empires in Mesopotamia and northern Africa. Sultan Mehmed V globalized the conflict in a different way when in November, he declared *jihad* (holy war) against his empire's enemies. *Jihad* was both a call to arms for his Muslim subjects to support the war effort at home as it was a call for Muslims globally to undermine the stability of the Russian French and British empires from within.[34]

When the Italian government chose to declare its neutrality in August 1914, despite a pre-existing alliance with both Germany and Austria-Hungary, it did so to protect the viability of its north African empire. It particularly feared the loss of Abyssinia (Ethiopia), where the local population was already waging a series of successful military campaigns to remove the Italian administration. At any rate, many Italians professed a distinct dislike for war and were particularly incensed at the German invasion of neutral Belgium. When the Italian government choose to join the war on the side of the Allies on 23 May 1915, it aimed at extending Italy's borders into Austria-Hungary and to augment its status as a major power in Europe.[35] Only in victory could it sustain that position. For remarkably similar reasons, Bulgaria joined the Central Powers in October 1915, aiming to extend its regional power, while neighbouring Romania became a belligerent on the side of the Allies in August 1916, although it soon succumbed to German occupation.[36]

The only great power that remained neutral by the end of 1914 was the United States. Its geographic distance from Europe helped its government's decision to remain neutral for the time being. From the outset, its business and governing elite recognized the advantages neutrality presented to maximize the United States' geostrategic location. The opening up of the Panama Canal on 15 August, within days of the onset of the war, made its neutrality even more lucrative: linking the east and west coasts of the United States more readily and giving easy access to the Asia-Pacific economy to all North and South American business ventures (see Figure 10.1). As a neutral with a growing merchant marine, it could also reach the belligerent economy of Great Britain and France relatively easily (at least until Germany's unrestricted U-boat campaign of 1917).[37] And until the Allies intercepted too much of its

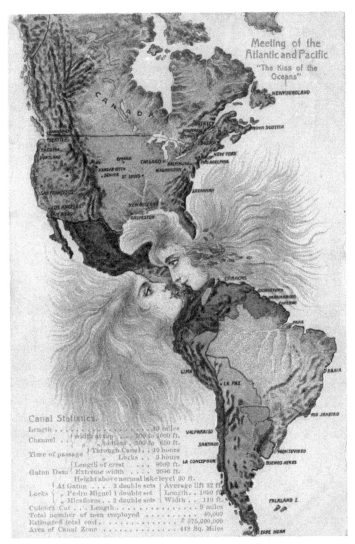

FIGURE 10.1 *The opening of the Panama Canal, 1914. This American postcard from 1914 advertised the key importance of the opening of the Panama Canal for connecting the Atlantic and Pacific Oceans. From this point on, ships no longer had to navigate around the treacherous Tierra del Fiego to get from the United States east coast to its west coast. The Panama Canal shortened the length of journeys and thus accelerated the growth of the United States economy. The (unexpected) congruence of the outbreak of the First World War with the Panama Canal's opening offered the neutral United States and ideal opportunity to maximize its access to the global economy and to supply the needs of the major power belligerents in the war.*

Source: 'Oceans kiss' postcard, 1914, Getty Images, 658649812.

trade going to the neutral countries bordering Germany, it could even expand its export market share in Germany and Austria-Hungary. Its banks and financial institutions happily extended credit to warring and neutral enterprises alike, its relative financial stability presenting an attractive alternative to the beleaguered British and French money and insurance markets.

The impact of United States neutrality in the years 1914 to 1917 cannot be overstated. Across those years, the United States turned from being a country that owed money to others (mainly the British), to becoming the world's primary creditor.[38] In 1916, 40 percent of all British war expenditure was spent in the United States, while 65 percent of American exports went to Britain.[39] By 1917, New York, not London, sat at the heart of the global economy. The United States' rise to superpower status in the twentieth century was propelled forward by this shift. Even when it did go to war in 1917, its position at the centre of the global economy only strengthened, making the fate of the world's neutrals even more dire. For without the diplomatic weight of the United States sustaining the principles of neutrality after April 1917, the smaller neutral states' claims to neutral rights were increasingly difficult to uphold. Neutrality may not have 'died' during the war (as some international lawyers and political commentators at the time argued), but its systemic functions had fundamentally altered.[40] In the post-war era, the newly established League of Nations would even try to outlaw neutrality, favouring the principle of collective security to protect the world from undesirable warfare.

Another way to describe the global implications of the First World War is to register the central role played by the conflict in the activities of the belligerents' subject peoples. In the nineteenth century, it was possible for contemporaries to separate at a conceptual level an interstate conflict from an imperial war or instance of state violence. The more astute among them, might also have recognized how each 'type' of warfare played a key role in sustaining the generic principles of the international system that protected the collective power of the industrializing empires. The frequent wars of this 'age of limited warfare' were contained in large part by the collective agreement of the great powers to avoid going to war with each other. In the context of the 1914–18 total war, however, those conceptual distinctions rarely held up, not least because the war between empires offered both opportunities and incentives for local communities to mould to their advantage and for the belligerent governments to use in aid of their own imperial ambitions.

Consider, for example, the stakes for Hutu and Tutsi peoples in central Africa. The context of the German–Belgian War enabled Tutsi cattle raiders to justify their activities against Hutu clans. In retaliation and with their own expansionism in mind, Hutu leaders supported the subsequent Belgian-led military campaigns in Burundi and Rwanda. For these Africans, the white people's war presented opportunities as well as costs. Tens of thousands of them became porters to the Belgian *Force Publique*, many of them subsequently died.[41] Along the borderlands of Persia and the Ottoman empire, the context of a global war and *jihad* pitted Muslims against Christians in the most violent ways. Kurdish chieftains also maximized the circumstances of the great power war to maximize their own fiefdoms in Persia and Azerbaijan.[42]

Meanwhile, other subject communities mobilized their governments' calls for material support as a rallying cry for greater political representation in their empire. French government promises to extend full citizenship to subject communities in Africa and Indo-China helped to recruit thousands of troops for the warfronts in Europe, Africa and the Middle East (see Figure 10.2). Vietnamese women even migrated to France to work in its weapons factories.[43] In India, the hope of greater independence and even self-rule, propelled many elites to support the British war effort.[44] Not only did more than half a million Indians serve in the British armed forces during the war, the vast Indian population supported the imperial war effort by subscribing to war loan schemes.[45] Furthermore, indigenous communities across the British empire used the language of imperial citizenship and the political opportunism of showing loyalty to the crown as a pathway to greater political representation and recognition.

FIGURE 10.2 *Algerians mobilize for war, 1914. This photograph from August 1914, captures the mobilization of French colonial troops in the North African port of Algiers at the outbreak of the First World War. These Algerian soldiers were destined to fight on the western front of the European theatre of war.*
Source: Getty Images, 481657727.

Many of these communities would be bitterly disappointed not only by the extreme costs of the war on their communities but also by the fact that they witnessed few improvements to their situation after 1918. By and large, disillusionment also accompanied the many promises and treaties the belligerent great powers initiated with other non-European communities during the war that aimed at helping one or other side defeat their enemies. This included agreements with Arab tribes, Palestinian communities and Zionists, who looked for a Jewish homeland in Palestine. In this respect, the First World War did not disrupt the 'global colour line' all that much. Still, the war marked a key shift in the willingness of subject peoples to accept the 'right to rule' of the imperial powers. The calls for political equality, self-determination and sovereignty only heightened in 1917 and 1918. They infused imperial politics and heightened outbreaks of rebellion and resistance, which only expanded after 1918. Decolonization and the break-up of the nineteenth-century's industrial empires were a marked feature of the 'second age of industrial globalization', although it would take another global total war to expedite these processes.

In the context of these non-European war experiences, the ongoing workings of a global press (much of it mobilized across neutral territory and communication channels) were also highly significant. They remind us that the world watched and assessed the war by reading and hearing about it. When Sanusiyya and Senussi Muslim communities rebelled against British and French authorities in northern Africa during the war, they did so as part of a long campaign against European power that had begun well before August 1914.[46] Still, their wartime efforts were particularly forceful given the context of global war, *jihad* and the opportunism it afforded for potential success.[47] The anti-imperial war declared by the Kuki people against the British crown in north-east India in 1917 was in part a protest against the recruitment of labourers for the war effort, a war which the Kuki understood to be foreign, dangerous and conducted by the most murderous of weapons. At any rate, as the Kuki explained it at the time, 'they had no quarrel with Germany and why should they go and fight the Germans? They said they would commit suicide rather than go [to Europe]'.[48]

When Irish revolutionaries rebelled against the British state in 1916 during what would become known as the Easter Rising, they did so hoping to capitalize on Britain's stressed position in the war. The point here is that the world of war between 1914 and 1918 displayed many faces of conflict and violence, all of which were representative of both local and imperial agency and global interconnections. The war years heightened the agency and alertness of many communities to define their lives in opposition to the imperial governments who were responsible for the continuation of the global war. As the historian Bill Nasson argues, the war context proved a rich fertilizer for identity politics and heightened anti-imperial activism everywhere.[49]

Neutral populations were as reflective about the war, its violence and local and global impacts as any belligerent community. In the cosmopolitan communities of the United States, for example, the war was a contested reality. As the historian Jennifer Keene explains, Americans 'engaged intellectually, politically and financially with the war's multiple fronts' and did so by foregrounding the issues and values that mattered most to them. Thus, American progressives fixated on the German invasion of Belgium and the threat Germany posed to undoing 'civilization' and the rule of international law; African Americans focused on the war in Africa and fought by Africans; while Jewish Americans fixated on the pogroms in Russia and on developments relating to Palestine.[50] In similar ways, the *émigré* populations of Argentina, which included Syrian Ottomans, Jews and Europeans of every nationality, also framed their wartime agency in terms of the conduct and progress of the war. As the historian Steven Hyland explains, 'The carnage meted out on the fields of Europe [and the Middle East] mobilised advocates and immigrants, politicians and intellectuals … to pursue a variety of responses, confront rival groups, and articulate competing demands.'[51] The complexity and range of their responses suggests not only how readily available information about the global war was but also how neutrals could impact the course of the war. After all, neutral trade and bank loans sustained the conflict as much as neutral humanitarian aid (in the form of ambulance units, Red Cross parcels, food transports and refugee and prisoner-of-war support) attempted to alleviate some its more adverse impacts.[52]

In this context, the exponential expansion of state violence around the world in the 1914–18 period is telling. On the battlefields of Europe and the Middle East, industrial warfare created veritable hell-scapes of artillery bombardments, gas attacks, machine-gun fire and barbed-wire entrapments to which millions of men (and a large number of women, who worked mainly in logistical support roles) succumbed. The production of faster and stronger aeroplanes revolutionized warfare: they were utilized for reconnaissance and surveillance and for the bombing of military and civilian targets. By 1918, 288,000 military aircraft had been built, where in 1914 there were only a thousand military planes in existence altogether.[53] These planes ensured that no population was now safe from war. Even some neutral countries had bombs 'accidentally' dropped on them with deadly results.[54] Treating the physical and psychological wounds of the victims of all these fronts also revolutionized modern medicine, surgical methods and psychiatry.

But even this military violence only presented the tip of a very large iceberg of destruction and violence that permeated the world between 1914 and 1918. The historian Annette Becker describes the First World War as the 'laboratory' for all twentieth-century state violence.[55] As an example, consider the wartime stakes for the subject peoples of the Ottoman empire. At the outset of the conflict, the Ottoman state forced 1.1 million Greeks to move from the empire's European border regions for fear they would start a fifth-column attack in support of the Allies.[56] As refugees many of these Greek families fell victim to police actions of the Ottoman state. The fate of the empire's Armenian subjects was equally dire. Given the geostrategic and historical significance which the empire's Turkish leadership placed on the Caucasus, removing any chance of political rebellion from its Armenian Christian population was a paramount concern. As of April 1915, Armenians were forcibly eradicated from the region. The ensuing violence, which included death marches, massacres, concentration camps and starvation tactics, equated to *genocide* (a word that would be invented in the aftermath of the war to describe the orchestrated mass slaughter of an ethnic or religious community) and resulted in the death of at least 1.5 million Armenians. That at least 2.5 million (and perhaps as many as 5 million) civilian subjects also died during the war due to the inability of the Ottoman government to distribute foodstuffs effectively reflected the serious and highly violent impact of this global total war. In Persia too, starvation and anarchy infused the war years. As the historian Mustafa Aksakal so powerfully describes it, the First World War incinerated the social fabric of the Middle East.[57] Meanwhile, the Russians initiated pogroms against the Jewish population of Galicia and the Muslim population in the Caucasus.

By 1917, the global war had skewed the global distribution of available goods and resources. The blockade of the European continent by the Allies and the expansion of German unrestricted submarine warfare, meant very little global shipping could get through. This economic warfare had an immediate impact on the well-being of all Europeans akin to developments in the Middle East and Africa. In Germany, Austria-Hungary, Russia and much of eastern and southern Europe, food and fuel shortages resulted in serious health defects and, in some places, starvation.[58] Even neutral European countries were affected resulting in their governments introducing new and higher taxes and greater controls over rationing and employment.

That belligerents and neutrals were jointly responsible for sustaining wartime suffering was also not lost on contemporaries. Furthermore, the war years inspired on-going consideration of what a post-war peace would look like and what values would underwrite a post-war international system.[59] How would global power be distributed at the end of the conflict? What impact would the rise of the United States as the world's new economic powerhouse have on the world order? What function would international law have in this global order given that so many laws of war were ignored during this conflict? As the war lengthened, the ability of the great power governments to understand or control its myriad impacts declined.

Above all, the 1914–18 war undid the power of the great power governments to micromanage global affairs. For one, as the costs of the war spiralled out of control even more pressure was brought to bear on belligerent communities to sacrifice even more of their people and resources. It also ensured that the European belligerents (as opposed to the United States and Japan) bankrupted themselves to pay for the war. In combination with their inability to effectively manage the global distribution of food and fuel stuffs, money and goods, the collective social impact was as revolutionary as it was global. These revolutions came to a head in 1917.

The historian Jay Winter describes 1917 as the 'climacteric' year of the war.[60] He argues that global developments during this year confirmed that the conflict, which in 1914 began as a war between states and empires and one in which subjects and citizens largely supported their governments, had turned into a revolutionary conflict, in which most communities were no longer willing to accept their governments' warmongering. Across the world, people took to the streets to protest the immense personal and societal costs of keeping the war effort going. It was this mass social movement 'from below', which was largely uncoordinated and reflective of a deep dissatisfaction among soldiers and civilians alike, that endangered the political cohesion of most of the world's empires. Few states and governments survived the ensuing years of political crisis and revolutionary violence unchanged.

Within the space of another twelve months, in fact, four of the world's great power empires collapsed completely including Russia, Austria-Hungary, the Ottomans and Germany. Britain and France had to accommodate major political changes as well. The April and October revolutions of 1917 in Russia exemplified the characteristics of this new age of global unrest. After October 1917, Russia descended into a lengthy civil war that lasted until 1923 and pitted Russians against Russians and the Red Army of the new Soviet regime against anti-communists, ethnic nationalists and numerous foreign governments. Ironically, more Russians died and suffered during this civil war than had done so between 1914 and 1917. The consolidation of the Soviet Union would, nevertheless, help to define the political dimensions of the 'second age of industrial globalization'. Soviet global power and economic precepts also distinguished this 'second age' from the political principles that defined the nineteenth-century global age of conservative monarchism, free trade liberalism and industrial imperialism.

The other reason why 1917 marked such a key divide in the war was the entry of the United States into the conflict as a belligerent. Alongside Japan, the United States was one of only a few states that came out of the war with its economy thriving and its global power on the rise. But even in the United States the social impact of the war registered as politically decisive. Real wages fell across the war years and inflation was of serious concern.[61] Moreover, the expansion of wartime industrial production occasioned a massive demographic shift mainly by African Americans from the southern states moving north into the growing industrial cities. By 1918, the United States experienced numerous strikes, race riots and urban protests in response to the socio-economic malaise of the times. Workers took to the streets demanding better pay and an end to war profiteering and inflation. In the neutral Netherlands, Switzerland and Spain, similar grievances also resulted in serious political upheavals in 1917 and 1918 leading to fundamental constitutional changes.[62] In the Latin American states, some of which had also declared war on Germany in 1917, the social and economic upheaval of the last two war years resulted in strikes, protests and political uncertainty. As the historian Olivier Compagnon describes them, their demands for change were 'explicitly associated' with the war and 'called for peace in Europe' as well as improved wages and better provisioning of essential food and fuel stuffs.[63]

Japanese society was also not immune to the socio-economic impacts of the war. Although the Japanese state grew its wealth, its banks became creditors to the Chinese and to the European powers and its trade and industry flourished, the country was not immune from rising inflation and its associated social costs.[64] As industrialization flourished, the war years witnessed a 17 percent growth in the size of Japanese cities. But their slums increased in size too.[65] The growth in Japanese rice production aimed to meet the rising demand of foreign buyers. But as rice was exported at the highest of prices, the cost of purchasing this staple grew for Japanese consumers as well. By 1917, the country suffered from a rice shortage and even with an increase of imports from Korea (at the cost of local Koreans) and the imposition of an Anti-Profiteering Law, its government could not prevent a series of strikes and 'rice riots' breaking out. These riots were not only a product of the heightened cost of living (which was 223 percent higher in 1918 than in 1914) but also a protest against the 'wantonly wasteful' lifestyles of the growing class of newly rich war profiteers and the rising disillusionment of the thousands of urban slum dwellers with their wartime lives.[66]

Meanwhile signs that the post-war global order would not tolerate the rule of the remaining industrial empires also grew. Anti-imperial resistance in India, Ireland, Senegal and the Middle East made the fate of the British and French empires increasingly uncertain. They nevertheless extended protectorates over much of the Middle East after 1918, eyeing up essential oil reserves and ensuring the ongoing instability of a region that continues to plague the world today. Their smaller European allies also faced serious challenges to their imperial power. The Italians, for example, lost any pretence of exercising control over Abyssinia, when Haile Selassie, heir to the Solomonic throne and revered messiah of the Rastafari movement, established himself as regent in 1916. In Italy, only protests met the disastrous military defeat at the battle of Caporetto in 1917. It is in the context of these disastrous campaigns and intense economic suffering among the Italian population that a new strain of militant nationalism came to dominate the Italian political landscape. Benito Mussolini's fascist party would rise to power in 1922 and inspire numerous radical populist movements across the world. Militant populist nationalism would feature brightly in the ensuing 'second age of industrial globalization'.

For China the whole 1914–18 period represented what many Chinese described as *weiji* (great crisis, literally 'danger opportunity').[67] Unlike the Napoleonic Wars, in which a non-belligerent Qing empire managed to sustain and grow its international power, the First World War saw China's government look anxiously outwards. Because the European great powers were fixated on the war, they did not have the resources or diplomatic ability to protect their 'open door' towards China (the policy that protected their collective right to access China's markets and uphold the sovereignty of the Chinese government). Instead, neutral China was left vulnerable to exploitation by its closest rival, Japan. The Japanese government maximized its empire's hegemonic position. Aside from acquiring the German possession of Qingdao, it also issued an invasive ultimatum – the Twenty-One Demands – in March 1915. According to the demands, China was to allow greater Japanese investment in and commercial access to its internal economy, the expansion of Japanese railways and industrial capacity in Manchuria and a measure of political influence in Beijing. The demands laid bare the potential seeds of China's destruction and resulted in widespread anti-Japanese activism among China's population. In response, the Chinese government recognized the need to sustain a working relationship with the United States and European belligerents. Only by joining the war could it imagine being offered a voice in shaping the contours of a post-war international system and protect its own sovereign independence. China joined the war on the side of the Allies in August 1917. Well before this date, however, it agreed to allow the French and British to recruit labourers for military service on Europe's western front. No fewer than 140,000 Chinese labourers served there after 1916.[68]

While China's formal entry into the war added another 440 million belligerents to the global tally, it would seem that its most important contribution to the disastrous course of the war in 1917 and 1918 was the spread of the deadly 'Spanish flu'.[69] After its outbreak in China late in 1917, the pandemic spread with the Chinese Labour Corps into Europe. From there it traversed the planet causing anywhere between 50 and 100 million deaths and leaving almost no community unscarred. The heights of global crisis were surely reached in 1918 when global warfare and global revolutions met global pandemic.[70]

The guns of western Europe finally quietened on 11 November 1918 after an armistice was signed between the great power belligerents. But revolutionary wars continued to rage in eastern and southern Europe (including in Germany), across the vast Russian hinterland, in the Middle East and Africa. The British and French overseas empires also faced numerous rebellions and revolts, many of which the imperial authorities repressed in the most brutal of ways.[71] The Amritsar massacre in April 1919, for example, witnessed the death of hundreds of Punjabi protestors who were shot by the British Punjabi Army when they broke a city-wide curfew. The massacre was one of many signs that India and Indians were even less willing to placidly accept British imperial authority than they had in the past.

From the perspective of the remaining great power governments, the world needed a workable treaty akin to the 1815 Congress of Vienna. It did not get it. Gone were many of the great powers that had collaborated in the managing of the first age of industrial globalization. Indeed, the nineteenth century's success in linking the global and local together had added many actively competing voices to the conversation. Powerful forces 'from below' were now mobilized by a range of political ideas based on class conflict, ethnic nationalism, democracy and anti-imperialism. None of their ideas were in themselves new, but in an environment in which the legitimacy and existence of many of the concepts and structures of the 1815 international order were critically weakened or gone, they had greater and enduring potency.

Out of the maelstrom of total global war between 1914 and 1918, then, a 'second age of industrial globalization' emerged that did not rest on the concepts of restraint, cooperation and war avoidance that had defined the international arena in the nineteenth century. Instead, the decades that followed the First World War were riven with hate-filled conflict. In the 'second age of industrial globalization' diplomatic agreements were hard to manufacture and the many newly created borders, states, treaties and structures were even harder to maintain.[72] None of these developments made another great war inevitable. Still, very few contemporaries would have argued against the notion that this 'second age of industrial globalization' was little more than a 'broken world' struggling to find some cohesion and a durable peace.[73]

Study questions

1. What is meant by the term 'total war'? Is it an appropriate descriptor for the First World War?

2. In what ways was the First World War a global war?

3. Assess the role and function of neutrals and neutrality in the war.

4. In what ways did subject peoples help to determine the global contours of the First World War?

5. Why might 1917 be considered such a pivotal year?

6. How did the First World War alter the systemic foundations of the 'first age of industrial globalization'?

Recommended readings

Bill Albert, *South America and the First World War: The Impact of the War on Brazil, Argentina, Peru and Chile*. Cambridge UP, 1988: Chapter 6 'The war and the workers', pp. 233–305.

Najwa al-Qattan, 'Historicising hunger: The famine in wartime Lebanon and Syria' in T. G. Fraser, *The First World war and Its Aftermath: The Shaping of the Middle East*. Gingko Library, 2015, pp. 111–26.

Stephane Audoin-Rouzeau, '1915' in Jay Winter, ed., *Cambridge History of the First World War*. Volume 1, Cambridge UP, 2014, pp. 65–88.

Mark Bailey, 'Supporting the wartime economy: Imperial maritime trade and the globalised maritime trade system, 1914–1916', *Journal for Maritime Research* 19, 1, 2017, pp. 23–45.

Annette Becker, 'The Great War: World war, total war', *International Review of the Red Cross* 97, 2015, pp. 1029–45.

Eric Dorn Brose, *A History of the Great War: World War One and the International Crisis of the Early Twentieth Century*. Oxford UP, 2010: Part Two 'The abyss', pp. 47–364.

Filipe Ribeiro de Meneses, 'The Portuguese empire' in Robert Gerwarth, Erez Manela, eds, *Empires at War 1911–1923*. Oxford UP, 2014, DOI:10.1093/acprof:oso/978 0198702511.003.0010.

Zachary J. Foster, 'Why are modern famines so deadly? The First World War in Syria and Palestine' in Richard P. Tucker, Tait Keller, J. R. McNeill, Martin Schmid, eds, *Environmental Histories of the First World War*. Cambridge UP, 2018, pp. 191–207.

Robert Gerwarth, Erez Manela, 'The Great War as a global war: Imperial conflict and the reconfiguration of world order, 1911–1923', *Diplomatic History* 38, 4, 2014, pp. 786–800.

Michael Howard, *The First World War: A Very Short Introduction*. Oxford UP, 2007

Steven Hyland Jr, 'The Syrian-Ottoman home front in Buenos Aires and Rosario during the First World War', *Journal of Migration History* 4, 2018, pp. 211–35.

Jennifer Keene, 'Americans respond: Perspectives on the global war, 1914–1917', *Geschichte und Gesellschaft* 40, 2, 2018, pp. 266–86.

Kathryn Meyer, 'Trade and nationality at Shanghai upon the outbreak of the First World War 1914–1915', *International History Review* 10, 2, 1988, pp. 238–60.

John Morrow, 'The imperial framework' in Jay Winter, ed., *Cambridge History of the First World War*. Volume 1, Cambridge UP, 2014, pp. 405–32.

Richard Roberts, 'A tremendous panic: The global financial crisis of 1914' in Andrew Smith, Simon Mollan, Kevin D. Tennent, eds, *The Impact of the First World War on International Business*. Routledge, 2017, pp. 121–41.

J. Charles Schenking, 'The imperial Japanese navy and the First World War' in Toshihiro Minohara, Tze-Ki Hon, Evan N. Dawley, eds, *The Decade of the Great War: Japan and the Wider World in the 1910s*. Brill, 2014, pp. 83–106.

Tim Stapleton, 'The impact of the First World War on African people' in John Laband, ed., *Daily Lives of Civilians in Wartime Africa: From Slavery Days to Rwandan Genocide*. Greenwood, 2007, pp. 113–37.

David Stevenson, 'From Balkan conflict to global conflict: The spread of the First World War 1914–1918', *Foreign Policy Analysis* 7, 2, 2011, pp. 169–82.

Alice Weinreb, 'Beans are bullets, potatoes are powder: Food as a weapon during the First World War' in Richard P. Tucker, Tait Keller, J. R. McNeill, Martin Schmid, eds, *Environmental Histories of the First World War*. Cambridge UP, 2018, pp. 19–37.

Notes

Chapter 1

1 Paul E. Lovejoy, 'The impact of the Atlantic slave trade on Africa: A review of the literature', *Journal of African History* 30, 3, 1989, pp. 365–94.

2 Alan Frost, *The Global Reach of Empire: Britain's Maritime Expansion in the Indian and Pacific Oceans 1764–1815*. Miegunyah Press, 2003.

3 Paul Kennedy, *The Rise and Fall of the Great Powers: Economic Change and Military Conflict from 1500 to 2000*. Vintage Books, 1987, p. 150.

4 Rein Taagepera, 'Expansion and contraction patterns of large polities: Context for Russia', *International Studies Quarterly* 41, 1997, pp. 475–504, esp. 484.

5 We prefer to use the term 'Anglo-European' as opposed to 'Western' here, as 'Western' can denote all communities 'Westernized' through the course of the nineteenth century (which for some scholars includes Japan). We wish to distinguish the English-speaking world (consisting of the United States, Greater Britain and all colonial outposts of the British empire) and the rest of the European continent and its colonial outposts as a distinct concept, while acknowledging how deeply embedded these regions were (and are) in the term 'Western'. For the history of the term 'the West': Alastair Bonnett, *The Idea of the West: Culture, Politics and History*. Palgrave MacMillan, 2004, esp. pp. 4–6.

6 There is some debate among historians about whether the early modern period constitutes the 'first age of globalization'. The 'first industrial revolution' and 'first agricultural revolution' are certainly situated in that period. Other scholars debate whether there was a 'second industrial revolution' around 1870, for example. We have chosen to describe the length of the nineteenth century (1815–1918) as the 'first age of industrial globalization' because it was in this period that the technological innovations of the industrial revolution directly impacted and shaped the contours of a globally connected world. There is also a well-established scholarly debate about the historical appropriateness of the term 'globalization', which is ably summarized in: Isabella Löhr, Roland Wenzlheumer, 'Introduction: The nation state and beyond', in Isabella Löhr, Roland Wenzlheumer, eds, *Governing Globalization Processes in the Nineteenth and Early Twentieth Centuries*. Springer, 2013, esp. pp. 1–5.

7 Eric Hobsbawm, *The Age of Revolution: Europe 1789–1848*. Cardinal, 1988 [1962]; Eric Hobsbawm, *The Age of Capital, 1848–1875*. Weidenfeld and Nicolson, 1975; *The Age of Empire 1875–1914*. Phoenix Press, 2000;

Eric Hobsbawm, *The Age of Extremes: A History of the World 1914–1991.* Pantheon Books, 1994.

8 Kennedy, *Rise and Fall*, p. 150.

9 Robert Gildea, *Barricades and Borders: Europe 1800–1914.* Oxford UP, 1996, p. 150.

10 Richard Evans, *The Pursuit of Power. Europe 1815–1914.* Viking, 2016, p. 293.

11 Steven C. Topik, Allen Wells, 'Commodity chains in a global economy' in Emily S. Rosenberg, ed., *A World Connecting, 1870–1945.* Belknap Press, 2012, p. 619.

12 Kathleen Burk, *Britain, America and the Sinews of War 1914–1918.* Allen & Unwin, 1985, p. 4.

13 The estimate for 1815 is taken from http://www.thuto.org/ubh/ub/h202/wpop1.htm (accessed December 2018) and is based on R. Cameron, *Concise Economic History of the World.* Oxford UP, 1993, p. 193. Figures for the twentieth century are more reliable and based on United Nations' data as found in http://www.ecology.com/population-estimates-year-2050/ (accessed December 2018).

14 T'an Ssu-T'ung, 'On the need for complete westernization' in Ssu-yin Teng, ed., *China's Response to the West: A Documentary Survey 1839–1923.* Harvard UP, 1965, p. 159.

15 Cf. Thomas Getz, *The Long Nineteenth Century 1750–1914: Crucible of Modernity.* Bloomsbury, 2018, pp. xvii–xviii.

16 Konrad H. Jarausch, *Out of the Ashes: A New History of Europe in the Twentieth Century.* Princeton UP, 2015, pp. 2–16.

17 Halford J. MacKinder, 'The geographical pivot of history', *Geographical Journal* 23, 4, April 1904, pp. 421–37.

18 Michael Adas, *Machines as the Measure of Men: Science, Technology and Ideologies of Western Dominance.* Cornell UP, 1989, p. 204.

19 Theodore H. von Laue, *The World Revolution in Westernization: The Twentieth Century in Global Perspective.* Oxford UP, 1989.

20 Evans, *Pursuit*, p. 27.

21 Maartje Abbenhuis, 'A most useful tool for diplomacy and statecraft: Neutrality and Europe in the "long" nineteenth century 1815–1914', *International History Review* 35, 1, 2013, pp. 1–22.

22 Maartje Abbenhuis, *An Age of Neutrals: Great Power Politics 1815–1914.* Cambridge UP, 2014.

23 W. T. Stead, *The United States of Europe on the Eve of the Parliament of Peace.* London, n.p., 1899.

24 Arno Mayer, *The Persistence of the Old Regime: Europe to the Great War.* Pantheon Books, 1981.

25 There is some scholarly debate about what constitutes 'new international history', which expands its analysis well beyond the state, governments and the ruling elite. For some excellent readings (in English) on the subject: Barbara Haider-Wilson, William D. Godsey, Wolfgang Mueller, eds, *Internationale Geschichte in Theorie und Praxis/International History in Theory and Practice*. Verlag der Österreichischen Akademie der Wissenschaften, 2017; J. A. Maiolo, 'Systems and boundaries in international history' and Patrick Finney, 'Narratives and bodies: Culture beyond the cultural turn' both in *International History Review* 40, 3, 2018, pp. 576–91, 609–30.

26 C. A. Bayly, *The Birth of the Modern World 1780–1914: Global Connections and Comparisons*. Blackwell, 2004, pp. 127–8, 230. For a history of technology and global networks that does take the political system into account: Per Högselius, Arne Kaijser, Erik van der Vleuten, *Europe's Infrastructure Transition: Economy, War, Nature*. Palgrave MacMillan, 2016, p. 24.

27 Brian Moloughney, 'S.A.M. Adshead on China, world institutions and world history', *Journal of World History* 27, 4, 2016, pp. 595–617.

28 Cf. Bayly, *Birth*, p. 1.

Chapter 2

1 Cf. Jürgen Osterhammel, *The Transformation of the World: A Global History of the Nineteenth Century*. Princeton UP, 2014, pp. 45–76; Charles S. Maier, 'Consigning the twentieth century to history: Alternate narratives for the modern era', *American Historical Review* 105, 3, 2000, p. 807.

2 Some historians typify the period 1850–1990 as the 'long' twentieth century on the basis of technological and/or institutional change: Johan Schot, Philip Scranton, 'Making Europe: An introduction' in Högselius, Kaijser, van der Vleuten, *Europe's Infrastructure*, p. xii; Charles S. Maier, 'Leviathan 2.0' in Emily Rosenberg, ed., *A World Connecting, 1870–1945*. Harvard UP, 2012, pp. 40–1.

3 Jonathan Israel, *The Expanding Blaze: How the American Revolution Ignited the World 1775–1848*. Princeton UP, 2017.

4 Marjolein 't Hart, Hilde Greefs, 'Sweet and sour: Economic turmoil and resilience of the sugar sector in Antwerp and Rotterdam 1795–1815', *Low Countries Historical Review* 133, 2, 2018, pp. 2–36.

5 See, for example, Kathleen Burk's most recent book: *The Lion and the Eagle: The Interaction of the British and American Empires 1783–1972*. Bloomsbury, 2018.

6 Odd Arne Westad, *Restless Empire: China and the World since 1750*. Basic Books, 2012, p. 38.

7 For a wonderful account of the Congress: David King, *Vienna 1914: How the Conquerors of Napoleon Made Love, War and Peace at the Congress of Vienna*. Broadway, 2008.

8 It actually lasted 110 days. After Waterloo, Napoleon was exiled to St Helena, a tiny island in the middle of the Atlantic Ocean.

9 Paul Schroeder, *The Transformation of European Politics 1763–1848*. Clarendon Press, 1994.

10 Hedley Bull, 'Order versus justice in international society', *Political Studies* 19, 3, 1971, pp. 269–83.

11 Paul Schroeder, 'The lost intermediaries: The impact of 1870 on the European system', *International History Review* 6, 1, 1984, pp. 4–8.

12 Abbenhuis, *Age of Neutrals*, pp. 46–53.

13 Jay Sexton, 'The Monroe doctrine in the nineteenth century' in Andrew Preston, Doug Rossinow, eds, *Outside In: The Transnational Circuitry of US History*. Oxford UP, 2017, pp. 19–23.

14 For more: Rafe Blaufarb, 'The western question: The geopolitics of Latin American independence', *American Historical Review* 112, 3, 2007, pp. 742–63.

15 Cf. Martin Lyons, *Post-Revolutionary Europe 1815–1856*. Palgrave MacMillan, 2006.

16 Israel, *Expanding Blaze*.

17 Ulrike Schmieder, 'Spain and Spanish America in the system of the Holy Alliance: The importance of interconnected historical events on the congresses of the Holy Alliance', *Review (Fernand Braudel Center)* 38, 1–2, 2015, pp. 147–69.

18 Evans, *Pursuit*, pp. 54–5.

19 Evans, *Pursuit*, pp. 54–5.

20 Alexis Heraclides, Ada Dialla, *Humanitarian Intervention in the Long Nineteenth Century: Setting the Precedent*. Manchester UP, 2015, pp. 105–33.

21 Lucien J. Frary, *Russia and the Making of Modern Greek Identity 1821–1844*. Oxford UP, 2015.

22 Cf. Matthew Rendall, 'Russia, the concert of Europe and Greece, 1821–29: A test of hypotheses about the Vienna system', *Security Studies* 9, 4, 2000, pp. 52–90.

23 Cf. Israel, *Expanding Blaze*, pp. 456–94.

24 James A. Sandos, 'Levantamiento! The 1824 Chumash uprising reconsidered', *Southern California Quarterly* 67, 2, 1985, pp. 109–33.

25 John Sedgwick, *Blood Moon: An American Epic of War and Splendor in the Cherokee Nation*. Simon & Schuster, 2018.

26 Atholl Anderson, Judith Binney, Aroha Harris, *Tangata Whenua: An Illustrated History*. Bridget Williams Books, 2014, p. 211.

27 J. A. de Moor, 'Warmakers in the archipelago: Dutch expeditions in nineteenth-century Indonesia' in J. A. de Moor, H. L. Wesseling, eds, *Imperialism and War: Colonial Wars in Asia and Africa* Brill, 1989, pp. 52–4.

28 De Moor, 'Warmakers', p. 71.

29 Kate Fullagar, Michael A. McDonnell, 'Empire, indigeneity and revolution' in Kate Fullagar, Michael A. McDonnell, eds, *Facing Empire: Indigenous Experiences in a Revolutionary Age*. Johns Hopkins UP, 2018, pp. 1–24.

30 Many historians argue that Dutch imperialism was protected by British naval power. They are not wrong, in so far as the British navy did protect the security of the seas. More powerfully, the international system of which Britain was a major guarantor and benefactor helped the Dutch sustain an overseas empire.

31 Evans, *Pursuit*, pp. 72–3.

32 Norman Rich, *Great Power Diplomacy, 1814–1914*. McGraw Hill, 1992, p. 61.

33 Evans, *Pursuit*, p. 208.

34 Rich, *Great Power*, pp. 109–10.

35 Jan Lemnitzer, *Power, Law and the End of Privateering*. Palgrave Macmillan, 2014.

36 Andrew C. Rath, *The Crimean War in Imperial Context 1854–1856*. Palgrave MacMillan, 2015.

37 Abbenhuis, *Age of Neutrals*, pp. 66–95.

38 In 1856, the United States was the only government that still formally accepted the right to privateering. It would give that up that right in the 1890s: Nicholas Parrillo, 'The de-privatization of warfare: How the US government used, regulated and ultimately abandoned privateering in the nineteenth century', *Yale Journal of Law and the Humanities* 19, 1, 2007, pp. 1–95.

39 Charles H. Stockton, 'The Declaration of Paris', *American Journal of International Law* 14, 3, 1920, p. 360.

Chapter 3

1 Korea opened its economy up to the world in 1876. Like Japan and much of the world, its development as an industrial capitalist society was dependent on the importation of technology and infrastructure concepts from abroad: C. J. Eckert, *Offspring of Empire: Koch'ang Kims and the Colonial Origins of Korean Capitalism 1876–1945*. University of Washington Press, 2014, p. 5.

2 For the military relevance of the United States acquisition of these Asia-Pacific coaling stations: Dirk Bönker, *Militarism in a Global Age: Naval Ambitions in Germany and the United States before World War 1*. Cornell UP, 2017, p. 133.

3 The Japanese were connected to the world in the early modern period, but the empire closely controlled who and what entered into its sovereign territory.

4 Joshua A. Fogel, *Maiden Voyage: The Senzaimaru and the Creation of Modern Sino-Japanese Relations*. University of California Press, 2014, p. 3. Also: Ian Nish, *The Iwakura Mission to America and Europe: A New Assessment*. Routledge, 2008.

5 Until 1871, Prussia was an independent state within the German Confederation (for which see Chapter 2). The Franco-Prussian War (1870–1) brought most, but not all, of the Germanic states in the Confederation together into a new nation, Germany (for more see Chapter 8).

6 Cf. Patrick O'Brien, 'A conjecture in global history or an Anglo-American construct: The British industrial revolution, 1700–1850', *Journal of Global History* 5, 3, 2010, pp. 503–9.

7 Hajo Brugmans, 'De beteekenis van 1813', *Onze Eeuw* 13, 3, 1913, p. 190.

8 Bo Stråth, *Europe's Utopias of Peace 1815, 1919, 1951.* Bloomsbury, 2016, p. 30.

9 Glenda Sluga, 'Who hold the balance of the world? Bankers at the Congress of Vienna and in international history', *American Historical Review* 122, 5, 2017, pp. 1403–30.

10 Maartje Abbenhuis, *An Age of Neutrals: Great Power Politics 1815–1914.* Cambridge UP, 2014, p. 35.

11 There is a large and vibrant literature about the importance of early modern industrialization (both the precursors to the nineteenth-century industrial revolution and as (proto-)industrial processes in their own right), which we do not have time to discuss here. One of the classic articles on the subject is Franklin F. Mendels, 'Proto-industrialization: The first phase of the industrialization process', *Journal of Economic History* 32, 1, 1972, pp. 241–61.

12 Frank Trentmann, *Free Trade Nation: Commerce, Consumption and Civil Society in Modern Britain.* Oxford UP, 2008.

13 There were, of course, many drivers for nineteenth-century imperialism as well, some of which will be discussed in the coming chapters. Both industrialization and imperialism were globalizing phenomena.

14 Jürgen Osterhammel, *The Transformation of the World: A Global History of the Nineteenth Century.* Princeton UP, 2014, p. 638.

15 Cf. Eric Hobsbawm, *The Age of Capital, 1848–1875.* Weidenfeld and Nicolson, 1975, chapter 8.

16 E. D. Langer, J. Tutino, 'Epilogue: Consolidating divergence: The Americas and the world after 1850' in J. Tutino, ed., *New Countries: Capitalism, Revolutions and Nations in the Americas 1750–1870.* Duke UP, 2016, p. 381.

17 Cf. Kathleen Burk, *Old World, New World: Great Britain and America from the Beginning.* Atlantic Monthly Press, 2008.

18 Antoinette Burton, Isabel Hofmeyr, 'Introduction: The spine of empire? Books and the making of an imperial commons' in Antoinette Burton, Isabel Hofmeyr, eds, *Ten Books That Shaped the British Empire: Creating an Imperial Commons.* Duke UP, 2014, p. 10.

19 Eric Hobsbawm, *Industry and Empire: From 1750 to the Present Day.* Penguin, 1968, p. 13.

20 Osterhammel, *Transformation*, p. 119.

21 Hobsbawm, *Industry and Empire*, pp. 326–7.

22 Peter N. Stearns, *The Industrial Revolution in World History.* Fourth edition, Westview Press, 2013, p. 13.

23 Richard Evans, *The Pursuit of Power. Europe 1815–1914.* Viking, 2016, pp. 113–14.

24 Bernard Semmel, *The Rise of Free Trade Imperialism: Classical Political Economy of Free Trade and Imperialism*. Cambridge UP, 2004, pp. 154–5.

25 Hobsbawm, *Industry and Empire*, p. 134.

26 Stearns, *Industrial Revolution*, p. 37.

27 Steven Bryan, *The Gold Standard at the Turn of the Twentieth Century*. Columbia UP, 2010, p. 18. The real price calculations were derived from *MeasuringWorth.com* (accessed November 2018).

28 Steven C. Topik, Allen Wells, 'Commodity chains in a global economy' in Emily Rosenberg, ed., *A World Connecting 1870–1945*. Belknap Press, 2012, pp. 620–1.

29 Doron S. Ben-Atar, *Trade Secrets: Intellectual Piracy and the Origins of American Industrial Power*. Yale UP, 2004.

30 Peter N. Stearns, *The Industrial Turn in World History*. New York: Routledge, 2017, p. 40; Trevor Getz, *The Long Nineteenth Century, 1750–1914: Crucible of Modernity*. Bloomsbury, 2018, pp. 132–3.

31 Odd Arne Westad, *Restless Empire: China and the World since 1750*. Basic Books, 2012, p. 36.

32 Westad, *Restless Empire*, p. 38.

33 Nick Robbins, *The Corporation That Changed the World: How the East India Company Shaped the Modern Multinational*. Pluto Press, 2012, p. 159.

34 Robbins, *Corporation*, p. 157.

35 As quoted in Robbins, *Corporation*, p. 7.

36 John Crawfurd, 1837, as quoted in Hans Derks, *History of the Opium Problem: The Assault on the East c. 1600–1950*. Brill, 2012, p. 51.

37 John Crawfurd, 1840, as quoted in Derks, *History of the Opium Problem*, p. 51.

38 For more on Indian economic agency: Christof Dejung, 'The boundaries of western power: The colonial cotton economy in India and the problem of quality' in Christof Dejung, Niels P. Peterson, eds, *The Foundations of Worldwide Economic Integration: Power, Institutions and Global Markets, 1850–1930*. Cambridge UP, 2013, pp. 133–57.

39 Westad, *Restless Empire*, p. 41

40 Westad, *Restless Empire*, p. 44.

41 Anne Reinhardt, *Navigating Semi-Colonialism: Shipping, Sovereignty and Nation-Building in China 1860–1937*. Harvard UP, 2018, p. 11.

42 Kirk W. Larsen, *Tradition, Treaties, and Trade: Qing Imperialism and Chosŏn, 1850–1910*. Harvard UP, 2008, pp. 12–13.

43 Marie-Claire Bergère, *Shanghai: China's Gateway to Modernity*. Stanford UP, 2009, pp. 50–83.

44 Aurora Gomez-Galvarriato, Jeffrrey G. Williamson, 'Was it prices, productivity or policy? Latin American industrialization after 1870', *Journal of Latin America Studies* 41, 4, 2009, pp. 670–1.

45 Valerii L. Stepanov, 'The Crimean War and the Russian economy', *Russian Studies in History* 51, 1, 2012, pp. 12–13.

46 John McKay, 'Foreign entrepreneurship in Russian industrialization, 1880–1914', *Journal of Economic History* 26, 4, 1966, pp. 582–3.

47 Stearns, *Industrial Revolution*, p. 127.

48 David Schimmelpennick van der Oye, *Toward the Rising Sun: Russian Ideologies of Empire and the Path to War with Japan*. Northern Illinois UP, 2006.

49 Jennifer Siegel, *Endgame: Britain, Russia and the Final Struggle for Central Asia*. I.B. Tauris, 2002, pp. 6–7.

50 John D. Grainger, *The First Pacific War: Britain and Russia, 1854–1856*. Boydell Press, 2008, p. xi.

51 Noriaki Hoshino, Qian Zhu, 'Histories of modern migration in East Asia: Studies of the first half of the twentieth century', *International Journal of Asian Studies* 14, 2, 2017, p. 183.

52 Stearns, *Industrial Revolution*, p. 40.

53 Miriam Kingsberg, *Moral Nation: Modern Japan and Narcotics in Global History*. University of California Press, 2014, pp. 16, 19.

54 Hoshina, Zhu, 'Histories', p. 174.

55 Austria-Hungary formed as a dual monarchy after Prussia defeated the Austrian Habsburg empire in the war of 1866.

56 Dominic Lieven, *Empire: The Russian Empire and Its Rivals*. Yale UP, 2000, p. 192.

57 Lieven, *Empire*, p. 192.

58 Lieven, *Empire*, p. 153.

59 Tony Ballantyne, Antoinette Burton, 'Empires and the reach of the global' in Emily Rosenberg, ed., *World Connecting*. Belknap Press, 2012, pp. 374–5.

Chapter 4

1 Nicholas Ruddick, 'Nellie Bly, Jules Verne and the world on the threshold of the American age', *Canadian Review of American Studies* 29, 1, 1999, pp. 5–6. Emily S. Rosenberg, 'Introduction' in Emily Rosenberg, ed., *A World Connecting, 1870–1945*. Harvard UP, 2012, p. 3.

2 Jules Verne, *Around the World in 80 Days*. n.p., 1873, chapter 3.

3 Joseph Conrad, *Heart of Darkness*. np, 1899; Maya Jasanoff, *The Dawn Watch: Joseph Conrad in a Global World*. HarperCollins, 2017, esp. chapter 8.

4 Arnold T. Wilson, *The Suez Canal: Its Past, Present and Future*. Second edition, Oxford UP, 1939, pp. 22, 31.

5 Valeska Huber, 'Multiple mobilities, multiple sovereignties, multiple speeds: exploring maritime connections in the age of empire', *International Journal of Middle East Studies* 48, 2016, pp. 763–6.

6 Valeska Huber, 'Connecting colonial seas: the "international colonization" of Port Said and the Suez Canal during and after the First World War', *European*

Review of History 19, 1, 2012, esp. pp. 145–9; Liat Kozma, 'Prostitution in Port Said' in J.-M. Chaumont, M. R. García, P. Servais, eds, *Trafficking in Women 1924–1926*. Volume 2, United Nations Publications, 2017, pp. 180–1; Ballantyne, Burton, 'Empires', pp. 352–7.

7 Prahsant Kidambi, *The Making of an Indian Metropolis: Colonial Governance and Public Culture in Bombay, 1890–1920*. Ashgate, 2007, p. 19.

8 Kidambi, *Making*, p. 22.

9 Pallavi V. Das, *Colonialism, Development and the Environment: Railways and Deforestation in British India 1860–1884*. Palgrave MacMillan, 2015, p. 18.

10 Das, *Colonialism*, pp. 18–20.

11 Britain's Representative in Paris telegram to the British Foreign Office, 28 June 1898, Foreign Office file 72/2096, National Archives, London.

12 Robert Griffeth, 'Economic change in colonial French West Africa 1900–1940' and Paul E. Pheffer, 'African influence on French colonial railroads in Senegal' both in G. Wesley Johnson, ed., *Double Impact: France and Africa in the Age of Imperialism*. Greenwood, 1985, pp. 17–29, 31–49.

13 Paul S. Reinsch, *Public International Institutions: Their Work and Organization*. Ginn and Company, 1911, p. 18. For more on the history of the telegraph: E. Thomas Ewing, 'A most powerful instrument for a despot: The telegraph as a trans-national instrument of imperial control and political mobilization in the Middle East' in Isabella Löhr, Roland Wenzlheumer, eds, *Governing Globalization Processes in the Nineteenth and Early Twentieth Centuries*. Springer, 2013, esp. pp. 83–100.

14 Daniel R. Headrick, *The Tools of Empire: Technology and European Imperialism in the Nineteenth Century*. Oxford UP, 1981, p. 167.

15 Topik, Wells, 'Commodity chains', p. 643.

16 Stephen Kern, *The Culture of Time and Space 1880–1918*. Harvard UP, 1983, pp. 213–14.

17 Jared Diamond, *Guns, Germs and Steel: The Fates of Human Societies*. W.W. Norton, 1997.

18 Kern, *Culture*, p. 12; Vanessa Ogle, *The Global Transformation of Time 1870–1950*. Harvard UP, 2015.

19 M. S. Anderson, *The Ascendancy of Europe: 1815–1914*. Third edition, Routledge, 2014, pp. 45–6, 286.

20 Mazower, *Governing*, p. 95.

21 Headrick, *Tools*, p. 171.

22 Reinsch, *Public International Institutions*, pp. 21–3.

23 Reinsch, *Public International Institutions*, pp. 15, 20.

24 Robert Gildea, *Barricades and Borders: Europe 1800–1914*. Oxford UP, 1996, p. 150.

25 Bernard Attard, 'The London stock exchange and the colonial market: The city, internationalisation and power' in Christof Dejung, Niels P. Peterson, eds, *The Foundations of Worldwide Economic Integration: Power, Institutions and Global Markets, 1850–1930*. Cambridge UP, 2013, pp. 89–111.

26 Stephen C. Neff, *Friends but No Allies: Economic Liberalism and the Law of Nations.* Columbia UP, 1990, pp. 5–6.

27 L. A. C. J. Lucassen, 'A many headed monster: The evolution of the passport system in the Netherlands and Germany in the long nineteenth century' in J. Caplan, J. Torpey, eds, *Documenting Individual Identity: The Development of State Practices in the Modern World.* Princeton UP, 2001, p. 237.

28 Mark B. Salter, *Rights of Passage: The Passport in International Relations.* Lynn Rienner, 2003, pp. 20–1, 25–6; Marilyn Lake, 'Lowe Kong Meng appeals to international law: Transnational lives caught between empire and nation' in Desley Deacon, Penny Russell, Angela Woollacott, eds, *Transnational Lives: Biographies of Global Modernity, 1700-Present.* Palgrave MacMillan, 2010, pp. 223–37.

29 Kern, *Culture*, p. 230.

30 Emily S. Rosenberg, Leviathan 2.0, 'Transnational currents in a shrinking world' in Emily Rosenberg, ed., *A World Connecting, 1870–1945.* Harvard UP, 2012, pp. 982–4.

31 Inis L. Claude Jr, *Swords into Plowshares: The Problems and Progress of International Organization.* Random House, 1956, p. 32.

32 Reinsch, *Public International Institutions*, pp. 28, 33.

33 Amos Hershey, 'History of international law since the peace of Westphalia', *American Journal of International Law* 6, 1, 1912, p. 54; Pierre-Yves Donzé, 'The international patent system and the global flow of technologies: The case of Japan, 1880–1930' in Christof Dejung, Niels P. Peterson, eds, *The Foundations of Worldwide Economic Integration: Power, Institutions and Global Markets, 1850–1930.* Cambridge UP, 2013, pp. 179–201.

34 Reinsch, *Public International Institutions*, pp. 56–60; Sunil S. Amrith, 'Internationalising health in the twentieth century' in Glenda Sluga, Patricia Clavin, eds, *Internationalisms: A Twentieth-Century History.* Cambridge UP, 2017, pp. 246–7.

35 Valeska Huber, 'The unification of the globe by disease? The International Sanitary Conferences on Cholera, 1851–1894', *Historical Journal* 49, 2, 2006, pp. 453–76.

36 Paul Reinsch lists all known international organizations in existence in 1911: Reinsch, *Public International Institutions*. See also: James H. Mills, *Cannabis Britannica: Empire, Trade and Prohibition.* Oxford UP, 2003, pp. 3–5.

37 Cf. Glenda Sluga, *Internationalism in the Age of Nationalism.* University of Pennsylvania Press, 2013, p. 14.

38 Mazower, *Governing*, p. 101.

39 Topik, Wells, 'Commodity chains', pp. 615–16.

40 Mazower, *Governing*, p. 104.

41 Norman Weiß, 'Institutionalised co-operation on international communication: The international administrative unions as a means of governing globalisation processes' in Isabella Löhr, Roland Wenzlheumer, eds, *Governing Globalization Processes in the Nineteenth and Early Twentieth Centuries.* Springer, 2013, pp. 65–82.

42 Tze-ki Hon, 'Global competition for power and wealth: The Chinese view of the world before and after the Great War' in Toshihiro Minohara, Tze-Ki Hon, Evan N. Dawley, eds, *The Decade of the Great War: Japan and the Wider World in the 1910s*. Brill, 2014, p. 504.

43 Laura Benton, Lisa Ford, *Rage for Order: The British Empire and the Origins of International Law 1800–1850*. Harvard UP, 2016. See also: Diane Kirkby, Catherine Coleborne, eds, *Law, History, Colonialism: The Reach of Empire*. Manchester UP, 2001.

44 Steven Press, *Rogue Empires: Contracts and Conmen in Europe's Scramble for Africa*. Harvard UP, 2017, quote on p. 8.

45 Cf. John Anthony Pella, 'World society, international society and the colonization of Africa', *Cambridge Review of International Affairs* 28, 2, 2015, pp. 210–28.

46 Joseph Conrad, *Heart of Darkness*. Roads, 1899 [2013], p. 101.

47 C. A. Bayly, *The Birth of the Modern World 1780–1914: Global Connections and Comparisons*. Blackwell, 2004, p. 230.

48 Cf. Michael Lobban, 'English approaches to international law in the nineteenth century' in Matthew Craven, Malgosia Fitzmaurice, Maria Vogiatzi, eds, *Time, History and International Law*. Martinus Nijhoff, 2007, p. 72.

49 Eric Yong-Joong Lee, 'Early development of modern international law in East Asia – with special reference to China, Japan and Korea', *Journal of the History of International Law* 4, 2002, pp. 46–8.

50 Gerrit W. Gong, *The Standard of 'Civilization' in International Society*. Clarendon Press, 1984, pp. 14–15.

51 Cf. Charles S. Maier, 'Leviathan 2.0' in Emily Rosenberg, ed., *A World Connecting, 1870–1945*. Harvard UP, 2012, pp. 30–1.

52 Heinhard Steiger, 'Peace treaties from Paris to Versailles' in Randall Lesaffer, ed., *Peace Treaties and International Law in European History: From the Late Middle Ages to World War I*. Cambridge UP, 2004, pp. 59–99; Cf. Jennifer Pitts, *Boundaries of the International: Law and Empire*. Harvard UP, 2018, esp. p. 3.

53 Kinji Akashi, 'Japanese "acceptance" of the European law of nations: A brief history of international law in Japan 1853–1900' in Michael Stolleis, Masaharu Yanagihara, eds, *East Asian and European Perspectives on International Law*. Nomos, 2004, pp. 17–21.

54 Marilyn Lake, Henry Reynolds, *Drawing the Global Colour Line: White Man's Countries and the International Challenge of Racial Equality*. Cambridge: Cambridge UP, 2012.

55 For more on cosmopolitanism and globalization: Margrit Schulte Beerbühl, 'Introduction' in Andreas Gestrich, Margrit Schulte Beerbühl, eds, *Cosmopolitan Networks in Commerce and Society 1660–1914*. German Historical Institute London, 2011, esp. pp. 2, 8–10.

56 Kidambi, *Making*, p. 1.

57 Angela Middleton, 'Maori and European landscapes at Te Puna, Bay of Islands, New Zealand 1805–1850', *Archaeologica Oceania* 38, 2003, pp. 110–24; Richard Wolfe, *Hell-Hole of the Pacific*. Penguin, 2005, p. 31.

58 Atholl Anderson, Judith Binney, Aroha Harris, *Tangata Whenua: An Illustrated History*. Bridget Williams Books, 2014, p. 220.

59 With thanks to Hazel Petrie.

60 Wolfe, *Hell-Hole*, pp. 191–2.

61 Ross Harvey, 'Establishing a goldfields newspaper: The *Inangahua Herald*, Reefton, New Zealand, 1872', *Studies in Newspaper and Periodical History* 1, 1–2, 1993, pp. 135–46.

62 Margaret McClure, *The Wonder Country: Making New Zealand Tourism*. Auckland, Independent Publishers, 2004, pp. 8–9.

63 McClure, *Wonder Country*, p. 26.

64 McClure, *Wonder Country*, p. 24.

65 Headrick, *Tools*, p. 168.

66 Noel Maurer, *The Empire Trap: The Rise and Fall of US Intervention to Protect American Property Overseas, 1893–2013*. Princeton UP, 2013, p. 27.

67 Richard Phillip Gilson, *Samoa 1830–1900: The Politics of a Multi-Cultural Community*. Oxford UP, 1970; Leilani Burgoyne, 'Redefining "the beach": The municipality of Apia 1879–1900', Master of Arts thesis, University of Auckland, 2006.

68 W. Boyd Rayward, 'Introduction: International exhibitions, Paul Otlet, Henri Fontaine and the paradox of the *belle époque*' in W. Boyd Rayward, ed., *Information beyond Borders: International Cultural and Intellectual Exchange in the Belle Époque*. Routledge, 2014, p. 9.

69 M. B. Iwinsky in J. H. de Vries, *Pour la Paix: Une Presse Mondiale*. Schleicher, 1911, p. 131.

70 Donald Read, *The Power of News: The History of Reuters, 1849–1989*. Oxford UP, 1992, p. 53; Volker Barth, 'The formation of global news agencies 1859–1914' in W. Boyd Rayward, ed., *Information beyond Borders: International Cultural and Intellectual Exchange in the Belle Époque*. Routledge, 2014, pp. 35–47.

71 Hon, 'Global competition', p. 508.

Chapter 5

1 Adam McKeown, 'Global migration, 1846–1940', *Journal of World History* 15, 2, 2004, pp. 155–89.

2 McKeown, 'Global migration', p. 156.

3 As noted at the end of Chapter 4.

4 James Belich, *Replenishing the Earth: The Settler Revolution and the Rise of the Anglo-World 1783–1939*. Oxford UP, 2009.

5 McKeown, 'Global migration', p. 157.

6 Nick Robbins, *The Corporation That Changed the World: How the East India Company Shaped the Modern Multinational*. Pluto Press, 2012, pp. 80–1.

7 The *Communist Manifesto* purposely separated industrial workers from agricultural workers, even when the latter produced the raw materials than enabled the former to do their jobs.

8 Richard Evans, *The Pursuit of Power: Europe 1815–1914.* Viking, 2016, pp. 331–2.

9 Sebastian Conrad, *German Colonialism: A Short History.* Cambridge UP, 2012, p. 18.

10 Dirk Hoerder, 'Migrations and Belongings' in Emily Rosenberg, *A World Connecting, 1870–1945.* Harvard UP, 2012, p. 498.

11 A. D. Hall, *Agriculture after the War.* John Murray, 1917, pp. 22–25.

12 Sevket Pamuk, Jeffrey G. Williamson, *The Mediterranean Response to Globalization before 1950.* Taylor & Francis, 2002, p. 8.

13 E. H. Carr, *What Is History?* Penguin, 1961, pp. 49–50.

14 Belich, *Replenishing*, esp. chapter 3.

15 McKeown, 'Global migration', pp. 158–9; Hoerder, 'Migrations', p. 527.

16 Robert Harms, 'Introduction' in Robert Harms, Bernard K. Freamon, David W. Blight, eds, *Indian Ocean Slavery in the Age of Abolition.* Yale UP, 2013, pp. 1–2.

17 Evans, *Pursuit*, p. 268.

18 Edward Alpers, *The Indian Ocean in World History.* Oxford UP, 2014, pp. 107–8.

19 Hoerder, 'Migrations', p. 516.

20 Hoerder, 'Migrations', p. 527.

21 Alan Lester, Zoë Laidlaw, 'Indigenous sites and mobilities: Connected struggles in the long nineteenth century' in Zoë Laidlaw, Alan Lester, eds, *Indigenous Communities and Settler Colonialism.* Palgrave MacMillan, 2015, pp. 1–23.

22 Jonas Fossli Gjersø, 'The scramble for East Africa: British motives reconsidered 1884–1885', *Journal of Imperial and Commonwealth History* 43, 5, 2015, pp. 831–60.

23 Tim Carmichael, 'British "practice" towards Islam in the East Africa Protectorate', *Journal of Muslim Minority Affairs* 17, 2, 1997, pp. 295–6.

24 In the end, Waiyaka Wa Hinga's Dagoretti people burnt down a British fort in 1890. W. Hinga was subsequently captured by British soldiers and buried alive as punishment: Peter Rogers, 'The British and the Kikuyu 1890–1905: A reassessment', *Journal of African History* 20, 2, 1979, pp. 255–69.

25 Dane K. Kennedy, *Islands of White: Settler Society and Culture in Kenya and Southern Rhodesia, 1890–1939.* Duke UP, 1987; William K. Storey, 'Big cats and imperialism: Lion and tiger hunting in Kenya and India', *Journal of World History* 2, 2, 1991, pp. 140–1.

26 Storey, 'Big cats', pp. 150–1.

27 Sugata Bose, Kris Manjapra, *Cosmopolitan Thought Zones: South Asia and the Circulation of Ideas.* Palgrave Macmillan, 2010, p. 113.

28 Niall Ferguson, *Empire: How Britain Made the Modern World.* Penguin Books, 2004, pp. 176–8.

29 Sharada Dwivedi, Rahul Mehrotra, *Bombay: The Cities within.* India Book House, 1995, p. 153.

30 Steven Press, *Rogue Empires: Contracts and Conmen in Europe's Scramble for Africa.* Harvard UP, 2017.

31 Press, *Rogue*, p. 19, and chapter 1.

32 For another example, this time in East New Guinea: Hans-Jürgen Ohff, *Disastrous Ventures: German and British Enterprises in East New Guinea.* Plenum, 2015, chapter 4.

33 Roger Knight, 'Family firms, global networks and transnational actors: The case of Alexander Fraser (1816–1904): Merchant and entrepreneur in the Netherlands Indies, Low Countries and London', *Low Countries Historical Review* 132, 2, 2018, pp. 27–51.

34 Robert Fitzgerald, *The Rise of the Global Company: Multinationals and the Making of the Modern World.* Cambridge UP, 2015, p. 24.

35 B. C. Schär, *Tropenliebe: Schweizer Naturforscher und niederländischer Imperialismus in Südostasien um 1900.* Campus Verlag, 2015.

36 Bradley D. Naranch, 'Between cosmopolitanism and German colonialism: Nineteenth-century Hanseatic networks in emerging tropical markets' in Andreas Gestrich, Margrit Schulte Beerbühl, eds, *Cosmopolitan Networks in Commerce and Society 1660–1914.* German Historical Institute London, 2011, pp. 108–9.

37 Daniel R. Headrick, *Power over Peoples: Technology, Environments and Western Imperialism, 1400 to the Present.* Princeton UP, 2010, p. 228.

38 Headrick, *Power*, pp. 232–4.

39 Press, *Rogue*, p. 91.

40 Press, *Rogue*, chapter 3.

41 Matthew G. Stanard, *Selling the Congo: A History of European Pro-Empire Propaganda and the Making of Belgian Imperialism.* University of Nebraska Press, 2011, p. 30.

42 Press, *Rogue*, pp. 127–30.

43 Joseph Conrad, *Heart of Darkness.* Roads, 1899 [2013], p. 116.

44 Adam Hochschild, *King Leopold's Ghost.* Houghton Mifflin, 1998, pp. 225–33.

Chapter 6

1 As quoted in Eric L. Jones, *Revealed Biodiversity: An Economic History of Human Impact.* World Scientific, 2014, p. 218.

2 Patrick Webb, 'Emergency relief during Europe's famine of 1817: Anticipated crisis-response mechanisms of today', *Journal of Nutrition* 132, 7, 2002, pp. 2092–5; Clive Oppenheimer, 'Climatic, environmental

and human consequences of the largest known historic eruption: Tambora volcano (Indonesia) 1815', *Progress in Physical Geography* 27, 2, 2003, pp. 230–59; K. E. Alexander, W. B. Leavenworth, T. V. Willis, et al., 'Tambora and the mackerel year: Phenology and fisheries during an extreme climate event', *Science Advances* 3, 1, 2017, doi: 10.1126/sciadv.160163; Ole Rössler, Stefan Brönnimann, 'The effect of Tambora eruption on Swiss flood generation in 1816/1817', *Science of the Total Environment* 627, 2018, pp. 1218–27.

3 Lord Byron, 'Darkness 1816', in Jelle Zeilinga de Boer, Donald T. Sanders, *Volcanoes in Human History: The Far-Reading Effects of Major Eruptions.* Princeton UP, 2002, pp. 151–2.

4 This event had equally destructive global consequences, not least in causing a series of major earthquakes in New Zealand, which destroyed the Te Otukapuarangi (Pink Terraces) and Te Tarata (White Terraces) discussed in Chapter 4.

5 Zielinga de Boer, Sanders, *Volcanoes*, p. 155.

6 Benjamin Lieberman, Elizabeth Gordon, *Climate Change in Human History: Prehistory to the Present.* Bloomsbury, 2018, p. 142.

7 Steven C. Topik, Allen Wells, 'Commodity chains in a global economy' in Emily Rosenberg, ed., *A World Connecting, 1870–1945.* Belknap Press, 2012, p. 693.

8 James Fairhead, Melissa Leach, 'Desiccation and domination: Science and struggles over environment and development in colonial Guinea', *Journal of African History* 41, 2000, pp. 35–6.

9 Sandip Hazareesingh, 'Your foreign plants are very delicate: Peasant crop ecologies and the subversion of colonial cotton designs in Dharwar, Western India, 1830–1880' in Sandip Hazareesingh, Harro Maat, eds, *Local Subversions of Colonial Cultures: Commodities and Anti-Commodities in Global History.* Palgrave MacMillan, 2016, pp. 97–8.

10 Lieberman, Gordon, *Climate Change*, p. 144.

11 Kathryn Edgerton-Tarpley, *Tears from Iron: Cultural Responses to Famine in Nineteenth-Century China.* University of California Press, 2008, p. 15.

12 Patrick Gage, 'A grande seca: El Niño and Brazil's first rubber boom' *Historical Climatology* 2017: https://www.historicalclimatology.com/blog/a-grande-seca-el-nino-and-brazils-first-rubber-boom (accessed November 2018).

13 Mike Davis, *Late Victorian Holocausts: El Niño Famines and the Making of the Third World.* Verso, 2001, examines these global tragedies in the context of a global political economy driven by industrial capitalism and exacerbated by imperialism.

14 Lieberman, Gordon, *Climate Change*, pp. 145–6.

15 Andrea Janku, 'The north-China famine of 1876–1879: Performance and impact of a non-event' in 'Measuring historical heat: Event, performance and impact in China and the West' Online symposium paper, 2001, pp. 127–34, http://www.sino.uni-heidelberg.de/conf/symposium2.pdf#page=127 (accessed November 2018).

16 As quoted in Heather D. Curtis, 'Evangelicals and the politics of pictorial humanitarianism in an imperial age' in Heide Fehrenbach, Davide Rodogno, eds, *Humanitarian Photography: A History*. Cambridge UP, 2015, pp. 36–7.

17 As quoted in Kathryn Edgerton-Tarpley, 'Tough choices: Grappling with famine in Qing China, the British empire and beyond', *Journal of World History* 24, 1, 2013, pp. 135–76.

18 W. H. McNeill, *Plagues and Peoples*. Anchor Books Doubleday, 1998 [1976], pp. 279–80.

19 Zielinga de Boer, Sanders, *Volcanoes*, p. 149.

20 McNeill, *Plagues*, pp. 276–8.

21 Ann Haley MacKenzie, 'An analysis of environmental issues in nineteenth-century England using the writings of Charles Dickens', *American Biology Teacher* 70, 4, 2008, p. 203.

22 Rosemary Ashton, *One Hot Summer: Dickens, Darwin, Disraeli and the Great Stink of 1858*. Yale UP, 2017, pp. 1–2.

23 David S. Barnes, *The Great Stink of Paris and the Nineteenth-Century Struggle against Filth and Germs*. Johns Hopkins Press, 2006.

24 McNeill, *Plagues*, pp. 279–80.

25 Andreas Malm, 'The origins of fossil capitalism: From water to steam in the British cotton industry', *Historical Materialism* 21, 1, 2013, p. 17.

26 *CAIT Climate Data Explorer* www.cait2.wri.org (accessed November 2018). In 2014, global emissions were more than sixteen times higher than 1900.

27 Elizabeth Sinn, *Pacific Crossing: California Gold, Chinese Migration and the Making of Hong Kong*. Hong Kong UP, 2013, pp. 1–2.

28 Raymond F. Dasmann, 'Environmental changes before and after the gold rush', *California History* 77, 4, 1998/9, pp. 105–22.

29 As quoted by Dasmann, 'Environmental', p. 109.

30 Conohar Scott, 'Photographing pollution in Gold Rush: California', *Photographies* 10, 2, 2017, pp. 189–209.

31 F. J. Broswimmer, *Ecocide: A Short History of the Mass Extinction of Species*. Pluto Press, 2002, p. 71.

32 Ryan Tucker Jones, 'A havock made among them: Animals, empire and extinction in the Russian North Pacific, 1741–1810', *Environmental History* 16, 2011, pp. 597–9.

33 Even as the first Battle of the Marne in France and the Russian campaign in Galicia raged in September 1914, newspapers such as the *El Paso Morning Times* noted Martha's death on 14 September 1914 alongside its war coverage.

34 Maya Jasanoff, *The Dawn Watch: Joseph Conrad in a Global World*. HarperCollins, 2017, pp. 188–9.

35 R. W. Beachey, 'The East African ivory trade in the nineteenth century', *Journal of African History* 8, 2, 1967, pp. 275–6.

36 N. Thomas Hakansson, 'The human ecology of world systems in East Africa: The impact of the ivory trade', *Human Ecology* 32, 5, 2004, pp. 570–1.

37 Hakansson, 'Human ecology', p. 579.

38 Lieberman, Gordon, *Climate Change*, p. 146.

39 Ingo Heidbrink, 'The First World War and the beginning of overfishing in the North Sea' in Richard P. Tucker, Tait Keller, J. R. McNeill, Martin Schmid, eds, *Environmental Histories of the First World War*. Cambridge UP, 2018, pp. 136–7.

40 Robert C. Allen, Ian Keay, 'Saving the whales: Lessons from the extinction of the Eastern Arctic Bowhead', *Journal of Economic History* 64, 2, 2004, p. 405.

41 Nancy Shoemaker, 'Whale meat in American history', *Environmental History* 10, 2, 2005, p. 270.

42 John T. Cumbler, *Cape Cod: An Environmental History of a Fragile Ecosystem*. University of Massachusetts Press, 2014, p. 83.

43 Emma L. Carroll, Jennifer A. Jackson, David Paton, Tim D. Smith, 'Two intense decades of nineteenth-century whaling precipitated the rapid decline of right whales around New Zealand and East Australia', *PLoS One* 9, 4, 2014, pp. 1–12; Allen, Keay, 'Saving'.

44 'Head-Smashed-In buffalo jump' UNESCO World Heritage Sites website, https://whc.unesco.org/en/list/158 (accessed December 2018).

45 M. Scott Taylor, 'Buffalo hunt: International trade and the virtual extinction of the North American Bison', *American Economic Review* 101, 7, 2011, p. 3163.

46 Dan Flores, 'Bison ecology and bison diplomacy: The southern plains from 1800 to 1850', *Journal of American History* 78, 2, 1991, p. 484.

47 Dale F. Lott, *American Bison: A Natural History*. University of California Press, 2003, p. 176.

48 Philip Weeks, *'Farewell My Nation': American Indians and the United States in the Nineteenth Century*. Third edition, Wiley Blackwell, 2016, p. 227.

49 For a moving portrait of the destruction of the bison and the Great Plains people, see: Dan O'Brien, *The Great Plains Bison*. University of Nebraska Press, 2017, chapter 3.

50 Weeks, *Farewell*, p. 231.

51 Jürgen Osterhammel, *The Transformation of the World: A Global History of the Nineteenth Century*. Princeton UP, 2014, p. 141.

52 Weeks, *Farewell*, pp. 259–65.

53 Maori brought kiore (Pacific rats) and kuri (Polynesian dogs) with them.

54 Te Ara Encyclopedia of New Zealand website https://teara.govt.nz/en/extinctions/print (accessed December 2018).

55 Thomas D. Isern, 'A good servant but a tyrannous master: Gorse in New Zealand', *Social Science Journal* 44, 2007, pp. 179–86.

56 James Beattie, 'The empire of the rhododendron: Reorienting New Zealand garden history' in Eric Pawson, Tom Brooking, eds, *Making a New Land: Environmental Histories of New Zealand*. Otago UP, 2013, pp. 241–57.

57 Nancy Langston, 'Global forests' in J. R. McNeill, Erin Stewart Mauldin, eds, *A Companion to Global Environmental History*. Wiley Blackwell, 2015, pp. 272–3.

58　The rubber was sourced from latex, the sap extracted from rubber trees that by the late nineteenth century grew in plantations around the world: Stephen L. Harp, *A World History of Rubber: Empire, Industry and the Everyday.* Wiley Blackwell, 2016, p. 1.

59　John Tully, 'A Victorian ecological disaster: Imperialism, the telegraph and gutta-percha', *Journal of World History* 20, 4, 2009, pp. 574–5.

60　Paul Warde, *The Invention of Sustainability: Nature and Destiny c.1500–1870.* Cambridge UP, 2018, p. 326.

61　As quoted in Paul Star, 'Ecology: A science of nation? The utilization of plant ecology in New Zealand 1896–1930', *Historical Records of Australian Science* 17, 2006, p. 198.

62　R. W. Stellars, *Preserving Nature in the National Parks: A History.* Yale UP, 1997, p. 7.

63　John Shultis, 'Improving the wilderness: Common factors in creating national parks and equivalent reserves during the nineteenth century', *Forest and Conservation History* 39, 3, 1995, pp. 121–3.

64　Bernhard Gissibl, Sabine Höhler, Patrick Kupper, 'Introduction: Towards a global history of national parks' in Bernhard Gissibl, Sabine Höhler, Patrick Kupper, eds, *Civilizing Nature: National Parks in Global Historical Perspective.* Berghahn, 2012, p. 2.

65　Karen Brown, 'Conservation and utilisation of the natural world: Silviculture in the Cape Colony, c.1902–1910', *Environment and History* 7, 2001, pp. 427–47.

66　Shultis, 'Improving', p. 124.

67　Mark Osborne Humphries, 'Paths of infection: The First World War and the origins of the 1918 influenza pandemic', *War in History* 21, 1, 2013, pp. 55–81.

68　Anne Rasmussen, 'The Spanish flu' in Jay Winter, ed., *The Cambridge History of the First World War.* Volume Three, Cambridge UP, 2014, pp. 233–357.

Chapter 7

1　Tony Ballantyne, Antoinette Burton, 'Empires and the reach of the global' in Emily S. Rosenberg, ed., *A World Connecting, 1870–1945.* Harvard UP, 2012, p. 389.

2　Antoinette Burton, *The Trouble with Empire: Challenges to Modern British Imperialism.* Oxford UP, 2015.

3　Michael Geyer, Charles Bright, 'Global violence and nationalizing wars in Eurasia and America: The geopolitics of war in the mid-nineteenth century', *Comparative Studies in Society and History* 38, 4, 1996, pp. 619–57.

4　Carl von Clausewitz, *On War.* N. Trübner, 1873 (translation of 1832 original in German).

5 'Soldiers of Empire: Garrison and Empire in the Nineteenth Century' website, http://www.soldiersofempire.nz/the-project.html (accessed August 2018); Charlotte MacDonald, Rebecca Lenihan, 'Paper soldiers: The life, death and reincarnation of nineteenth-century military files across the British empire' *Rethinking History* 22, 3, 2018, pp. 375–402.

6 Burton, *Trouble*, p. 44.

7 Emmanuel Kreike, 'Genocide in the Kampongs? Dutch nineteenth-century colonial warfare in Aceh, Sumatra', *Journal of Genocide Research* 14, 3–4, 2012, pp. 297–315.

8 As opposed to the frequent wars of the early modern period (up to 1815) or the 'global total wars' of the 1914–45 period.

9 Cf. Dominic Eggel, 'Quo vadis diplomatic history? Reflections on the past and present of writing the history of international relations' in Barbara Haider-Wilson, William D. Godsey, Wolfgang Mueller, eds, *Internationale Geschichte in Theorie und Praxis/International History in Theory and Practice*. Verlag der Österreichischen Akademie der Wissenschaften, 2017, pp. 220–3.

10 Sergiusz Michalsky, 'War imagery between the Crimean campaign and 1914' in Joanna Bourke, ed., *War and Art: A Visual History of Modern Conflict*. Reaktion, 2017, pp. 44–79.

11 Joseph J. Matthews, *Reporting the Wars*. University of Minnesota Press, 1957, pp. 34, 52–4.

12 Lynn McDonald, 'Florence Nightingale, statistics and the Crimean War', *Journal of the Royal Statistics Society* 177, 3, 2014, p. 569.

13 Maartje Abbenhuis, *An Age of Neutrals: Great Power Politics 1815–1914*. Cambridge UP, 2014, p. 95.

14 Michael Paris, *Warrior Nation: Images of War in British Popular Culture 1850–2000*. Reaktion, 2000, pp. 13–48.

15 Maartje Abbenhuis, 'A most useful tool for diplomacy and statecraft: Neutrality and Europe in the "long" nineteenth century 1815–1914', *International History Review* 35, 1, 2013, pp. 1–23.

16 Richard Bach Jensen, 'Daggers, rifles and dynamite: Anarchist terrorism in nineteenth-century Europe', *Terrorism and Political Violence* 16, 1, 2004, p. 116.

17 Jonathan W. Jordan, 'Hiram Maxim's machine gun probably claimed more lives than any other weapon every made', *Military History* 19, 4, 2002, pp. 16–20.

18 The first war of Italian unification occurred during the revolutionary years of 1848 and 1849.

19 For an excellent account of the Wars of German Unification, including the Franco-Prussian War, see: Dennis E. Showalter, *The Wars of German Unification*. Second edition, Bloomsbury, 2015.

20 Cf. Christopher Ernest Barber, 'Nineteenth-century statecraft and the politics of moderation in the Franco-Prussian War', *European Review of History* 21, 1, 2014, pp. 1–17.

21 David Wetzel, *A Duel of Nations: Germany, France and the Diplomacy of the War of 1870–1871*. University of Wisconsin Press, 2012, pp. 41–66.

22 Abbenhuis, *Age of Neutrals*, pp. 122–43.

23 William Mulligan, *The Origins of the First World War*. Second edition, Cambridge UP, 2018.

24 Douglas Howland, 'Sovereignty and the laws of war: International consequences of Japan's 1905 victory over Russia', *Law and History Review* 29, 1, 2011, p. 54.

25 Maartje Abbenhuis, *The Hague Conferences and International Politics 1898–1915*. Bloomsbury, 2018.

26 Steven M. Harris, 'The global construction of international law in the nineteenth century: The case of arbitration', *Journal of World History* 27, 2, 2016, pp. 307–8; Kathryn Greenman, 'Aliens in Latin America: Intervention, arbitration and state responsibility for rebels', *Leiden Journal of International Law* 31, 2018, pp. 617–39.

27 Abbenhuis, *Age of Neutrals*, pp. 144–77. Also: Julia F. Irwin, *Making the World Safe: The American Red Cross and a Nation's Humanitarian Awakening*. Oxford UP, 2013, esp. pp. 1–13.

28 Elizabeth van Heyningen, 'The South African war as humanitarian crisis', *International Review of the Red Cross* 97, 900, 2015, pp. 999–1028.

29 Raymond Probst, *'Good Offices' in the Light of Swiss International Practice and Experiences*. Martinus Nijhoff, 1989, p. 148.

30 For an excellent overview: Jean H. Quataert, 'A new look at international law: Gendering the practices of humanitarian medicine in Europe's "small wars" 1879–1907', *Human Rights Quarterly* 40, 3, 2018, pp. 547–69.

31 Lindsay Schakenbach Regele, 'Industrial manifest destiny: American firearms manufacturing and antebellum expansion', *Business History Review* 92, 2018, pp. 57–83; Keith Krause, *Arms and the State: Patterns of Military Production and Trade*. Cambridge UP, 1992, pp. 58–9.

32 Krause, *Arms*, p. 59.

33 Elizabeth Chadwick, *Traditional Neutrality Revisited: Law, Theory and Case Studies*. Springer, 2002, pp. 83–5.

34 Matthias Schultz, 'Did norms matter in nineteenth-century international relations? Progress and decline in the "culture of peace" before World War I' in Holger Afflerbach, David Stevenson, eds, *An Improbable War: The Outbreak of World War I and European Political Culture before 1914*. Berghahn, 2007, pp. 43–60.

35 Joanna Bourke, 'Barbarization vs civilization in time of war' in George Kassimeris, ed., *The Barbarization of Warfare*. New York UP, 2006, pp. 19–38, quote on p. 37.

36 Tom Pessah, 'Violent representations: Hostile Indians and civilized wars in nineteenth-century USA', *Ethnic and Race Studies* 37, 9, 2014, pp. 1631–2.

37 Cf. Will Smiley, 'Lawless wars of empire? The international law of war in the Philippines, 1898–1903', *Law and History Review* 36, 3, 2018, pp. 511–50.

38 Thomas H. Reilly, *The Taiping Heavenly Kingdom*. University of Washington Press, 2004, pp. 3–6.

39 Al Nofi, 'Statistical summary America's major wars' 2007, website https://web.archive.org/web/20070711050249/http://www.cwc.lsu.edu/other/stats/warcost.htm (accessed August 2018).

40 C. A. Bayly, *The Birth of the Modern World 1780–1914: Global Connections and Comparisons*. Blackwell, 2004, p. 162.

41 Pessah, 'Violent', pp. 1628–45.

42 James Belich, *The New Zealand Wars and the Victorian Interpretation of Racial Conflict*. Third edition, Auckland UP, 2015, p. 15.

43 For a useful subaltern reflection on the events in India in 1857–9: Darshun Perusek, 'Subaltern consciousness and historiography of the Indian rebellion of 1857', *Economic and Political Weekly* 28, 37, 1993, pp. 1931–6.

44 Lyndall Ryan, 'Settler massacres on the Australian colonial frontier, 1836–1851' in Philip G. Dwyer, Lyndall Ryan, eds, *Theatres of Violence: Massacre, Mass Killing and Atrocity throughout History*. Berghahn, 2012, pp. 94–109.

45 A. Dirk Moses, *Genocide and Settler Society: Frontier Violence and Stolen Children in Australian History*. Berghahn, 2005, statistics on p. 26.

46 Ross E. Dunn, *Resistance in the Desert*. University of Wisconsin Press, 1977, p. 19.

47 Elizabeth Elbourne, 'Race, warfare and religion in mid nineteenth-century Southern Africa: The Khoikhoi rebellion against the Cape Colony and its uses, 1850–1858', *Journal of African Cultural Studies* 13, 1, 2000, pp. 17–42, quotes on pp. 26 and 27.

48 Robert Aldrich, *Greater France: A History of French Overseas Expansion*. St Martin's Press, 1996, pp. 204–5.

49 Jürgen Osterhammel, *The Transformation of the World: A Global History of the Nineteenth Century*. Princeton UP, 2014, pp. 140–1.

50 Antje Missbach, 'The Aceh War (1873–1913) and the influence of Christiaan Snouck Hurgronje' in Arndt Graf, Susanne Schröter, E. P. Wieringa, eds, *Aceh: History, Politics and Culture*. Institute of Southeast Asian Studies, 2010, p. 58.

51 B. Kiernan, *Blood and Soil: A World History of Genocide and Extermination from Sparta to Darfur*. Yale UP, 2007, pp. 382–7.

52 Fehrenbach, Rodogno, *Humanitarian Photography*.

53 Daniel Laqua, *The Age of Internationalism and Belgium 1880–1930: Peace, Progress and Prestige*. Manchester UP, 2013, pp. 56–62; Andrew G. Bonnell, 'Social Democrats and Germany's war in South-West Africa, 1904–7: The view from the socialist press' in Matthew P. Fitzpatrick, Peter Monteath, eds, *Savage Worlds: German Encounters Abroad, 1798–1914*. Manchester UP, 2018, pp. 206–29.

54 Dominic Lieven, *Empire: The Russian Empire and Its Rivals*. Yale UP, 2000, p. 198.

55 Antoinette Burton, Isabel Hofmeyr, 'Introduction: The spine of empire? Books and the making of an imperial commons' in Antoinette Burton,

Isabel Hofmeyr, eds, *Ten Books That Shaped the British Empire: Creating an Imperial Commons*. Duke UP, 2014, p. 14; Ballantyne, Burton, 'Empires' pp. 385–6.

56 Cf. Daniel Gorman, *International Cooperation in the Early Twentieth Century*. Bloomsbury, 2017, pp. 20–1.

Chapter 8

1 C. A. Bayly, *The Birth of the Modern World 1780–1914: Global Connections and Comparisons*. Blackwell, 2004, p. 1.

2 Jürgen Osterhammel, *The Transformation of the World: A Global History of the Nineteenth Century*. Princeton UP, 2014, pp. 744–7.

3 For a useful description of the various types of nineteenth-century nationalism: Thomas Getz, *The Long Nineteenth Century 1750–1914: Crucible of Modernity*. Bloomsbury, 2018, pp. 87–94.

4 Cf. Christopher Bayly, 'European political thought and the wider world during the nineteenth century' in G. S. Jones, G. Claeys, eds, *Nineteenth-Century Political Thought*. Cambridge UP, 2011, pp. 835–63.

5 Sebastian Conrad, 'Enlightenment in global history: A historiographical critique', *American History Review* 117, 4, October 2012, pp. 999–1027.

6 Osterhammel, *Transformation*, pp. 756–7.

7 For an overview of the many forms of nineteenth-century liberalism: Alan S. Kahan, *Liberalism in Nineteenth-Century Europe: The Political Culture of Limited Suffrage*. Palgrave MacMillan, 2003, pp. 1–20.

8 For a British perspective: Frank Trentmann, 'Political culture and political economy: Interest, ideology and free trade', *Review of International Political Economy* 5, 2, 1998, pp. 217–51.

9 For an enlightening discussion of the issues involved in Latin America in the immediate aftermath of their wars of independence: Diego Acosta, *The National Versus the Foreigner in South America: 200 Years of Migration and Citizenship Law*. Cambridge UP, 2018, pp. 31–3.

10 Robert Gildea, *Barricades and Borders: Europe 1800–1914*. Oxford UP, 1996, pp. 304–5.

11 Getz, *Long Nineteenth Century*, pp. 168–9.

12 K. Steven Vincent, 'Visions of stateless society' in G. S. Jones, G. Claeys, eds, *Nineteenth-Century Political Thought*. Cambridge UP, 2011, p. 434.

13 Ian Tyrrell, 'International aspects of the woman's temperance movement in Australia: The influence of the American WCTU 1882–1914', *Journal of Religious History* 12, 3, 1983, pp. 284–304; Tomoko Seto, 'Organizing Meiji women: The role of the Japanese chapter of the Woman's Christian Temperance Union for individual activists, 1900–1905', *Women's History Review* 26, 6, 2017, pp. 975–93.

14 Nicole A. N. M. van Os, 'They can breathe freely now: The International Council of Women and Ottoman Muslim women (1893–1920s)', *Journal of Women's History* 28, 3, 2016, pp. 17–32.

15 F. Ugbaoaja Ohaegbulam, *West African Responses to European Imperialism in the Nineteenth and Twentieth Centuries*. University Press of America, 1984, pp. 239–67.

16 S. K. B. Asante, 'Neglected aspects of the activities of the Gold Coast Aborigines Rights Protection Society', *Phylon* 36, 1, 1975, pp. 32–45.

17 Denis Vovchenko, 'Gendering irredentism? Self and other in Russian Pan-Orthodoxy and Pan-Slavism (1856–1885)', *Ethnic and Racial Studies* 34, 2, 2011, pp. 248–74.

18 Stuart A. Cohen, 'How shall we sing of Zion in a strange land? East European immigrants and the challenge of Zionism in Britain 1897–1918', *Jewish Social Studies* 1, 2, 1995, pp. 101–22.

19 Benedict Anderson, *Imagined Communities: Reflections on the Origin and Spread of Nationalism*. Revised edition, Verso, 2006.

20 Constance Bantman, Ana Cláudia Suriani da Silva, eds, *The Foreign Political Press in Nineteenth-Century London: Politics from a Distance*. Bloomsbury, 2018.

21 Bayly, *Birth*, p. 349.

22 Bayly, *Birth*, pp. 345–7; Antoinette Burton, *The Trouble with Empire: Challenges to Modern British Imperialism*. Oxford UP, 2015, p. 32.

23 Bayly, *Birth*, p. 341; Conrad, 'Enlightenment', pp. 1019–20.

24 Isabel Hofmeyr, 'Gandhi's printing press: Indian Ocean print cultures and cosmopolitanisms' in Sugata Bose, Kris Manjapra, eds, *Cosmopolitan Thought Zones: South Asia and the Circulation of Ideas*. Palgrave Macmillan, 2010, pp. 113–14.

25 Rachel Chrastil, 'The French Red Cross, war readiness and civil society, 1866–1914', *French Historical Studies* 31, 3, 2008, pp. 445–76.

26 Caroline Reeves, 'Developing the humanitarian image in late nineteenth- and early twentieth-century China' in Heide Fehrenbach, Davide Rodogno, eds, *Humanitarian Photography: A History*. Cambridge UP, 2015, pp. 115–39.

27 Sho Konishi, 'The emergence of an international humanitarian organization in Japan: The Tokugawa origins of the Japanese Red Cross', *American Historical Review* 119, 4, 2014, p. 1129.

28 Kris Manjapra, 'Communist internationalism and transcolonial recognition' in Sugata Bose, Kris Manjapra, *Cosmopolitan Thought Zones: South Asia and the Circulation of Ideas*. Palgrave Macmillan, 2010, pp. 161–3.

29 Also published as Benedict Anderson, *The Age of Globalization: Anarchists and the Anticolonial Imagination*. Verso, 2013.

30 Anderson, *Globalization*, p. 2.

31 The best history of the Second International remains: James Joll, *The Second International 1889–1914*. Weidenfeld & Nicolson, 1955.

32 Ian Tyrrell, 'New comparisons, international worlds: transnational and comparative perspectives', *Australian Feminist Studies* 16, 36, 2001, p. 355; Julie Carlier, 'Forgotten transnational connections and national contexts: An "entangled history" of political transfers that shaped Belgian feminism, 1890–1914', *Women's History Review* 19, 4, 2010, pp. 503–22.

33 Megan Hutching, 'Mothers of the world: Women, peace and arbitration in early twentieth-century New Zealand', *New Zealand Journal of History* 27, 2, 1997, pp. 173–85.

34 Anti-suffrage campaigners also worked trans- and internationally: Sharon Crozier-de Rosa, 'The national and transnational in British anti-suffragists' views of Australian women voters', *History Australia* 10, 3, 2013, p. 53.

35 Maartje Abbenhuis, *The Hague Conferences and International Politics 1898–1915*. Bloomsbury, 2018, pp. 136–7.

36 M. Krajewski, 'Organizing a global idiom: Esperanto, Ido and the world auxiliary language movement before the First World War' in R. W. Boyd, ed., *Information beyond Borders: International Cultural and Intellectual Exchange in the Belle Époque*. Taylor and Francis, 2014, pp. 97–122.

37 Laqua, *Age of Internationalism*.

38 Emily Rosenberg, 'Exhibitionary nodes' in E. Rosenberg, ed., *World Connecting, 1870–1945*, Belknap Press, 2012, pp. 886–918.

39 As quoted in Bernard Porter, *Absent-Minded Imperialists: Empire, Society and Culture in Britain*. Oxford UP, 2004, p. 91.

40 Pascal Blanchard, Nicolas Bancel, Gilles Boëtsch, Eric Deroo, Sandrine Lemaire, Charles Forsdick, eds, *Human Zoos: Science and Spectacle in the Age of Empire*. Liverpool UP, 2008.

41 Abbenhuis, *Hague*, p. 15.

42 Warren Kuehl, *Seeking World Order: The United States and International Organization to 1920*. Vanderbilt UP, 1969, pp. 48–9.

43 Cf. Desley Deacon, Penny Russell, Angela Woollacott, 'Introduction' and Penny van Toorn, 'Writing the entrapped nations of indigenous Australia into being' both in Desley Deacon, Penny Russell, Angela Woollacott, eds, *Transnational Lives: Biographies of Global Modernity, 1700-Present*. Palgrave MacMillan, 2010, pp. 1–2, 42–4.

Chapter 9

1 Sanford Fleming, 1886, in Stephen Kern, *The Culture of Time and Space 1880–1918*. Harvard UP, 1983, p. 11.

2 Glenda Sluga, *Internationalism in the Age of Nationalism*. University of Pennsylvania Press, 2013, p. 14.

3 Robert Fitzgerald, *The Rise of the Global Company: Multinationals and the Making of the Modern World*. Cambridge UP, 2015, pp. 154–5.

4 For two excellent overviews of the historiographical debate on the origins of the First World War: William Mulligan, *The Origins of the First World War* Second edition, Cambridge UP, 2018, pp. 1–23; Annika Mombauer, *The Origins of the First World War: Controversies and Consensus*. Taylor and Francis, 2013.

5 Vladimir Lenin, *Imperialism the Highest Form of Capitalism: A Popular Outline*. Second edition. Lawrence and Wishart, 1934.

6 Mulligan, *Origins*.

7 Michael Neiberg, *Dance of the Furies: Europe and the Outbreak of World War I*. Harvard UP, 2013.

8 Cf. Norman Davies, *Europe: A History*. Random House, 1996, p. 896.

9 Paul W. Schroeder, 'International politics, peace, and war, 1815–1914' in T. C. W. Blanning, ed., *Nineteenth Century: Europe 1789–1914*. Oxford UP, 2000, pp. 115–49.

10 Christopher Clark, *The Sleepwalkers: How Europe Went to War in 1914*. Penguin, 2012.

11 Rachel G. Hoffman, 'The age of assassination: Monarchy and nation in nineteenth-century Europe' in Jan Rüger, Nikolaus Wachsmann, eds, *Rewriting German History: New Perspectives on Modern Germany*. Palgrave MacMillan, 2015, pp. 121–41.

12 Clark, *Sleepwalkers*, esp. pp. 77, 99.

13 Cf. Dominic Lieven, *Empire: The Russian Empire and Its Rivals*. Yale UP, 2000, pp. 192, 198.

14 Which is the reason some historians claim that the 'concert system' no longer functioned in 1914: Paul Schroeder, 'World War I as galloping Gertie: A reply to Joachim Remak', *Journal of Modern History* 44, 3, 1972, pp. 320–45.

15 For more on Russia and the origins of the war: David Alan Rich, 'Russia' in Richard F. Hamilton, Holger H. Herwig, eds, *The Origins of World War I*. Cambridge UP, 2003, pp. 188–226.

16 For a recent interpretation: Volker Berghahn, 'Origins' in Jay Winter, ed., *Cambridge History of the First World War*. Volume 1, Cambridge UP, 2014, pp. 16–38.

17 Cf. David Stevenson, *1914–1918: The History of the First World War*. Penguin, 2012, pp. 14–19.

18 Mulligan, *Origins*, p. 216.

19 For more on France and Britain and the origins of the war: Eugenia C. Kiesling, 'France' and J. Paul Harris, 'Britain' in Richard F. Hamilton, Holger H. Herwig, eds, *The Origins of World War I*. Cambridge UP, 2003, pp. 227–65, 266–99.

20 Richard F. Hamilton, Holger H. Herwig, *War Planning 1914*. Cambridge UP, 2010.

21 Stevenson, *1914*, p. 22.

22 Catriona Pennell, *A Kingdom United: Popular Responses to the Outbreak of the First World War in Britain and Ireland*. Oxford UP, 2012, pp. 23–35.

23 Jürgen Osterhammel, *The Transformation of the World: A Global History of the Nineteenth Century*. Princeton UP, 2014, p. 119.

24 David Lloyd George, *War Memoirs*. Volume 1, Odhams Press, 1938, p. 32; Andrew Suttie, *Rewriting the First World War: Lloyd George, Politics and Strategy 1914–1918*. Palgrave MacMillan, 2005, pp. 27–33.

25 Cf. David Stevenson, 'Militarization and diplomacy in Europe before 1914', *International Security* 22, 1, 1997, pp. 125–61.

26 Cf. Jörn Leonhard, *Pandora's Box: A History of the First World War*. Belknap, 2018, pp. 102–3.

27 For more on the international history of the Balkan Wars: Dominik Geppert, William Mulligan, Andreas Rose, eds, *The Wars before the Great War: Conflict and International Politics before the Outbreak of the First World War*. Cambridge UP, 2015.

28 For more: Robert A. Bickers, R. G. Tiedemann, eds, *The Boxers, China and the World*. Rowman & Littlefield, 2007.

29 Maartje Abbenhuis, *An Age of Neutrals: Great Power Politics 1815–1914*. Cambridge UP, 2014, p. 185.

30 David Stevenson, *Armaments and the Coming of War: Europe 1904–1914*. Clarendon Press, 1996.

31 Jonathan A. Grant, *Rulers, Guns and Money: The Global Arms Trade in the Age of Imperialism*. Harvard UP, 2007.

32 Elizabeth Chadwick, *Traditional Neutrality Revisited: Law, Theory and Case Studies*. Springer, 2002, pp. 83–4.

33 David Stevenson, echoing Leon Trotsky, in Ian F. W. Beckett, *The Great War 1914–1918*. Longman, 2001, p. 25.

34 Cf. Frank Ninkovich, *The United States and Imperialism*. Wiley Blackwell, 2001, p. 201.

35 Maartje Abbenhuis, *The Hague Conferences and International Politics 1898–1915*. Bloomsbury, 2018, esp. pp. 97–120.

36 Dan L. Morrill, 'Nicholas II and the call for the first Hague conference', *Journal of Modern History* 46, 2, 1974, pp. 296–313.

37 Abbenhuis, *Hague*.

38 Neville Wylie, 'Muddied waters: The influence of the first Hague conference on the evolution of the Geneva Conventions of 1864 and 1906' in Maartje Abbenhuis, Christopher Ernest Barber, Annalise Higgins, eds, *War, Peace and International Order: The Legacies of the Hague Conferences of 1899 and 1907*. Routledge, 2017, pp. 52–68.

39 Abbenhuis, *Hague*, p. 154.

40 Neiberg, *Dance*.

41 Frederick R. Dickinson, 'The view from Japan: War and peace in Europe around 1914' in Holger Afflerbach, David Stevenson, eds, *An Improbable War? The Outbreak of World War I in European Political Culture before 1914*. Berghahn, 2012, p. 305.

Chapter 10

1 Bill Albert, *South America and the First World War: The Impact of the War on Brazil, Argentina, Peru and Chile.* Cambridge UP, 1988, pp. 1–2.

2 Richard Roberts, 'A tremendous panic: The global financial crisis of 1914' in Andrew Smith, Simon Mollan, Kevin D. Tennent, eds, *The Impact of the First World War on International Business.* Routledge, 2017, pp. 121–41.

3 Albert, *South America*, p. 1.

4 Mark Bailey, 'Supporting the wartime economy: imperial maritime trade and the globalised maritime trade system, 1914–1916', *Journal for Maritime Research* 19, 1, 2017, pp. 23–45.

5 Albert, *South America*, p. 177.

6 Albert, *South America*, p. 296.

7 Cf. Phillip A. Dehne, *On the Far Western Front: Britain's First World War in South America.* Manchester UP, 2009.

8 Maartje Abbenhuis, *The Art of Staying Neutral: The Netherlands in the First World War, 1914–1918.* Amsterdam UP, 2006, pp. 65–8.

9 Kathryn Meyer, 'Trade and nationality at Shanghai upon the outbreak of the First World War 1914–1915', *International History Review* 10, 2, 1988, pp. 238–60.

10 Joshua A. Sanborn, *Drafting the Russian Nation: Military Conscription, Total War and Mass Politics 1905–1925.* Illinois UP, 2003, p. 31.

11 M. L. Sanders, P. M. Taylor, *British Propaganda during the First World War 1914–1918.* MacMillan, 1982, p. 19.

12 Byron Farwell, *The Great War in Africa 1914–1918.* Viking, 1987, p. 25.

13 Charles Stephenson, *Germany's Asia-Pacific Empire.* Boydell Press, 2009, p. 100.

14 Richard Hough, *Falklands 1914: The Pursuit of Admiral von Spee.* Periscope, 2003, p. 47.

15 Tim Stapleton, 'The impact of the First World War on African people' in John Laband, ed., *Daily Lives of Civilians in Wartime Africa: From Slavery Days to Rwandan Genocide.* Greenwood, 2007, p. 117.

16 Stapleton, 'Impact', pp. 123–4.

17 Dirk Hoerder, 'Migrations, free and bound' in Emily Rosenberg, ed., *A World Connecting 1870–1945.* Belknap Press, 2012, p. 556.

18 Léon Daudet, *La guerre totale.* Nouvelle Librairie Nationale, 1918, p. 8.

19 Stephen Broadberry, Mark Harrison, 'The economics of World War One: An overview' in Stephen Broadberry, Mark Harrison, eds, *The Economics of World War One.* Cambridge UP, 2005, p. 5.

20 C. Paul Vincent, *The Politics of Hunger: The Allied Blockade of Germany 1915–1919.* Ohio UP, 1985, p. 14.

21 Albrecht Ritschl, 'The pity of peace: Germany's economy at war, 1914–1918 and beyond' in Stephen Broadberry, Mark Harrison, eds, *The Economics of World War One.* Cambridge UP, 2005, p. 62.

22 Stephen Broadberry, Peter Howlett, 'The United Kingdom during World War I: Business as usual?' in Stephen Broadberry, Mark Harrison, eds, *The Economics of World War One*. Cambridge UP, 2005, p. 219.

23 Max-Stephen Schulze, 'Austria-Hungary's economy in World War I' and Sevket Pamuk, 'The Ottoman economy in World War I' both in Stephen Broadberry, Mark Harrison, eds, *The Economics of World War One*. Cambridge UP, 2005, pp. 94, 127.

24 Eric Hobsbawm, *The Age of Extremes: A History of the World 1914–1991*. Pantheon Books, 1994.

25 Bailey, 'Supporting', p. 23.

26 For more: Maartje Abbenhuis, Ismee Tames, *Global War, Global Catastrophe: Neutrals, Belligerents and the Transformation of the First World War*. Bloomsbury, forthcoming.

27 Marjorie Milbank Farrar, *Conflict and Compromise: The Strategy, Politics and Diplomacy of the French Blockade 1914–1918*. Martinus Nijhoff, 1974, pp. 18–19.

28 For a useful overview of the impact of the war on neutrals: Johan den Hertog, Samuël Kruizinga, eds, *Caught in the Middle: Neutrals, Neutrality and the First World war*. Aksant, 2011.

29 Homa Katouzian, 'Ahmad Kasrari on the revolt of Sheikh Mohammad Khiyabani' in Touraj Atabaki, ed., *Iran and the First World War: Battleground of the Great Powers*. I.B. Tauris, 2006, pp. 95–119.

30 J. Charles Schenking, 'The imperial Japanese navy and the First World War' in Toshihiro Minohara, Tze-Ki Hon, Evan N. Dawley, eds, *The Decade of the Great War: Japan and the Wider World in the 1910s*. Brill, 2014, pp. 83–106; A. Morgan Young, *Japan under Taisho Tenno 1912–1926*. George Allen, 1928, pp. 73–4.

31 Young, *Japan*, p. 111.

32 Schenking, 'Imperial', p. 96.

33 Masato Kimura, 'Securing maritime trade' in Tosh Minohara, Tze-ki Hon, Evan Dawley, eds, Toshihiro Minohara, Tze-Ki Hon, Evan N. Dawley, eds, *The Decade of the Great War: Japan and the Wider World in the 1910s*. Brill, 2014, p. 127.

34 Mustafa Aksakal, 'The Ottoman Empire' in Jay Winter, ed., *Cambridge History of the First World War*. Volume 1, Cambridge UP, 2014, pp. 473–4.

35 Alan Kramer, *Dynamic of Destruction: Culture and Mass Killing in the First World War*. Oxford UP, 2007, p. 50.

36 Glen E. Torrey, ed., *Romania and the First World War: A Collection of Studies*. Center for Romanian Studies (Iasi), 1999.

37 Eric W. Osborne, *Britain's Economic Blockade of Germany 1914–1918*. Frank Cass, 2004, p. 85.

38 Kathleen Burk, *Britain, America and the Sinews of War, 1914–1918*. George, Allen & Unwin, 1985.

39 Burk, *Sinews of War*, p. 5; Jennifer D. Keene, 'North America' in Jay Winter, ed., *Cambridge History of the First World War*. Volume 1, Cambridge UP, 2014, p. 512.

40 Maartje Abbenhuis, 'On the edge of the storm? Situation Switzerland's neutrality in the context of the First World War' in Michael M. Olsansky, ed., *Am Rande des Sturms: das Schweizer Militär im Ersten Weltkrieg/En marge de la tempête: les forces armées suisses pendant la Première Guerre Mondiale.* Hier und Jetzt, 2018, pp. 33–5.

41 Ingeborg Vijgen, *Tussen Mandaat en Kolonie: Rwanda, Burundi en het Belgisch Bestuur in Opdracht van de Volkenbond (1916–1932).* Acco, 2004, p. 72.

42 Martin van Bruinessen, 'A Kurdish warlord on the Turkish-Persian frontier in the early twentieth century: Isma'il Aqa Simko' in Touraj Atabaki, ed., *Iran and the First World War: Battleground of the Great Powers.* I.B. Tauris, 2006, pp. 69–93.

43 Guoqi Xu, 'Asia' in Jay Winter, ed., *Cambridge History of the First World War.* Volume 1, Cambridge UP, 2014, p. 503.

44 Guoqi Xu, *Asia and the Great War: A Shared History.* Oxford UP, 2016, p. 59.

45 Xu, *Asia and the Great War* p. 75; Radhika Singha, 'India's silver bullets: War loans and war propaganda, 1917–1918' in Maartje Abbenhuis, Neill Atkinson, Kingsley Baird, Gail Romano, eds, *The Myriad Legacies of 1917: A Year of War and Revolution.* Palgrave MacMillan, 2018, pp. 77–102.

46 Jason Pack, 'The antecedents and implications of the so-called Anglo-Sanussi War 1915–1917' in T. G. Fraser, *The First World war and Its Aftermath: The Shaping of the Middle East.* Gingko Library, 2015, pp. 41–62.

47 Bill Nasson, 'Africa' in Jay Winter, ed., *Cambridge History of the First World War.* Volume 1, Cambridge UP, 2014, pp. 447–8.

48 Jangkhomang Guite, Thongkholal Haokip, 'Introduction' in Jangkhomang Guite, Thongkholal Haokip, eds, *The Anglo-Kuki War, 1917–1919.* Routledge, 2018, pp. 16–17.

49 Nasson, 'Africa', pp. 454–7; Xu, 'Asia', p. 487.

50 Jennifer Keene, 'Americans respond: Perspectives on the global war, 1914–1917', *Geschichte und Gesellschaft* 40, 2, 2018, pp. 267–8.

51 Steven Hyland Jr, 'The Syrian-Ottoman home front in Buenos Aires and Rosario during the First World War', *Journal of Migration History* 4, 2018, pp. 211–35, quote on p. 212.

52 Julia Irwin, 'Taming total war: Great War-era American humanitarianism and its legacies' in Thomas W. Zeiler, David K. Ekbladh, Benjamin C. Montoya, eds, *Beyond 1917: The United States and the Global Legacies of the Great War.* Oxford UP, 2017, pp. 122–55.

53 Enzo Angelucci, *Illustrated Encyclopedia of Military Aircraft*, Chartwell, 2001, as quoted by: 'The aircraft of World War 1' *The Aerodrome*, website: http://www.theaerodrome.com/aircraft/statistics.php (accessed November 2018).

54 Hans van Lith, *Plotseling een Vreselijke Knal: Bommen en Mijnen Treffen Neutraal Nederland 1914–1918.* Europese Bibliotheek, 2001.

55 Annette Becker, 'The Great War: World war, total war', *International Review of the Red Cross* 97, 2015, pp. 1029–45.

56 Kramer, *Dynamic*, pp. 139–40.

57 Aksakal, 'Ottoman', p. 459.

58 Vincent, *Politics*, pp. 21–2.

59 William Mulligan, *The Great War for Peace*. Yale UP, 2014.

60 Jay Winter, 'War and anxiet in 1917' in Maartje Abbenhuis, Neill Atkinson, Kingsley Baird, Gail Romano, eds, *The Myriad Legacies of 1917: A Year of War and Revolution*. Palgrave MacMillan, 2018, pp. 13–33.

61 Hugh Rockoff, 'Until it is over: The United States economy in World War I' in Stephen Broadberry, Mark Harrison, 'The economics of World War One: An overview' in Stephen Broadberry, Mark Harrison, eds, *The Economics of World War One*. Cambridge UP, 2005, p. 335.

62 Hans A. Schmitt, *Neutral Europe between War and Revolution 1917–1923*. University Press of Virginia, 1988.

63 Olivier Compagnon, 'Latin America' in Jay Winter, ed., *Cambridge History of the First World War*. Volume 1, Cambridge UP, 2014, p. 545.

64 Xu, 'Asia', p. 503.

65 Susan C. Townsend, 'The Great War and urban crisis: Conceptualizing the industrial metropolis in Japan and Britain in the 1910s' in Toshihiro Minohara, Tze-Ki Hon, Evan N. Dawley, eds, *The Decade of the Great War: Japan and the Wider World in the 1910s*. Brill, 2014, pp. 301–22.

66 Young, *Japan*, pp. 114–22.

67 Xu, 'Asia', p. 483.

68 R. A. Rogers, N. R. Daut, 'China in the First World War: A forgotten army in search of international recognition', *Contemporary Chinese Political Economy and Strategic Relations* 3, 3, 2017, pp. 1237–69.

69 Mark Osborne Humphries, 'Paths of infection: The First World War and the origins of the 1918 influenza pandemic', *War in History* 21, 1, 2013.

70 Jörn Leonhard, *Pandora's Box: A History of the First World War*. Belknap, 2018, p. 721.

71 Robert Gerwarth, Erez Manela, 'The Great War as a global war: imperial conflict and the reconfiguration of world order, 1911–1923', *Diplomatic History* 38, 4, 2014, pp. 786–800.

72 For the economic consequences of the war and the global shift away from Europe: Christof Dejung, Niels P. Peterson, 'Introduction: Power, institutions and global markets – actors, mechanisms and foundations of worldwide economic integration, 1850–1930' in Christof Dejung, Niels P. Peterson, eds, *The Foundations of Worldwide Economic Integration: Power, Institutions and Global Markets, 1850–1930*. Cambridge UP, 2013, pp. 12–17.

73 Raymond Sontag, *A Broken World, 1919–1939*. HarperCollins, 1971.

Index